Adulterous Nations

Adulterous Nations

Family Politics and National Anxiety in the European Novel

Tatiana Kuzmic

NORTHWESTERN UNIVERSITY PRESS
EVANSTON, ILLINOIS

the modern language initiative

THIS BOOK IS MADE POSSIBLE BY A COLLABORATIVE GRANT FROM THE ANDREW W. MELLON FOUNDATION.

Northwestern University Press
www.nupress.northwestern.edu

Printed in the United States of America

10 9 8 7 6 5 4 3 2 1

Library of Congress Cataloging-in-Publication Data

Names: Kuzmic, Tatiana, author.
Title: Adulterous nations : family politics and national anxiety in the European novel / Tatiana Kuzmic.
Description: Evanston, Illinois : Northwestern University Press, 2016. | Includes bibliographical references and index.
Identifiers: LCCN 2016007596| ISBN 9780810133976 (pbk. : alk. paper) | ISBN 9780810133983 (cloth : alk. paper) | ISBN 9780810133990 (e-book)
Subjects: LCSH: European fiction—History and criticism. | Adultery in literature. | Nationalism in literature.
Classification: LCC PN56.A29 K89 2016 | DDC 809.933543—dc23
LC record available at http://lccn.loc.gov/2016007596

To my parents,
who imparted to me
—through both nature and nurture—
their love of books and languages

Beauty and the Beast

The deceiving beauty
Slammed the door
Finally
Like the Homeland
And disappeared
Into History.

Therefore, the deceiving beauty
And the Homeland
Have something in common:
Both leave behind
Boys
Who will die
For them.

war 1991

—Ferida Duraković, Sarajevo

CONTENTS

Acknowledgments *xi*

Note on Translation, Transliteration, and Dates *xv*

Introduction *3*

PART I: EMPIRES

Chapter 1
Middlemarch: The English Heroine and the Polish Rebel(lions) *27*

Chapter 2
Effi Briest: German Realism and the Young Empire *57*

Chapter 3
Anna Karenina: The Slavonic Question and the Dismembered Adulteress *92*

PART II: NATIONS

Chapter 4
The Goldsmith's Gold: The Origins of Yugoslavism and the Birth of the Croatian Novel *131*

Chapter 5
Quo Vadis: Polish Messianism and the Proselytizing Heroine *155*

Conclusion *181*

Notes *189*

Bibliography *213*

Index *223*

ACKNOWLEDGMENTS

In many of the workshops I attended about publishing one's first book, the project was frequently compared to a firstborn child. If it takes a village, as the saying goes, to raise the latter, the same can be said for completing the former. I will begin with the people most recently involved in seeing *Adulterous Nations* through to its fruition and proceed backwards. Mike Levine, acquisitions editor for Northwestern University Press, first expressed interest in the project and continued to express interest as I struggled on chapter by chapter. Comments from all three readers for the press were helpful in making the final rendition substantially better than it was in its original form, but I wish to extend special thanks to Reader 3 for a particularly attentive reading (and for using the adjective "outrageous" as a compliment).

At the University of Texas at Austin, the Center for Women's and Gender Studies, where I first had the opportunity to "test-drive" the book project in front of an interdisciplinary audience, the British Studies Society, which hosted the intellectually invigorating Friday lunches, and the Humanities Institute, where I worked on chapter 3 of the book, offered inspiration, feedback, and occasional research financing, the last of which came with the all-important teaching release. The book has also benefited from the dedicated work of my two graduate student research assistants. Nadya Clayton plowed through Tolstoy's letters in search of references to the Russo-Turkish War, alerted me to relevant entries in Sofya Tolstaya's diary, and forwarded to me the news about Anatoly Lebed', the Russian colonel who fought in Serbia in the 1990s. Katya Cotey also plowed through Tolstoy's writings as well as writings about Tolstoy; she is an inexhaustible source of information with an extraordinary gift for locating everything, including a nineteenth-century article on Polish beggars, which enriched my reading of *Middlemarch*. Over the many hours of conversation we have spent on our shared love of the nineteenth-century novel I have also come to regard her as a dear friend.

The book has also been enriched by the faculty book club that I led for two years, and I wish to thank everybody who was involved in it. Most of the participants were in the stressful pre-tenure phases of their careers when they read Tolstoy's *Anna Karenina* and (even more amazingly) *War and Peace*, as well as George Eliot's *Middlemarch*, with me. Thanks to Lisa Neff for coming up with the idea, to Jenni Beer for teaching with me a course on psychology in the Russian novel that was a direct consequence of the book club, and to all of the following for their involvement: Ted and Chris Huston, Deborah Beck, Angie Littwin, Cristine Legare, Rebecca Callahan, Marie Monfils, and Paige Harden. To all of the psychologists in the group, a special thanks for making me appreciate Tolstoy all the more for your valuable insights and connections.

Outside of the university, I wish to thank Ellen-Elias Bursać for always and quickly answering my e-mail questions about August Šenoa and *Vienac* and for putting me in touch with Ferida Duraković, whom I heartily thank for permission to use her poem as an epigraph. I also thank Irina Rubis for permission to use the image from her and Katerina Venzhik's *Ne dai Russkomu* campaign. Shorter versions of chapters 1 and 3 were previously published elsewhere, the former as "'The German, the Sclave, and the Semite': Eastern Europe in the Imagination of George Eliot" in *Nineteenth-Century Literature* 68 (2014): 513–541, and the latter as "'Serbia—Vronsky's Last Love': Reading *Anna Karenina* in the Context of Empire" in the *Toronto Slavic Quarterly* 43 (2013): 40–66. *NCL* editor Jonathan Grossman and the anonymous reviewers not only sharpened my thinking about George Eliot but also made me into a better writer overall and taught me skills I have continued to use in other projects.

I cannot say that I did not realize while in graduate school how fortunate I was to have landed in such a supportive environment, but over the years my gratitude only grew. My committee chair, Harriet Murav, can only be described by that wonderful German word for one's adviser—*Doktormutter*; Lilya Kaganovsky was always generous with both intellectual and practical advice; and Valeria Sobol has been a delightful source of inspiration in my Tolstoy scholarship, all the more for answering every one of my calls to participate in a conference panel. Among the graduate students whose friendship has withstood the test of time and distance, Dheepa Sundaram and Karen Lukrhur were always and still are willing to "talk theory," whip up an amazing meal, and offer pet-sitting services, all of which supported my research.

There are aspects of this book that date back to my undergraduate days and the two professors who influenced me most. Elaine Phillips taught me the wonders of the Hebrew Bible, and at a random piano recital that we both happened to attend years after I graduated, when I told her about my dissertation, she introduced me to the term "porno-prophetics." The chapter on *Anna Karenina* would have been seriously impoverished without that concept. My favorite psychology professor, Bert Hodges, claimed that Tolstoy and Dostoevsky were the best psychologists he had ever read and so, albeit unintentionally, steered me into a different field of study. (He also pointed out the beautiful mowing scenes in *Anna Karenina* as the perfect depiction of the famous social psychologist Mihály Csíkszentmihályi's notion of *flow*, which came in very handy fifteen years later when I taught Russian Literature and Psychology with Jenni Beer.)

Last and most important of all, I wish to thank my family. The credit for the catchy phrase that is the main title of this book goes to my uncle—*ujo*—Miroslav Volf, who came up with it when I shared with him my first thoughts about the project, before it was even a dissertation draft. My sisters, Kristina and Petra, shared their kids with me, sometimes even across continents, as when Kristina allowed me to fly her Luka and Matea all the way from L.A. to Croatia several times over the summers. Petra made her home my home during those summers, a few holidays, and one semester that I spent completing the book; she cooked all of my favorite meals and pushed me to write when, more often than not, I preferred to play the role of aunt rather than scholar. As I have often told her, her idyllic life with her husband and their four beautiful children in the Croatian countryside would make Tolstoy proud.

I owe the deepest level of gratitude to my parents, Vlasta and Peter Kuzmič, to whom this book is dedicated. One of my earliest memories is that of my dad creating rhyming songs for me in order to teach me to count (*ti i ja—to smo dva; mama, ja i ti—to smo tri . . .*) or help me remember the names of our numerous relatives (starting with himself—*tata Petar, brz k'o vjetar*). The hours and hours I spent listening to my mom read aloud to me—everything from the international children's favorite *The Chronicles of Narnia* to the Croatian masterpiece of children's literature, Ivana Brlić-Mažuranić's *Šegrt Hlapić*—remain my favorite childhood memories.

NOTE ON TRANSLATION, TRANSLITERATION, AND DATES

All translations of the non-English quotes used in this book (as well as the poem that serves as the epigraph), unless otherwise noted, are my own. I have attempted to remain as literal as meaningful English permitted.

In transliterating names of Russian authors and fictional characters, I have used the Library of Congress system, except for those last names whose endings are typically rendered with a *y* in English-language publications, both male—Tolstoy and Vronsky, for example, instead of Tolstoi and Vronskii—and female—Tolstaya and Kovalevskaya instead of Tolstaia and Kovalevskaia. In addition, in order to avoid the orthographical awkwardness of the apostrophe in the middle of Tolstoy's wife's first name—Sof'ia—I have spelled it Sofya. I have also used English spelling for the English nicknames—popular at the time—of Russian first names, so that Kiti, for example, is Kitty, and Dolli is Dolly.

In the original *Quo Vadis* Henryk Sienkiewicz rendered the ancient Roman names in Polish; thus, Petronius is Petroniusz, Vinicius Winicjusz, and so on. I have used the Latin spelling for easier readability in English, except for when it does not make a difference, mainly with Ligia, whom English translators tend to spell Lygia.

The prerevolutionary calendar in Russia was Julian or Old Style, and its dates remain as such in the official collected works of Tolstoy and in his secretary Gusev's *Annals of the Life and Work of Tolstoy.* I have not changed them to Gregorian dates in my work, which means that they are 12 days (and from February 17, 1900, 13 days) behind the Gregorian calendar.

Finally, most novels discussed in the following pages were, as was typical in the nineteenth century, serialized in literary journals before becoming books, and I have strived to be clear about which of the two modes I refer to when listing their publication dates. When no explanation is given, the year listed refers to the book.

Adulterous Nations

Introduction

"Adultery is not just the favorite, but also the only theme of all novels."[1] So writes the great Lev Tolstoy in 1898, exactly twenty years after his own, enormously successful *Anna Karenina* had come out in book form. What Tolstoy detects—rather bitterly, since at this point he has parted with high culture and renounced his former masterpieces as yet another source of pleasure for the idle wealthy classes—is the prevalence of the novel of adultery in the second half of the nineteenth century, when it had practically become a subgenre within realism. The inaugural novel of this subgenre is typically considered to be Gustave Flaubert's *Madame Bovary*, to which all subsequent novels of adultery have been compared. Its serialization in 1856 was followed by a lawsuit against the author on account of "outrage to public and religious morals and to morality,"[2] which only made the sales of the 1857 book version skyrocket. Although *Madame Bovary* was, obviously, not the world's first novel to take up the theme of the unfaithful wife, it did establish a particular pattern for addressing this theme. The aforementioned Russian *Anna Karenina*, for example, the American *The Awakening* (1899), and the somewhat lesser known German *Effi Briest* (1896) all feature, like the French masterpiece, an attractive and energetic young woman, who, feeling stifled in a marriage to a dull and significantly older man, cheats on him and subsequently commits suicide. The eponymous heroine of *Effi Briest*, to be precise, dies a natural death but one that is occasioned by the stresses of her unenviable situation. Although volumes have been written about the various nineteenth-century novels of adultery and the politics of gender that are inherent in them, none have as of yet analyzed the adultery plots from the perspective of nationalism and imperialism that imbued the time period of these novels' literary dominance. Relying on the long history of gendering nations as female, the present volume offers a reading of the adulterous woman of nineteenth-century European fiction as a symbol of national anxieties.

The notion of adultery as an international crisis played out in miniature within the confines of a nuclear family becomes almost obvious if we consider the fact that some of the world's best-known novels of adultery portray the home-wrecking lover figure as a national outsider. As the subsequent chapters show, the triangular love constellations depicted in these novels are not random, but rather they reflect the political tensions taking place between different European nations at the time. The first part of this book, "Empires," examines three masterpieces that belong to the canon of world literature: England's beloved *Middlemarch*, the novel par excellence of German realism, *Effi Briest*, and Russia's famous *Anna Karenina. Middlemarch* is a novel in which no actual sexual betrayal occurs, but it is as close to the novel of adultery as the nineteenth-century English literary tradition gets and, as such, is frequently compared to *Anna Karenina* and *Effi Briest* in the critical literature.[3] The heroines of both the English and the German novel are tempted by a lover of Polish origins, while Anna's lover, Count Vronsky, embodies everything that the author considers inauthentic (i.e., westernized) about Russian aristocracy, including its desire to liberate the South Slavs from Ottoman rule. If Russia's war against the Ottoman Empire forms the political backdrop—and even interferes with the publication, as chapter 3 shows—of *Anna Karenina*, *Middlemarch* unfolds in the wake of England's support of Polish insurrections against Russia, while *Effi Briest* operates in the context of hostile neighbor relations between the newly unified Germany and its Polish provinces. All three of the authors included in the first part of this study had written other novels that have been considered each author's major work on the nation and, by extension, the empire that it oversees. While I address these, more straightforwardly national novels as well, the book as a whole is an invitation to read in George Eliot's case not only *Daniel Deronda* but also *Middlemarch*, in Theodor Fontane's not only *Vor dem Sturm* (though this novel is hardly known even in Germany) but also *Effi Briest*, and, finally, in Tolstoy's case not only *War and Peace* but also *Anna Karenina* as novels of empire.

Looking at the adultery novels of empires from the perspective of national tensions naturally calls for a corresponding examination of the literary output from the occupied territories that subsisted in between and on the fringes of those empires and generated those tensions. The second part of the book, "Nations," complements the first part by turning to the novels of the very regions that spawn—or are otherwise associated with, as in the case of Vronsky—the lover figures who disturb the peace of respectable English, German, and Russian families. Serbia, Croatia, and Poland had their own thriving if not always internationally recognized realist traditions and canonical works that defined them. Moreover, unlike the literary fiction composed in the centers of empires, the works emerging from subjugated nations played indispensable political roles in raising the national consciousness of their reading populace and bolstering their national liberation movements. Although neither the South Slavic nor the Polish realist movements produced the typical novel of adultery with the plot conventions established by *Ma-*

dame Bovary, their key works nevertheless rely on the trope of adultery to convey their patriotic message. Precisely because these novels utilize adultery in a politically significant way, they provide a necessary answer to the more mainstream novels whose adultery plots I contextualize politically for the first time.

The two novels of stateless nations that I analyze in this book are the inaugural novel of Croatian realism, *The Goldsmith's Gold*, and Poland's international best seller, *Quo Vadis*, both of whose plots are propelled by a love triangle that, as in the novels of empires, reflects the political crisis of their age. Rather than present a sexually tempted or transgressing heroine, each novel associates adultery with the heroine's nemesis, who comes from the ruling caste. The heroine herself—unlike Dorothea Brooke of *Middlemarch*, Effi Briest, or Anna Karenina, all of whom inhabit the upper echelons of society—comes from the impoverished class or belongs to a conquered people. The social status of the heroines of all five novels, then, is indicative of the political status of their respective geographic regions. If in the novels of empires it is the ethnically dubious lover figure who endangers the marital bonds of the aristocratic couple, then in the novels of stateless nations it is the heroine's adulterous nemesis who threatens her romantic union with the novel's hero. In both the Croatian and the Polish novel the role of the adulterous woman is played by the unfaithful wife of a ruling male figure, which makes her comparable to Effi Briest and Anna Karenina, since both of them are married to highly placed government officials. Even the scholarly project of Dorothea Brooke's vicar husband, a book titled *The Key to All Mythologies*, implies a sort of world dominance. It is important to note, however, that the difference between the two types of adulterous women is the difference between the pursued in the "Empires" section and the pursuer in "Nations." Ladislaw fantasizes of rescuing Dorothea from the "dragon who had carried her off to his lair,"[4] Crampas is known as a notorious womanizer around town in *Effi Briest*, and seducing Anna becomes the "исключительно одно желанье" (one exclusive desire) of Vronsky's life (*PSS* 18:157). Conversely, in the literatures of the "nations in waiting"[5] the empire is evil and its immorality is highlighted through its sexually aggressive female representative. She uses both her beauty and her political clout to attempt to woo the hero away from his beloved and into doing the bidding of the empire, thereby diverting his energies from improving the lot of the subjugated nation.

While a Serbian work may have made for a better complement to the Russian novel that sends its heroine's seducer to fight the Turks in Serbia, the case is such that no suitable Serbian novel exists. To be sure, there is no dearth of Serbian realist novels, but none stands out as a work employing the trope of adultery in the way I analyze it in this project. The reason for this absence must, at least partially, be the fact that the Ottoman Empire was never anthropomorphized as a bewitching woman in the literature of the South Slavs, as the western empires were. Even in the literature of Serbian realism, the temptress is, as revealed in the title of a short story by Laza Lazarević, which I discuss at the end of chapter 4, a "Švabica" (German girl). The history of Croatia, like that of other South Slavic regions, involves numerous battles against the Ottoman Empire and the accompanying national epics that celebrate their heroism. August Šenoa is especially significant in the latter regard for his turning away from the popular literary genre and developing the novel, in which he warns against the nation's reliance on Austria and its use of Croatian soldiers as Turkish cannon fodder. His work also presents a valuable follow-up to the Russian novel because he promoted an alternative to the Slavophile/Westernizer binary that dominated Russian intellectual thought of the nineteenth century by calling for the South Slavs scattered among the Habsburg and Ottoman Empires to unite into their own state. The solution to statelessness as advocated by Šenoa, then, not only for Croatia, but also for the neighboring nations whose autonomy was secured by Russian intervention, was not a reliance on a powerful big brother, but a strengthening by means of sheer numbers based on a common cultural and linguistic identity.

As the subsequent chapters inevitably demonstrate, compared to the plethora of secondary material that is available for informing the discussion of the three novels of empires, the Croatian and the Polish novel have engendered meager scholarship. The Croatian novel, which has only recently been translated into English for the first time,[6] has been examined mostly by Croatian scholars working at Croatian universities. More surprisingly, the Polish novel, which secured its author international fame and a Nobel Prize, and was even the subject of a hugely successful Hollywood motion picture in the early 1950s, also yields very little by way of critical engagement. The vast disparity between the amount of mainstream critical attention devoted to the key works of English, German, and Russian literature and to those of Croatian and Polish literature accurately reflects the inequality between those countries in terms of their political and economic power. A mere glance at the theories of realism and the novel reveals that what they group under those categories are the realist movements and the novels of empire. Georg Lukács's definition of the "historico-philosophical" milieu of the novel as one of "transcendental homelessness" is one very telling example,[7] since the Polish and South Slavic realists lived and wrote under conditions of literal homelessness, in the sense that their nations were not possessed of a state. Including the two lesser-known novels here alongside the three world classics provides an initial step toward filling that gap. The tactic is also necessary for bringing my study thematically full circle, as the last two chapters examine the novels produced in the regions whose characters and political upheavals cause familial strife in the novels examined in the first three chapters. In addition, it allows a couple of key works from "minor" or "peripheral" literatures to speak back to both the canon and the empire, with adultery as the point of convergence.

The most frequently cited monograph on the topic of the unfaithful wife remains Tony Tanner's *Adultery in the Novel: Contract and Transgression* (1979), and I use it as my point of departure. Other articles and books on individual novels of adultery, needless to say, have been published since, and I refer to many of them here. When it comes to taking up the subject across different national literatures, however, despite a couple of more recent comparative treatises, Tanner's still stands out as the most widely recognized one.[8] His study covers about a century's worth of time just before adultery became, as Tolstoy put it, "the favorite . . . theme of all novels" and the plot sequence in which adultery leads to death was established; it begins with Jean-Jacques Rousseau's 1761 *Julie, ou la nouvelle Héloïse* (Julie, or the New Heloise), continues with Johann Wolfgang von Goethe's 1809 *Wahlverwandtschaften* (Elective Affinities), and ends with the trendsetting *Madame Bovary*. Tanner's most valuable suggestion for the study of adultery in fiction is to examine "the connections or relationships between a specific kind of sexual act, a specific kind of society, and a specific kind of narrative."[9] His take on the sexual act of adultery privileges the category of class, specifically the bourgeoisie and its mores, which is why an analysis of *Madame Bovary* constitutes the appropriate ending for his book. The placement of Rousseau's *La nouvelle Héloïse* and Goethe's *Wahlverwandtschaften* under the bourgeoisie umbrella, it ought to be noted, has not gone unnoticed, and at least one reviewer took issue with this grouping.[10] The overarching theme that holds the three novels together in Tanner's framework is the compulsion to order. This compulsion is evident in the bourgeois society's tendency to "enforce unitary roles on its members," which means that adultery becomes a "bad multiplicity within the requisite unities of social order."[11] Tanner emphasizes the bourgeoisie's obsession with "taxonomy and categorization,"[12] which is why Eduard and Charlotte's never-ending improvements to their estate in *Elective Affinities* support his central argument so well, even though the couple is of a much higher economic crust. If the bourgeois reading is misapplied to the novels of adultery that precede *Madame Bovary*, it cannot be applied to those that follow either. The central characters of *Madame Bovary*'s most famous successor, *Anna Karenina*, belong to the enormously wealthy Russian landed gentry and the family of *Effi Briest* inhabits the upper echelons of Prussian society. Even *Middlemarch*, whose subtitle is *A Study of Provincial Life*—similar in that vein to *Madame Bovary*'s *Moeurs de province* (Provincial Manners)—informs us regarding its heroine on the first page of the first chapter that "the Brooke connections, though not exactly aristocratic, were unquestionably 'good': if you inquired backward for a generation or two, you would not find any yard-measuring or parcel-tying forefathers—anything lower than an admiral or clergyman" (7). The rise of the bourgeoisie, however, had enormous consequences for the development of national identity with its concomitant anxieties, and these are reviewed below.

In tracing the literary history of adultery in his introduction, Tanner observes that the first stories on the theme portray the act as threatening to entire civilizations (such as Paris and Helen's) and societies (such as Launcelot and Gwenyver's), whereas in the nineteenth-century novel the destruction is focused on the nuclear family and typically on the adulteress herself. My own reading of the nineteenth-century novel of adultery in a way returns to the ancient theme of threatened civilizations, which is why Ferida Duraković's poem, though written about the dissolution of Yugoslavia at the end of the twentieth century, is the appropriate epigraph for a study of nineteenth-century national anxieties as rendered through a sexual metaphor. While heroines of Anna's or Effi's ilk do not provoke war—or launch a thousand ships, to use Christopher Marlowe's poetic phrase—like Helen of Troy does, they are linked, through their lovers, with the wars their nations do fight, whether it be to liberate another people (such as the South Slavs in Anna's case) or to subjugate them (such as the Poles in Effi's). Dorothea's second husband, as the grandson of a Polish refugee, is connected to the country's partitions and its subsequent uprisings, which England supported. In the Croatian and Polish novel the link between adultery and threatened civilizations is even stronger, since the adulteress herself, a symbol of the overpowering empire, actually threatens the survival of the subjugated nation, her ire inflamed by the hero's rejection of her in favor of a woman with an inferior pedigree.

Other kinds of social anxieties can be detected in the portrayal of other kinds of sexual breaches, as Tanner remarks, though he does not develop the idea further: "Earlier fiction, particularly in the eighteenth century, abounds in seduction, fornication and rape, and it would be possible to show how these particular modes of sexual 'exchange' were related to differing modes of economic exploitation or simply different transactional rules between classes or within any one class."[13] Building on this insight, I wish to point out that the very rise of the novel as a literary genre in eighteenth-century England did, in fact, coincide with a major shift in class structure, that is, as Ian Watt has famously shown, with the rise of the middle class. This structural shift, together with the anxieties it generated, is mirrored in the topics those first novels address. It is not coincidental that all three authors in the subtitle of Watt's work, *The Rise of the Novel: Studies in Defoe, Richardson and Fielding*, depict impoverished protagonists—such as the eponymous heroines in Daniel Defoe's *Moll Flanders* and Samuel Richardson's *Pamela*, as well as the eponymous hero in Henry Fielding's *Tom Jones*—who transgress class boundaries through sexual relations and marital unions with members of the aristocracy. The rise of the middle class, the very demographic whose literary imagination came to subsist on these works, threatened the previously firmly established class demarcations and, more specifically, the width of the gap between them. The fears associated with the narrowing of this gap are embedded in the stories where the wider gap is crossed through sexual liaisons and, most terrifyingly of all, liaisons that elevate a servant girl to the status of an aristocrat's wife. The seduction or rape of a servant girl by one of her male employers was not an uncommon occurrence—this is precisely what Pamela Andrews's parents fear when they learn from her letters of Mr. B's attentions—but a marriage between the two indicated a collapse in class structure and suggested class mobility, which is precisely the kind of threat that the rise of the middle class posited.

As various scholars of nationalism have amply demonstrated, "the formal universality of nationality as a socio-cultural concept"[14] was made possible by the rise of the middle class and, in fact, replaced class as the operative form of identification. In outlining what he sees as the necessary precursor to the birth of nationalism, Ernest Gellner describes "a path from the agrarian world, in which culture underwrites hierarchy and social position, but does not define political boundaries, to the industrial world in which culture *does* define boundaries of states, but where it is standardized, and hence insensitive, non-discriminating with respect to social position."[15] "It was thus natural," Eric Hobsbawm argues regarding the half century leading up to World War I, "that the classes within society, and in particular the working class, should tend to identify themselves through nation-wide political movements or organizations ('parties'), and equally natural that de facto these should operate essentially within the confines of the nation."[16] Commenting on the period preceding this shift, Hannah Arendt describes eighteenth-century "nobles who did not regard themselves as representatives of the nation, but as a separate ruling caste which might have much more in common with a foreign people of the 'same society and condition' than with its compatriots."[17] One of these eighteenth-century nobles, the famous German poet, playwright, and philosopher Friedrich von Schiller encapsulated the idea in a footnote to the fifteenth of his *Letters on the Aesthetic Education of Man* (1795). Recounting the various national pastimes in cities like London and Madrid, he observes that "there is far less uniformity among the amusements of the common people in these different countries than there is among those of the refined classes in those same countries."[18] The eventual faltering of class boundaries necessitated national identity as a new means of social cohesion, since, as Hobsbawm shows, "from the 1870s onwards it became increasingly obvious that the masses were becoming involved in politics and could not be relied upon to follow their masters."[19] Hobsbawm's choice of the 1870s as the point of demarcation coincides with the publication dates of the novels under my consideration, whose heroines come under threat from a national outsider rather than an unscrupulous master, as they do in the novels that comprise Watt's study. Arendt's observation, somewhat humorous in its bluntness, that the newly emerged "bourgeoisie from the very beginning wanted to look down not so much on other lower classes of their own, but simply on other peoples,"[20] is evident in the transition from the eighteenth-century predominantly class-oriented novels to those of the nineteenth and especially later nineteenth century, in which national concerns predominate.

Hobsbawm's choice of the 1870s as the point of demarcation is also significant for my lack of inclusion of the foundational modern novel of adultery, *Madame Bovary*, in the present study. Tanner's evaluation of this 1857 masterpiece as "the most important and far-reaching novel of adultery in Western literature" might cause one to wonder whether the English, German, and Russian classics on the same topic could have even been possible without it.[21] Yet the key difference between the first and the three that followed in its wake is that Emma Bovary does not have a foreign lover or even one connected to a foreign cause, so neither of her two adulteries translates into a compromise of French national purity. At one point in the novel she even "retrouvait dans l'adultère toutes les platitudes du mariage" (rediscovered in adultery all the banality of marriage),[22] thus obliterating the difference between the two, between husband and lover, insider and outsider.

Hobsbawm's and, preceding his, Arendt's assessment of the difference between French and German nationalism is useful in shedding further light on the difference between *Madame Bovary* and its successors. According to Arendt, French nationalism was born out of class struggle, as opposed to a competitiveness with other nations, culminating in the storming of the Bastille and the French Revolution of 1789. Arendt invokes the writings of the Comte de Boulainvilliers, who "interpreted the history of France as the history of two different nations of which the one, of Germanic origin, had conquered the older inhabitants, the 'Gaules,' had imposed its laws upon them, had taken their lands, and had settled down as the ruling class."[23] Consequently, "the French brand of race-thinking [w]as a weapon for civil war," whereas, by contrast, "German race-thinking was invented in an effort to unite people against foreign domination" and was based on "a consciousness of common origins."[24] This "foreign domination" refers to Napoleon, whose conquests, needless to say, inspired other nationalisms all over Europe, including Russia, where it subsequently generated Tolstoy's other mammoth classic, *War and Peace*. Hobsbawm echoes Arendt when he identifies "the founding acts of the new régime" as the French Revolution for the French and the Franco-Prussian War for the Germans.[25]

Emma Bovary's adulteries turn out to be concomitant with the class-based nature of French nationalism. The bourgeois heroine engages in her first extramarital relationship with the wealthy Rodolphe, carries out a prolonged yet unconsummated romance with the merchant Lheureux, and has one more affair with the office clerk Léon. Her suicide, it is also important to remember, is not occasioned by guilt or shame over her infidelities, or because she sees no way out of a love triangle, but because she sees no way out of the monetary debt she has accrued.[26] The novel, therefore, both in its choice of Emma's lovers and in its reason for her tragic ending, reflects the peculiar, class-inflected "French brand of race-thinking," while the novels that follow in its path negotiate the boundaries of belonging vis-à-vis a lover figure whose national authenticity is in question.

The latter half of the nineteenth century witnessed what in 1878 George Eliot, the author of *Middlemarch*, described and welcomed as "the modern insistance on the idea of Nationalities."[27] It witnessed the height of imperialism and colonialism, as well as the national uprisings that inevitably followed, and it witnessed the rise of the modern nation-state, the unification of Italy in 1861 and the unification of Germany in 1871. Replacing class, uniformity began to be viewed on the level of nationality and distinction as existing between various nationalities, which now, like individual humans, each acquired its own "character." My inquiry into the role that gender and gender relations play in defining the concept of nation and negotiating its boundaries has partly been inspired by the observation that prominent scholars of nationalism have employed the former to emphasize the importance of the latter. Benedict Anderson, for example, postulates that "in the modern world everyone can, should, will 'have' a nationality, as he or she 'has' gender."[28] The analogy is pertinent to my examination of the novel of adultery because the subgenre flourished at a time when "having" a nationality first grew to unprecedented importance but also at a time when mending the inequality between the genders first became a matter of serious debate. If the proliferation of the novel of adultery revealed the anxieties associated with the burgeoning Woman Question, then the concomitant "insistance on the idea of Nationalities" reverberated in those novels where the lover who lures the heroine away from home and hearth also happens to be of the "wrong" nationality. In defining the nation as the marriage of state and culture, Gellner creates an analogy even more pertinent to both the theme of the unfaithful wife and that of the anxious nation: "Just as every girl should have a husband, preferably her own, so every culture must have its state, preferably its own."[29] The conflict that propels the plots in the novels of empires is created by the girl who is unhappy with the husband that is her own and, therefore, vulnerable to the advances of one who is not. (Incidentally, both Effi's and Anna's unhappy marriage is the direct consequence of their society's strong conviction that every girl should have a husband, as each is pushed into a union with a man she barely knows, let alone loves, Effi by her parents and Anna by an aunt.) In the case of *Middlemarch* and *Effi Briest*, the other man comes from a culture that does not have a state but is desperately trying to acquire one, which in turn makes the empire vulnerable to political disasters. Anna Karenina's lover, on the other hand, is guilty of fully embracing the foreign culture that had been imposed by the state since the time when Peter the Great westernized Russia, and further guilty of joining the movement that pushes the empire into war, one whose purpose is to grant other oppressed cultures their own states. The novels emerging from the stateless cultures, finally, allegorize their political woes through the figure of the wicked woman who has a husband of her own but pursues another's husband-to-be and, by implication, further thwarts the subjugated culture's strivings for a state of its own.

Returning to Tanner's invitation to seek out the "relationships between a specific kind of sexual act, a specific kind of society, and a specific kind of narrative," it is worth considering that the political relationship between the European empires and their overseas colonies has frequently been sexualized through the trope of rape. Rape has been employed both in narratives justifying colonial oppression, by depicting the native male population as a threat to white womanhood, and in narratives critiquing imperial conquest, by depicting the subjugated land as metaphorically raped by the European invaders.[30] While the relationship between the European empires and their colonies has generated an enormous amount of scholarship and defined the field of postcolonial studies, the so-called semicolonialism occurring on the European continent—such as the Polish partitions by Austria, Prussia, and Russia or the Habsburg and Ottoman occupations of South Slavic lands—has begun to be explored only in the last couple of decades, the scholarship seemingly spurred by the end of the Cold War. *Adulterous Nations* belongs in this newer category and brings to it a gendered inflection, one that has heretofore only been explored in classic, that is, global-scale East versus West, postcolonial theory.

I borrow the term "semicolonialism" from Maria Todorova's work on the Balkans. Hers is one of the two monographs that were published shortly after the Cold War ended, in the 1990s, and have addressed, taking their lead from Edward Said's famous *Orientalism*, conceptions of otherness between East and West on the European continent itself. While Larry Wolff's *Inventing Eastern Europe* encompasses a larger geographic swath and, therefore, plays a greater role in chapter 1, which discusses English attitudes toward both Poland and Russia, Todorova's *Imagining the Balkans* is valuable for the entire scope of the book. Although her area of investigation is the Balkan peninsula, some of her key conclusions can easily be applied to Poland, such as "the issue of the Balkans' semicolonial, quasi-colonial, but clearly not purely colonial status"[31] and the observation that "unlike orientalism, which is a discourse about an imputed opposition, balkanism is a discourse about an imputed ambiguity."[32] The difference between "opposition" and "ambiguity" is the difference between "colonial" and "semicolonial," between a European empire's subjects in Africa or the Indian subcontinent and those in Poland or the Balkan provinces of southeastern Europe. Todorova notes the prevalence of the prefix "semi-" in popular descriptions of the Balkans–"semideveloped, semicolonial, semicivilized, semioriental"[33]—and these are, again, equally applicable to the perception of Poland by Western Europe, especially by Germany, whose close proximity to its Polish semicolony made the need for differentiation all the more urgent. In addition, Germany's dearth of overseas colonies and the resulting insecurity vis-à-vis England, as chapter 2 shows, marks the last term on Todorova's list–semioriental—especially significant in the adultery tale of *Effi Briest.* Both Effi's lover and Dorothea's second husband are semicolonial in the sense that they are perceived as European-yet-not-quite-European by the Prussians and the English among whom they live.

Although an imperial equal, Russia also endured, as Larry Wolff shows, using phrasing similar to Todorova's, "demi-Orientalization" by the West, whose diplomats wrote about the "demi-savages" they encountered there.[34] The Russians' self-definition was divided in the nineteenth century, as stated previously in regard to Šenoa's alternative vision, between the Slavophile and the Westernizer camp. The Slavophiles emphasized Russia's uniqueness and promoted a return to its autochthonous culture, while the Westernizers promoted reform and progress based on the English and French models. It is within this divide that the notion of *semi* becomes useful in my reading of *Anna Karenina*. The heroine's westernized lover, insofar as he falls short of Tolstoy's national ideal, is semi-Russian or, to rephrase an earlier construction, Russian-yet-not-quite-Russian. He is, therefore, appropriately sent off to fight—and, we are led to believe, die—for the liberation of the Balkan semicolonies from Ottoman rule.

Just as the term "colonialism" does not seem entirely fitting for describing the conquests and exploitation that took place within Europe, so rape as a sexual metaphor does not seem quite appropriate for capturing the relationship between European empires and their semicolonies. Rape is not commonly utilized in the fiction of the era, whether it be fiction produced by the oppressor or by the oppressed, nor has it been employed as a theoretical tool in the scholarly literature. Rather, it seems to be adultery, based on its prevalent use in the nineteenth-century novels of both the empires and their semicolonies, that constitutes the suitable sexual metaphor for the political relationship between the two. Tanner's most fruitful observation for my work in this regard is the etymological link he notes between "adultery" and "adulteration," the latter implying that something—a family unit at face value, but the nation in my reading—has been polluted or contaminated.[35] The fear of adulteration is especially relevant to nations inhabiting the same continental space and was felt acutely by those empires that ruled contiguous territories, which placed them in close proximity to their subjects. The overseas colonies were not only separated by geographic distances from the centers that governed them; their inhabitants could also be conceptually distanced from those centers based on racial differences. The inhabitants of the semicolonized regions on the European continent, on the other hand, did not look all that different from those in power, although efforts were certainly made to differentiate, orientalize, and even simianize them. A look at the relations between contiguous regions of unequal power reveals that vague similarity is often experienced as much more threatening than clearly delineated difference. This was not only the case for those in power, since, as the last two chapters of this book show, the fear of adulteration went both ways. The oppressed nations fighting for independence also had to fight the many temptations to "sell out," especially when currying favor with one empire seemed to promise protection from another or when belonging under the umbrella of a particular empire afforded one the veneer of being more "civilized" than one's neighbors. Todorova also brings up the notion of pollution, as used by Mary Douglas, in discussing Western perceptions of the Balkans. If "objects or ideas that confuse or contradict cherished classifications provoke pollution behavior that condemns them,"[36] then this conclusion holds true as much for the odd in-between status of a semicolony as it does for a third person in a marriage. Both defy classification; both adulterate set categories.

A point of clarification in the terminology *empire* and *nation* is in order. An empire, by definition, consists of multiple nations, but only one of those is in an incontestable position of privilege, while the others are disadvantaged to various degrees. The example of the British Empire, with the English in charge, is probably the most widely familiar. The case of the German Empire is slightly different. Prussia, whose three successful wars—against Denmark in 1864, Austria in 1866, and France in 1870—secured German unification, was clearly in charge and could, in that sense, be compared to England in the British Empire. There is no question, however, that Bavaria, even during Bismarck's vehement anti-Catholic campaign, fared immeasurably better than Ireland did under English rule; in fact, a comparison of the two seems rather ridiculous. Poland in respect to Prussia would make for a much more apt comparison with Ireland in respect to England, including the efforts of the dominant nation to draw racial distinctions between itself and the nation that it subjugated. Austria is yet another differing example as its empire's internal problems led to the *Ausgleich* with Hungary in 1867, which resulted in the creation of the Austro-Hungarian Empire. The nations on both sides of that hyphen were a source of threat or "adulteration" for nineteenth-century Croatians, as shown in chapter 4. Russia stands out among all of these as a nation whose territory was significantly larger—because of, to quote from *Anna Karenina*, the "огромные незанятые пространства" (vast unoccupied spaces) (*PSS* 18:362) that Siberia comprises—than the sum of the colonies it possessed, though its centers of power and culture were located in its smaller, European part.

If both the center and the periphery fear national adulteration, then the "national" in that phrase refers both to the nations without states and to the ruling nations within empires. The multiethnic empire is by definition adulterated, and it is its privileged nation that fears adulteration from the periphery, as the independence-seeking periphery does from the center. The appearance of the quarter Polish Will Ladislaw in *Middlemarch*, for example, does not threaten the British Empire, but rather his pursuit of the English heroine threatens England, which she embodies. *Effi Briest*'s half Polish Major Crampas does not threaten the German Empire, as he lives under and supports its dominion. He crosses both ethical and ethnic lines, however, and contaminates Prussia when he seduces the novel's eponymous Prussian heroine. Conversely, when the cuckolded Karenin drafts a solution to a rebellion occurring in one of Russia's colonies—significantly, as chapter 3 argues, in the same evening that he writes a letter to his unfaithful wife—he is dealing with a problem that belongs to the empire and to the Russian nation as its primary agent. Even when I write of empires, then, the fears I analyze as expressed in their novels of adultery are national fears.

I use the term "nationalism" to indicate both the concern of the dominant nation within the empire to protect its advantageous position and the desire of the subjugated nations to win independence. Since Poland plays a large role in the book, I also wish to heed the warning of one of America's great Polonists, Andrzej Walicki, that in Poland "nationalism" is "a pejorative term, meaning, approximately, the same as chauvinism, narrow national egoism, state expansionism, intolerant attitudes towards national minorities, and so forth." Walicki points out that nineteenth-century Poles used the term "patriotism" and that today "the average educated Pole would be surprised and indignant if he were told that Adam Mickiewicz was not only the greatest Polish poet but also one of the greatest Polish 'nationalists.'"[37] Therefore, when discussing Poland, I have taken care to employ the terms "patriots" and "patriotism." Nationalism has acquired especially negative connotations among the South Slavs over the past few decades, when it occasionally became synonymous with ethnic cleansing because of the violent disintegration of Yugoslavia. Since the critical literature on the national awakening of nineteenth-century South Slavs employs the term "nationalism," however, I continue to use it in chapter 4.

The Woman Nation, the Chosen Nation, and the Adulterous Nation

The anthropomorphizing of nations, empires, and the earth itself as female has a long history, evident in expressions ranging from "Mother Earth" to

"Mother Russia." This latter expression—*mat' Rossiia*—might be the best known and most widely used example of gendered nations; as chapter 3 elaborates, it is closely related to the veneration of the Mother of God in Russian Orthodoxy. The case is the same for Catholic countries. The medieval Polish knights sang the anthem "Gaude Mater Polonia" (Rejoice, Mother Poland) at a time when Poland was a European force to be reckoned with, while Poland's favorite romantic poet, Adam Mickiewicz, mourned its death in the 1830 poem "Do Matki Polki" (To Mother Poland) as well as in the 1834 epic poem *Pan Tadeusz*, which contains the following poignant line: "O Matko Polsko! Ty tak świeżo w grobie / Złożona—nie ma sił mówić o tobie!" (O Mother Poland! Thou wast so lately laid in the grave. No man has the strength to speak of thee!).[38] One of Croatia's most popular patriotic songs is titled and begins with the words, "Rajska Djevo, Kraljice Hrvata" (Heaven's Virgin, Queen of the Croats). Composed by a Catholic priest who was murdered during World War II by the pro-Yugoslav *partizani*, it quickly regained its popularity after Communism fell and Croatia declared independence.[39] Anglican England is also known as "Mother England" and the British Isles as "Mother Britannia."[40] Germany, of the countries addressed in the current project, is the only one more commonly known as *das Vaterland* (the fatherland), but even so, its anthropomorphized embodiment is Germania. When Theodor Fontane, the author of *Effi Briest*, had a discussion about Bismarck's unification of Germany with fellow writer Friedrich Theodor Vischer, the latter expressed his dislike of the chancellor thus: "It pains me that it should be precisely Bismarck who succeeded. I wrote recently that Germany, after the German Michel had wooed her in vain with his songs, fell finally to the boldness of a Prussian Junker. He grabbed and had her."[41]

"The German Michel" is the male personification of Germany, as John Bull is of England or Uncle Sam of the United States of America, and these male images need to be addressed as well. They may be as ubiquitous as the female images, but they are less compelling, especially when it comes to rallying cries and mobilizing people on behalf of a nation. Uncle Sam may "want you," but a distressed Lady Liberty is more likely to stir men to action. And this—stirring *men* to action—is where the crux of the difference lies. Patriotic rhetoric is imbued with (hetero)sexual allusions. A nation, like a woman, is an entity for which men will live and die—as do, for example, Anna Karenina's husband and lover, respectively—and whose honor they will pledge to defend. Traditionally, and still overwhelmingly, it has been men who have built, conquered, and defended, as well as theorized, the nation, from statesman to soldier to scholar. The last category brings to mind the tireless efforts of the aforementioned Polonist Andrzej Walicki to make Polish history better known in the West. In the introduction to his *Philosophy and Romantic Nationalism: The Case of Poland*, he writes, "Poland was for centuries the most important country of this area [East Central Europe] and *her* intellectual history provides many keys to a better understanding not only of *her* own history, but of European history as a whole. . . . [A] true Slavist, even if *he* specializes in Russian history, should be able to see *his* subject in an all-Slavonic perspective."[42] Walicki merely follows the long-established convention of referring to a nation in the feminine and a human professional in the masculine, but it is hard to deny that the particular gender distribution increases the emotional potency of the appeal, as it calls upon (male) scholars to rescue (female) Poland from oblivion. Walicki's book was published in 1982, but even as recently as 2008, there was a vigorous debate on the listserv for Slavic scholars, SEELANGS, on whether Russia should be referred to as "she" or "it." [43] Compared to the female images of the nation, the male images tend to be caricatures, as is immediately apparent in the contrast between visual representations of Uncle Sam and Lady Liberty, or the chubby John Bull and the regal Britannia. And, when the nation is in danger, she is usually a woman being attacked by a male and in need of male defense. As formulated by Vischer, Michel "wooed" Germany, whereas Bismarck "grabbed and had her." To use an example closer to home, a popular nineteenth-century U.S. Southern secessionist banner depicts the federal government as the bald eagle, aiming his beak at two women who represent the Southern states. The caption placed between the eagle and the woman next to him reads, "touch her if you dare," which is undoubtedly the utterance of the Southern armies, proclaiming their readiness to defend "her."

In discussing "the invention of tradition" that supported the rise of the nation-state, Eric Hobsbawm offers a valuable distinction between male and female images of the nation, using France and Germany as examples. The French Marianne, he claims, is "the image of the Republic itself" and separate from, though usually accompanied by, "the bearded civilian figures of whoever local patriotism chose to regard as its notables, past and present."[44] In the same vein, the German Michael "belongs to the curious representation of the nation, not as a country or state, but as 'the people', which came to animate the demotic political language of the nineteenth-century cartoonists, and was intended (as in John Bull and the goateed Yankee—but *not* in Marianne, image of the Republic) to express national character, as seen by the members of the nation itself."[45] The female images, then, embody the nation "as a country or a state" or "the Republic," whereas the male images embody the nation's subjects, either as a whole or through individual representations of famous men who brought her glory.

Hobsbawm's distinction in meanings behind the male and female images of the nation illuminates my analysis of the role of gender in the novelistic expression of national anxieties, specifically in the novels of empires, which are, after all, the immediate subject of Hobsbawm's inquiry in the chapter I have been referencing. The sympathetic, even beloved female protagonist, who functions in my reading as the embodiment of the nation, finds herself stifled from the one end by the lackluster husband, typically one who in some shape or form works on the empire's behalf, and pursued from the other end by an outsider, who is perceived as a national threat. The gender distribution is different in the novels of stateless nations because the imminent threat comes from the dominant empire, which is appropriately embodied in another female figure. The hero in that case, as the expression of "national character," to use Hobsbawm's phrase, is the one pulled in opposite directions, between fighting for the subjugated nation's sovereignty and serving the evil empire.

Parenthetically, my observation of the female images of the nation as regal and the male as caricatures—the latter supported by Hobsbawm's reference to "the demotic political language of the nineteenth-century cartoonists"—is visible in the portrayal of some of the characters in the novels of empires. Dorothea Brooke, for example, is compared in the very opening of *Middlemarch* to "the Blessed Virgin" as depicted by "Italian painters," and her simple yet dignified appearance is contrasted to "provincial fashion" as "a fine quotation from the Bible—or from one of our elder poets,—in a paragraph of to-day's newspaper" (7). Dorothea's first husband, on the other hand, truly is merely the caricature of a scholar with his never-ending book project, while her second husband, at least in the beginning of the novel, is a romantic wanderer with no firm purpose in life. Anna Karenina is, before the affair unravels her, the epitome of class, grace, and poise, while the fleshless and bumbling Karenin is prone to being the object of mockery in his government committee meetings and Vronsky, who worries very much about appearing "смешным" (ridiculous) (*PSS* 18:136) in high Russian society, appears exactly so as soon as he lets his guard down and attempts to be a painter while traveling with Anna in Italy.[46]

The long history of gendering nations and similar collectivities as female can be traced all the way back to traditions that are considered foundational to modern European literatures and cultures. The ancient Greek myth of Europa's abduction by Zeus is one example. Another is the ancient Hebrew prophets' personification of Israel as a woman, often, more significantly for the project at hand, an adulterous woman. The biblical examples are especially relevant to the novels covered here because their authors were citizens of countries that were (and to a large extent still are) steeped in the Judeo-Christian tradition. The sacred Hebrew texts provided European Christian nations with the validation for considering themselves exceptional and with the conviction that they were the new Israel, a view that was used to justify not only a nation's right to exist but also its right to acquire the "promised land" and expel others from it. The term associated with this line of thinking is "replacement theology" or "supersessionism"—the idea that, since the ancient Jews rejected Jesus as the Messiah, the church has become the new

Israel and, hence, God's new chosen people. The idea was easily co-opted by imperialist rhetoric and is still alive and well today in American conservative Christian circles.[47]

The Puritans leaving England for Massachusetts in the seventeenth century were as convinced that they were establishing the new Israel as were the English back at home regarding their ancestors' settlement of the British Isles. The idea in England even reached a bizarre point over the course of the nineteenth century in the form of British or Anglo-Israelism—the notion that the Anglo-Saxons were the direct descendants of the lost tribes of Israel, who migrated to the Isles across Europe—which culminated in the founding of the Anglo-Israel Association in 1874. Examples of less extreme adaptations are numerous, but to offer just one from each side of the Atlantic, the English Diggers founder, Gerard Winstanley, pronounced that "the last enslaving conquest which the enemy got over Israel was the Norman over England,"[48] while the American Thomas Jefferson concluded his second inaugural address by calling upon "the favor of that Being . . . who led our fathers, as Israel of old, from their native land and planted them in a country flowing with all the necessities and comforts of life."[49] The ever perspicacious George Eliot commented on the tendency of both nations to appropriate Israel's history to suit their own political objectives in "The Modern Hep! Hep! Hep!," the same essay in which she described "the modern insistance on the idea of Nationalities":

> The Puritans, asserting their liberty to restrain tyrants, found the Hebrew history closely symbolical of their feelings and purpose; and it can hardly be correct to cast the blame of their less laudable doings on the writings they invoked, since their opponents made use of the same writings for different ends, finding there a strong warrant for the divine right of kings and the denunciation of those who, like Korah, Dathan, and Abiram, took on themselves the office of the priesthood which belonged of right solely to Aaron and his sons, or, in other words, to men ordained by the English bishops.[50]

While critical of the English and their belief in "a peculiar destiny as a Protestant people," in soliciting sympathy for the Jews Eliot still found it necessary to employ the same creed: "There is more likeness than contrast between the way we English got our island and the way the Israelites got Canaan."[51] Far from being unique to England or the United States, replacement theology, with its concept of the new Israel and the idea of exceptionalism that it fostered, was part and parcel of nationalist rhetoric across Europe. The empires that occupied the dominant positions on the continent and ruled other parts of the globe saw their political and economic advantage over others as proof of their chosenness. The subjugated nations, on the other hand, expected a future deliverance, a vanquishing of their enemies, and the full possession of their "promised land."

If the Old Testament portrays Israel as God's wife, and when "she" fails to obey God's law as an adulteress, then the New Testament carries on the gendered imagery by depicting the church as the bride of Christ. An especially potent New Testament female image, due to her role of mother, as stated previously, is the Virgin Mary, whose sexual purity bears relevance for the (desired) purity of the nation. An important antipodal image is one that is not typically opposed to the Virgin, the prostitute Mary Magdalene, but rather the Whore of Babylon from the last book of the New Testament, Revelation. Biblical scholars agree that the moniker was used as a code phrase for Rome by its persecuted Christians, which is why many a subjugated nation has employed it since. The Bible, then, has been a fecund source of national metaphors in European politics, and its various female images play a role in the novels discussed in this book. Male images of the Bible were also used for national purposes; there is the Hebrew Bible's Moses delivering his people from Egyptian bondage and his successor, Joshua, as well as the New Testament's figure of the Antichrist that was widely associated with Napoleon in the early nineteenth century. It was the female images, however, as already established, that symbolized the nation as an entity and effected the more potent patriotic emotions, from the revered Mother of God to the reviled Whore of Babylon.

The Geography of the Book

The novels that are the focus of the next five chapters were published in the 1870s (*Middlemarch*, *Anna Karenina*, *The Goldsmith's Gold*) and the 1890s (*Effi Briest* and *Quo Vadis*). I have opted to proceed in a particular geographic fashion instead of a straightforward chronological line for a couple of reasons. The more practical one is that I contextualize all of these novels in their authors' larger oeuvres and sometimes even in their national traditions, which would make it impossible to proceed chronologically without skipping back and forth from country to country. The chapter on *Effi Briest* includes the largest amount of discussion of the author's other novels because Fontane wrote several with adultery as the central topic; he also wrote a number that include Germany's Slavs in their plots and a couple in which the two threads are intertwined. The reading of his crowning masterpiece, therefore, would be impoverished if it were not preceded by the works that led up to it. Since August Šenoa, the author of *The Goldsmith's Gold*, supported the unification of the South Slavs into their own state, chapter 4 begins with a discussion of the preceding romantic period in which the movement was born and ends with a reading of a Serbian realist author whose portrayal of the Germanic West is comparable to Šenoa's.

The other reason for the geography of the book is that it felt appropriate for a study of national anxieties to follow the path of prejudice known as orientalism, or, more suitable for the spaces in the European continent, nesting orientalisms. This latter concept was developed by Milica Bakić-Hayden, who originally employed it for discussing the relationship between the republics of the former Yugoslavia. It describes the "gradation of 'Orients'" within a more geographically circumscribed area than Edward Said had in mind, that is, "a pattern of reproduction of the original dichotomy upon which Orientalism is premised."[52] Before the breakup of Yugoslavia inspired Bakić-Hayden's amendment of Said's famous notion, Julia Kristeva had already described a similar gradation of othering in *Strangers to Ourselves*. Although her geography does not proceed in a smooth West-to-East fashion, the idea is the same, especially in its iteration of the dichotomies between civilized and barbarian, rich and poor: "In France, Italians call Spaniards foreigners, the Spaniards take it out on the Portuguese, the Portuguese on the Arabs or the Jews, and the Arabs on the blacks and so on."[53] The way in which nesting orientalisms function among the empires covered in the present volume is that Germany, as a new competitor on the colonial scene, looked up to England, but the sentiment was not returned, since England perceived the unification of Germany as a threat and ridiculed its imperial aspirations. Both countries looked down on Russia, and, even though the English expressed sympathy with the Poles seeking independence from Russia as well as with the South Slavs seeking independence from the Ottoman Empire, all of these nations in the eastern half of Europe constituted for the West that barbaric remnant whose ethnic designation—Slav—is etymologically related to "slave" and other denigrating terms, such as "slovenly." It thus seemed logical to begin part 1, "Empires," with the novel from the most powerful empire of the time, the English, and from there to proceed eastward, from England to Germany and from Germany to Russia.

As discussed previously in reference to the work of Maria Todorova and Larry Wolff, Eastern Europe has been theorized as Europe's *other* within, and these theories play a role in the first two chapters of the book. The contrast posited in the previous sentence, between Eastern Europe and Europe, is typical of the idea that what we mean by Europe is really Western Europe, though the end of the Cold War and the gradual entry of the formerly Eastern Bloc states into the European Union has begun to change that. Wolff notes the appearance of the term "Central Europe," whose advocates, he claims, "are committed to shattering intellectually the oppressive idea of Eastern Europe, to redeeming the Czech Republic and Hungary, maybe Poland, even perhaps Slovenia."[54] Since the publication of Wolff's book in 1994 the advocates of "Central Europe" have undeniably accomplished their goal as Poles, Slovenes, and Croatians not only firmly identify themselves as Central Europeans, but feel offended at being called Eastern European and are quick to correct anyone who puts that label on them. The strong reaction testifies to the negative connotations the term "Eastern Europe" has acquired and shows, more generally, just how politically and socially loaded our geographic designations are. Since my book examines novels written in the last third of the nineteenth century, the period preceding by more than a century the invention of Central Europe (about which an entire follow-up to Wolff's seminal work could be written, as an analysis of the post–Cold War response to the West's invention of Eastern Europe), employing the new term would be anachronistic, so I use "Eastern Europe" when discussing both Poland and the South Slavic lands, even though I understand that it might grate on the ears of contemporary readers. It was the term in use during George Eliot's and Theodor Fontane's milieu, and using the "softer" variant would attenuate the meaning of the reaction elicited by the Slavic lover figures in their novels. Because of the ethnicity of those outsider lover figures, a review of each author's general attitude toward the Slavic world also forms an integral part of the first two chapters.

Poland, as it turns out, figures in all three chapters of "Empires" because, even though Poland is not the "problem" in *Anna Karenina*, *War and Peace*, which occupies a substantial portion of chapter 3, was written during the time of Poland's second insurrection against Russia. Poland may seem an odd choice for the chapter on the English novel, but it just so happens that the English novel most comparable to *Anna Karenina* and *Effi Briest* casts a Polish character in the lover's role. And while, as mentioned earlier, Ireland to England makes a better analogy for what Poland was to Germany (as well as to Russia), an English novel of adultery with an Irishman was not produced until D. H. Lawrence penned *Lady Chatterley's Lover* in 1928, that is, after the age of empires, the realist movement in literature, and the general novelistic fascination with adultery had already passed.

Part 2, "Nations," turns from Russia to the southwest and then moves north as it meanders through the provinces at the mercy of the empires discussed in part 1. Since chapter 3 discusses Russia's war with the Ottoman Empire on behalf of the South Slavs, South Slavic literature is the subject of chapter 4, and chapter 5 closes the circle with Poland, whose characters cause havoc in the novels of the first two chapters. Although the Ottoman Empire plays a role in both chapter 3 and chapter 4, its literature does not merit a chapter of its own because the Ottoman Empire did not participate in European culture in the way that Russia and its authors did. This difference between the two empires also accounts for why Russia was perceived as a greater threat to England. As summed up in a review of David Urquhart's *The Progress of Russia in the West, North, and South* for the *Westminster Review* in 1853, when George Eliot was its deputy editor: "The Russians are more insidious than the Ottomans three centuries before, because they are culturally and diplomatically involved with Europe."[55] While part 1 and part 2 are meant to complement one another, I attempt throughout the book to rub the various novels against one another, so to speak, and to put their authors in conversation, not only because their themes overlap, but also because some of the authors thought highly of one another, as Tolstoy did of Eliot and Fontane of Tolstoy.

Last, the Slavic theme that is common to all five chapters of this study is somewhat accidental, at least in the sense that the book was not originally conceived as one with a broad Slavic focus. With *Anna Karenina* as one of the world's best-known novels of adultery and with Poland playing a prominent role through the lover figure in the English and German novels of the same category, the Slavic theme emerged and spread. The theme is not so accidental, however, when one considers these novels in the larger political context of nineteenth-century imperialism and nationalism, which *was* the original intention of the book. German unification entailed a reconfiguring of the meaning of Poland in Prussian politics, which resulted in the reinterpretation of Poland as an acquired colony. In Russian politics Slavophilism, with its image of Russia as the leader, unifier, and protector of all Slavs, began to play a prominent role. The Poles were not sold on the idea as they launched two insurrections, the merciless quashing of which presented a crisis for Slavophilic rhetoric of magnanimity and inclusiveness. Conversely, the South Slavs under Ottoman rule found Slavophilism incredibly useful when they rebelled against their colonizer with the full expectation of Russia's aid, which was swiftly delivered. Other voices, suspicious of Russia's imperial designs, advocated the unification of South Slavs into their own separate state. From the western end of Europe England observed all these political upheavals and, fearing both German unification and Russian expansion, ardently supported Poland while wishing that South Slavic liberations would be less entangled with Russia. The age of empires and national revivals, then, was to a great extent a Slavic age. On the literary scene, those Slavic authors whose nations were struggling for independence employed the trope of adultery to symbolize their oppression, and the Slavic theme in the empires' novels of adultery reverberated as far as England.

Part I

Empires

Chapter 1

✦

Middlemarch

The English Heroine and the Polish Rebel(lions)

George Eliot's authorial trajectory mirrors the general historical shift of the novel's focus from class to nation that was described in the introduction. Deborah Nord, a scholar whose work on George Eliot I elaborate on below, identifies this trajectory as the author's shift of focus "from disinherited individual to disinherited nation."[1] Eliot's first novel, *Adam Bede* (1859), echoes the story lines of Defoe's and Richardson's well-known works as it depicts the seduction of a naive servant girl by a spoiled young squire. *Silas Marner* (1861) and *Felix Holt, the Radical* (1866) both engage class issues by featuring a person of humble origins who turns out to be an inheritor of a great fortune. It is not until Eliot's last two novels, *Middlemarch* (1871) and *Daniel Deronda* (1876), that ethnic outsiders become determining protagonists in the story—the first Polish and the second Jewish—and present romantic possibilities for the English heroines. The eponymous hero of *Daniel Deronda*, in fact, in a reversal of the typical plots mentioned above, is an English aristocrat who discovers and accepts his humble Jewish origins.

A possible reason for this shift in Eliot's focus may be the Second Reform Bill, which was passed in 1867, that is, after the writing of *Felix Holt* and before *Middlemarch*. The First Reform Bill, which was passed in 1832 and on which the actions in both these novels are centered, was largely a disappointment. Although it did almost double the franchise by extending it to the majority of the middle class and thus ending the aristocracy's exclusive hold on power, it ensured that political control remain tied to the land and its owners. The bill gave any adult male who owned or leased £10 worth of land the right to vote, but a tenant's dependence on his landlord still made him likely to vote the same way as his boss. The Second Reform Bill, which tripled the electorate and extended democracy to urban England, relieved a lot of the tensions that were the focus of Eliot's earlier novels.[2] Although *Felix Holt* and *Middlemarch* both cover the events surrounding the First Reform Bill, *Middlemarch* has the advantage of double hindsight as a work written after passage of the Second Reform Bill, which rectified the shortcomings of the First. *Middlemarch* addresses the Reform Bill and highlights class disparity by portraying the heroine's concern for the upgrading of tenants' cottages, but the main event that stirs up unrest in the novel is the appearance of a man of "foreign extraction" (336), who arouses suspicion among both the rich and the poor.

Although national concerns inform the latter part of George Eliot's career, her entire oeuvre demonstrates her ongoing interest in the Slavic world, an interest that has heretofore been grossly overlooked by George Eliot scholarship. While inquiries into her position vis-à-vis English colonialism abound, several excellent studies of her relationship to Germany exist, and there is even a monograph on her view of Italy, with the exception of one chapter on *Middlemarch* at the end of a book cleverly titled *The Other East and Nineteenth-Century British Literature*, not one major publication has been devoted to her portrayal of Europe's eastern half.[3] The western Slavs especially occupy Eliot's imagination, starting with Countess Czerlaski's dead husband in her first work of fiction, "The Sad Fortunes of the Rev. Amos Barton" (1857), and ending with Herr Klesmer and Mirah Lapidoth in her last novel, *Daniel Deronda*. It is *Middlemarch*, however, her best-known work, that features Will Ladislaw, a man marked by his "queer genealogy" (676) due to his Polish ancestry, as one of its main protagonists.

Middlemarch stands out from the rest of the novels discussed in this part of the book as one with a happy ending. In comparison to the unhappily married young women of *Anna Karenina*, *Effi Briest*, and *Madame Bovary*, the heroine of *Middlemarch*—Miss Dorothea Brooke, who becomes the unfortunate Mrs. Casaubon—not only survives the end of the novel, but her stifling old husband conveniently dies of a heart condition, which frees her to enjoy a happy second marriage without committing adultery. This observation must be tempered, however, with the reminder that the incriminating codicil to her first husband's will taints her second marriage with the aura of betrayal. The jealous Edward Casaubon, suspicious of his young wife's feelings for his younger cousin, decides to divest her of his fortune should she marry Will Ladislaw after his death. When her family members discuss Casaubon's dishonorable act and face their own fears as to the gossip that is about to ensue, her brother-in-law and former suitor, Sir James Chettam, worries that "the world will suppose that she gave him some reason" (455) for the will's codicil. Nevertheless, as far as the laws of church and state are concerned, Dorothea engages in no official breach in entering into her second, happy marriage. Her chief fault, as encapsulated by Sir James, is marrying "a man so marked out by her husband's will, that delicacy ought to have forbidden her from seeing him again—who takes her out of her proper rank—into poverty" (766). The disturber of marital and societal peace in *Middlemarch* also fares immeasurably better than his fictional counterparts; whereas Major Crampas gets shot in *Effi Briest* and Count Vronsky is sent off to war with Turkey in the epilogue of *Anna Karenina*, Will Ladislaw not only wins the girl but also a seat in Parliament. The primacy of *Middlemarch* in the English literary canon gives us all the more reason to investigate the novel's incorporation of a Pole of "dangerously mixed blood" (435) so intimately—sexually and politically—into its fabric.

Contemporary Scholarship on Eastern Europe

The opening of the Prelude to *Middlemarch* reads thus: "Who that cares much to know the history of man, and how that mysterious mixture behaves under the varying experiments of Time, has not dwelt, at least briefly, on the life of Saint Theresa" (3). Relying on this captivating first line in her introduction to *Middlemarch in the Twenty-First Century*, Karen Chase invites critics and readers to submit the novel itself to "the varying experiments of Time."[4] *Middlemarch* has, since its first appearance, primarily been associated with "the Woman Question," as has been typical for novels of adultery.[5] The novel's emphasis on reform, both political and medical, is another of its important topics that still lends itself to fruitful rereadings.[6] Finally, Eliot's interest in science, combined with her close relationship to Herbert Spencer, is inseparable from her fiction.[7] Ladislaw's mixed Polish blood will be shown to bear on all of the novel's major considerations just reviewed, and these will be addressed in light of recent scholarship on Eastern Europe, as well as scholarship from Eastern Europe. The changes wrought by "the varying experiments of Time" in Eastern Europe in the past couple of decades have yielded scholarship on the region that can illuminate not only Ladislaw's role in Middlemarch, both town and novel, but also the mostly negative reception he has encountered among both readers and critics.

Just as Edward Said makes a convincing claim that orientalism "has less to do with the Orient than it does with 'our' world,"[8] so Larry Wolff declares that "it was Western Europe that invented Eastern Europe as its complementary other half."[9] (Incidentally, beginning with Said is apropos, since in the introduction to his seminal work he recalls *Middlemarch* as a novel conscious of the role of German scholarship in the rise of orientalism and quotes Ladislaw's remark to Dorothea regarding her husband's scholarly limitations—specifically, his lack of knowledge of German—"He is not an Orientalist, you know.")[10] Wolff demonstrates how the conceptual boundary between civilization and barbarism in Europe was redrawn during the Enlightenment, from an axis separating the north from the south to one separating the west from the east. When the cultural centers of Europe were located in classical Greece and Rome, and later in Renaissance Italy, countries such as Poland and Russia were imagined as northern in European cultural geography. The rise of the French Empire and the influence of French philosophy in the eighteenth century shifted the axis as the philosophes began corresponding with Russian royalty and testing their political theories in the "experimental domain" of Eastern Europe.[11] Wolff's book offers a fascinating account of Voltaire's and Catherine the Great's admiration for each other, as well as Denis Diderot's visit to the (in)famous German empress of All the Russias. In contrast to these two French Russophiles, Wolff shows that Rousseau wrote essays in support of Poland, which was under Catherine's thumb at the time, while Catherine's famous lover, Grigory Orlov, invited the father of romanticism to discover the modern-day "noble savage" in Russia's peasants. Since Wolff shows that "Eastern Europe" is not a Cold War term but rather dates back to the eighteenth century, this means that it was influential in George Eliot's historical milieu and not merely a later designation that can retroactively be projected onto her fiction. The French and German Enlightenment thinkers, who played the major role of "inventing" Eastern Europe, did not depict the place so much as Western Europe's opposite—that function was fulfilled by non-Europeans—but rather, in the words of Wolff (borrowing from Honoré de Balzac's *La Cousine Bette*), as "the geographic frontier between Europe and Asia" and "the philosophical frontier between civilization and barbarism."[12] Although English intellectuals do not figure large in Wolff's work, they were undoubtedly influenced by their continental neighbors. George Eliot, as has been well established, was especially influenced by German thought, and I demonstrate in this chapter how this influence affected her portrayal of Ladislaw and other Eastern Europeans.

While English colonialism, as Said has shown, rested on a discourse of racial otherness that delineated a firm line between the empire and those of its subjects who lived outside of Europe's boundaries, Will Ladislaw, a descendant of "a Polish refugee who gave lessons for his bread" (343), muddles those categories. An offspring of a people whose Europeanness, whiteness, and other signifiers of power are unclear, he presents a curious epistemological problem for his fictional contemporaries. Neither a proper Englishman nor a colonial subject, he is marked by his already mentioned "dangerously mixed blood" and "queer genealogy," a topic of much debate among his Middlemarch neighbors. Ladislaw has been equally epistemologically problematic for Eliot's readers and critics, who have found him difficult to classify at best and just plain distasteful at worst. In a letter to John Blackwood dated September 19, 1873, Eliot relates the following humorous encounter she had with a couple of *Middlemarch* readers: "When I was at Oxford in May, two ladies came up to me after dinner: one said, 'How could you let Dorothea marry *that* Casaubon?' The other: 'O I understand her doing that; but why did you let her marry the other fellow, whom I cannot bear?'"[13] The latter of the two ladies, as it appears, could not even "bear" to mention Ladislaw's name; her substitution of the term "*other* fellow" is as apt for his reception as it is theoretically productive.

When it comes to Eliot's fellow authors, Henry James seemed downright offended by Ladislaw, famously pronouncing him, in his review of *Middlemarch* for the *Galaxy*, Eliot's "only eminent failure in the book." Ladislaw was, for James, "a woman's man"; he "lacks sharpness of outline and color" and "remains vague and impalpable to the end."[14] When it comes to more contemporary literary scholars, Jerome Beaty read him as a mere precursor to Daniel Deronda,[15] about whom later, and Deborah Nord has more recently assessed him within Eliot's oeuvre as a "transition from the largely figurative strangeness of Maggie Tulliver—and Silas Marner before her—to the actual, although hidden, foreign origins of both Fedalma and Daniel Deronda."[16] All of these assessments, ranging from the earliest responses to the novel to twenty-first-century scholarship, focus on the ambiguity of Will Ladislaw. They use a vocabulary reflective of the liminal identity that has characterized Eastern Europe, the space described as a philosophical and geographic "frontier" by Wolff and one endowed with, we recall from the introduction, "imputed ambiguity" according to Todorova.

It is surprising that neither the Cold War era of the twentieth century nor the more recently burgeoning age of cultural studies inspired more interest in the significance of Will Ladislaw's national heritage. The issue has been highlighted, as I discuss, by two scholars writing from a Polish university and for a Polish journal, but the "much abused young man"[17] has yet to come into his own in the mainstream Anglo-American academic conversation. The pervasive dislike of Ladislaw, George Eliot's most prominent character with connections to Eastern Europe, may be a possible reason for this neglect, as well as the neglect of the role of Eastern Europe more broadly in George Eliot scholarship.

Marrying a man of "bad origin" (766) and one for whom she must give up her widow's inheritance allows Dorothea Brooke to live out a smaller, domesticated version of the "epic life" (3) of St. Theresa within the limits—even if they are the outer limits—of Victorian decorum. It is a compromise with which her readers and critics could never quite come to terms. Although the author herself anticipates this when she writes of Dorothea in the Finale that "many who knew her, thought it a pity that so substantive and rare a creature should have been absorbed into the life of another, and be only known in a certain circle as a wife and mother" (783), Dorothea's becoming a wife and mother per se has not been so much in question as her becoming the wife of Will Ladislaw. Yet it is precisely Ladislaw's lack of roots, suitable to the romantic aesthetic of the 1830s in which the novel is situated, that makes him the right kind of match for the overly zealous Dorothea. By extension, this also makes him the right kind of match for a country in dire need of the reforms that provide the immediate political context of the novel. If his foreign origins satisfy the heroine's desire "to lead a grand life here—now—in England"

(27), they are also enmeshed in the solving of the nation's most pressing political problems, as I show later.

"Polish Fever" and Will Ladislaw

In an article candidly titled "What Is a Pole Doing in *Middlemarch*?," David Malcolm makes a case that the political goings-on in nineteenth-century Europe would have made Eliot's contemporaries keenly aware of the significance of Ladislaw's Polish heritage. Malcolm reminds us that Poland ceased to exist after its third partition between Russia, Prussia, and Austria in 1795. Two Polish rebellions against Russia, which gained the largest area of Poland in the partitions, took place during the course of the following century, in 1830–31 and in 1863–64. The first one, although never directly referred to in *Middlemarch*, happened during the period covered by the novel (1829–32); the second one occurred eight years prior to its publication, being thus within the experience of the author and the audience. Malcolm points out that both rebellions provoked "international sympathy with the Poles, and outrage against Tsarist Russia,"[18] which a closer look into the history of Anglo-Polish relations at the time confirms. Before reviewing those relations, it is worth pausing to reflect on the fact that Malcolm's article was written at the University of Gdansk during the time of the rising Solidarity movement. The late twentieth-century anti-Russian resistance movement must have provided a poignant context for discussing the country's nineteenth-century political woes, including their relevance to England and one of its most famous novels.

The Russian quashing of the first rebellion spawned a wave of Polish emigration to Western Europe and the United States. This coincided with the movement toward the First Reform Bill in England, where Polish patriots inspired those pleading the cause of the English working classes. The greater freedoms accorded by the bill were favorable to Polish emigrants working to garner international support, and those who were thrown out of France and Belgium for these activities not only found shelter but also received an exile's allowance in England.[19] By the 1863 rebellion, the Polish cause was propagated diligently by the emigrants of the 1830s and again found a receptive ear among their English audience, who read reports and letters from Warsaw in the newspapers and attended public support meetings. The country seemed unanimously in favor of Poland, while the government was reluctant to wage another war against Russia, the Crimean War having been fought in the preceding decade. The issue was discussed in Parliament, which was aided by France and Austria in its attempt at diplomatic interventions, but Russia was ultimately left unfettered in brutally quashing the second rebellion and russifying Poland even further.[20]

The "Polish fever" that swept England in the 1830s reached such a pitch that beggars from other countries craftily exploited the nation's sympathies and, counting especially on the romantic fantasies of the "fair sex," managed to obtain money and lodgings by passing themselves off as impoverished Polish princes. The popular Victorian journalist Andrew Halliday, writing in the 1862 supplemental volume of Henry Mayhew's *London Labour and the London Poor*, recalls these events in a section titled "Foreign Beggars" and warns his audience that "it will not do to mistake every vagabond refugee for a noble exile."[21] "To be a Pole and in distress, was almost a sufficient introduction," Halliday states, as well as "so excellent an opportunity for that class of foreign swindlers which haunt roulette tables and are the pest of second-rate hotels abroad."[22] He writes:

> Crowds of adventurers, 'got up' in furs, and cloaks, and playhouse dresses, with padded breasts and long moustachios, flocked to England, and assuming the title of count, and giving out that their patrimony had been sequestered by the Emperor of Russia, easily obtained a hearing and a footing in many English families, whose heads would not have received one of their own countrymen except with the usual credentials.[23]

He also describes a certain imprisoned Adolphus Czapolinski, "one of the most extraordinary of the beggars of the present day."[24] Czapolinski was actually Polish, as Halliday informs his readers, but passed himself off as Captain Noodt, another real person, whose identity he stole.

The last name Czapolinski bears a close resemblance to the last name of a character from George Eliot's very first work of fiction, the countess Caroline Czerlaski from the first story in *Scenes of Clerical Life*. "The Sad Fortunes of the Rev. Amos Barton" was first published in *Blackwood's Magazine* in 1857, and it reveals the same kind of mistrust of Polish exiles and their potential impersonators as seen in Halliday's article . Chapter 4 of the story begins with the following observation by the narrator: "I am by no means sure that if the good people of Milby had known the truth about the Countess Czerlaski, they would not have been considerably disappointed to find that it was very far from being as bad as they imagined."[25] The narrator's further observation that one of these considerable disappointments would come from the fact that "her husband had been the veritable Count Czerlaski, who had had wonderful escapes, as she said" (33), insinuates that her Milby neighbors were, indeed, doubtful of Czerlaski's aristocratic status. The other side of the life of an émigré count, one that his widow "did *not* say," is that he "had subsequently given dancing lessons in the metropolis" (34), which anticipates Will Ladislaw's "musical" Polish grandfather, who "got his bread by teaching all sorts of things" (343). Farther on in the chapter, the narrator assures us that the widowed countess "had had seven years of sufficiently happy matrimony with Czerlaski, who had taken her to Paris and Germany, and introduced her there to many of his old friends with large titles and small fortunes" (34). Such a description of the count's friends is a clear allusion to the impoverished Polish nobility seeking exile in Western European countries. The countess herself ends up an exile of sorts in the home of the Bartons—as well as a major drain on their finances—after the shock of her brother marrying her maid causes her to leave his house and the financial support it guaranteed in a huff.

Will Ladislaw's Middlemarch neighbors are as distrustful as "the good people of Milby," although their suspicions are of a slightly different nature, since Ladislaw claims no pretensions to noble roots. That he is working for a liberal paper at the same time that Polish emigrants are cooperating with English radicals, however, explains the "stories going about him as a quill-driving alien, a foreign emissary, and what not" (356). The provincial Cadwallader, Hackbutt, and Hawley families guard themselves not only against Mr. Brooke's liberal politics, but against their town's entertaining of aliens and foreigners. As far as Ladislaw's actual roots are concerned, the account of his grandfather as a "refugee" and a "patriot" (343) prompts Gordon S. Haight to estimate that if Ladislaw is around twenty-five years old in 1830, his grandfather would have been a "patriot" and a "refugee" of the first partition of Poland in 1772.[26]

Writing in 1992 for the journal *Polish Anglo-Saxon Studies*, David L. Smith reviews the same important Polish elements of *Middlemarch* as David Malcolm and reiterates that "Ladislaw is not a generic foreigner, introduced into the novel merely to highlight English narrowmindedness." But Smith takes it too far—perhaps carried away with zeal for the newly sovereign and democratic Poland of the early 1990s—by insisting in the next sentence that Ladislaw is "Polish by design, created by George Eliot to embody the spirit of Polish Romanticism."[27] The problem with this argument is that, although we can be confident of Eliot's acquaintance with the political goings-on in Europe, neither her letters nor her journals indicate any interest in Poland beyond the manner in which it briefly affected her family life. As both Malcolm and Smith point out, George Henry Lewes's son (and Eliot's stepson), Thornton, wanted to join the fight against Russia in Poland after failing his Indian Civil Service exam for the second time in 1863. But a closer look into the one journal entry and one letter that record this family episode reveals no political concerns or opinions on Eliot's part. The journal entry, made on August 22, 1863, merely mentions Thornie failing the exam and "having set his mind on going out to Poland to fight the Russians."[28] Writing to François d'Albert-Durade on November 28 of the same year, Eliot mentions the "hated Russians" and describes the Polish rebels as "coarse men engaged in a guerrilla warfare,"[29] but these are echoes of broader public opinion and private maternal concern, and her assessment of the Polish rebels could not be further from her portrayal of the culturally refined Will Ladislaw.

The only Polish person that appears in Eliot's personal writings is "Klackzo" [*sic*] from the April 10, 1870, journal entry, made in Vienna: ". . . lively well-informed man. Conversations always general and easy. Many *bons mots* and stories."[30] Smith identifies the man as Julian Klaczko, "a Polish journalist and patriot . . . who was attached to the Austrian Ministry,"[31] and points out that this meeting took place during the writing of *Middlemarch*, yet Klaczko's political allegiances appear of no significance in Eliot's note. His attachment to the Austrian Ministry, however, along with his meeting of Eliot and Lewes in Vienna, does point to Poland's close association with the Germanic lands, which is explored in more detail below.

The search for possible real-life models for Will Ladislaw, though tantalizing, has proven to be a futile exercise, but I will still indulge in it briefly for the sake of offering an additional perspective on the novel. There is, for example, his namesake, Count Ladislas Zamoyski, director of the London Bureau for publicity founded by Polish exiles after the first uprising.[32] Major Bartłomiej Beniowski is another example; he was born in Poland around 1800, which is Ladislaw's approximate birth year, and settled in England around 1836. In Poland he belonged to the same romantic youth movement as the most famous representative of Polish romanticism, the poet Adam Mickiewicz, while in England he became the only Pole to actively participate in English radical politics.[33] Yet since neither the journals and letters of George Eliot nor the letters of George Henry Lewes contain a single reference to any of these figures, we can only speculate whether Eliot might have read about them in the newspapers.

There are also a couple of famous medieval Ladislaws, rulers who achieved great feats for Poland. King Władysław Łokietek I, for example, led the country in regaining its independence from the Holy Roman Empire in 1308. Władisław Jagiellończyk II beat out the Habsburgs in ascending to the vacated Bohemian throne in 1471, followed by the Hungarian throne in 1490, and thus secured for his dynasty the domination of a significant portion of Europe.[34] Haight makes a note of this connection in his defense of "the much abused young man" by referring, most likely, to the latter Władysław when describing Will's grandfather as "bearing the name of the greatest Polish king."[35] For stateless nations like Poland, as I elaborate in the last two chapters of this book, remembering past glories was a way of keeping national consciousness and the hope of a future restoration alive.

It is a pity we have no information regarding Eliot's possible knowledge of the famous Poles, either from her own century or from the past, when Poland was a European force to be reckoned with. Nor do we know if she was aware that she used a Polish first name for the last name of her Polish character. She certainly could not have been aware of the *meaning* of the name, since she did not know Slavic languages, yet this is a hugely significant and utterly overlooked aspect—perhaps because Slavic scholars do not usually examine English novels—of the character she fashioned. One wonders if Eliot was even aware of the fact that the last syllable of Ladislaw's name contains his ethnicity. It is likely that she was not because of the English pronunciation of the name. David Malcolm is the only critic to point out the correct pronunciation, which in phonetic English spelling would be rendered "Ladislav," since the Polish (just as the German) letter *w* is pronounced like the English *v*. Malcolm also correctly surmises that the proper pronunciation would be lost on the native English speaker, which both the BBC miniseries of the novel and university English department professors confirm with the pronunciation that makes the *w* silent and the last syllable sound like the dinner side dish "cole slaw." Even more significant, in combination with the Slavic ethnicity, is the first part of Ladislaw's name, a derivative of "wladanie," which in varied forms in different Slavic languages means "reign" or "rule." The name as a whole, then, for those familiar with Slavic languages, evokes the image of a reign of Slavs. Eliot had, as it turns out, unintentionally chosen a name for her Polish protagonist that accentuates the fears he triggers in Middlemarch. His work on behalf of reform—especially in the broader historical context of Polish patriots inspiring English radicals—and his eventual engagement in Parliament but most significantly his winning the hand of an English lady all introduce a certain degree of a reign of Slavs in the novel.

More personal and poignant reasons for Eliot's fashioning of Ladislaw—as well as Rex Gascoigne of *Daniel Deronda*—but ones devoid of those characters' national significance have been explored by Rosemarie Bodenheimer and Nancy Henry. After failing his Indian Civil Service exam in 1863 and being dissuaded from going to fight in Poland, Eliot's stepson Thornton went to South Africa, where his older brother, Herbert (Bertie), joined him six years later. The Middlemarch residents express the same wishes for Ladislaw on two separate occasions. First, in chapter 38, when Ladislaw first moves into town in order to join Mr. Brooke in his political endeavors—but really to be close to Brooke's niece—the ever-meddlesome Mrs. Cadwallader wonders why Casaubon did not "use his interest to get Ladislaw made an *attaché* or sent to India," since "that is how families get rid of troublesome sprigs" (357). And second, in chapter 49, after hearing the news of Casaubon's codicil that incriminates Dorothea, her brother-in-law, Sir James, attempts to talk Brooke into getting Ladislaw "a post": "He could go in the suite of some Colonial Governor!" (456).

Thornie returned from South Africa in May 1869, "financially and physically broken,"[36] and died in October of the same year, a couple of months after Eliot commenced the writing of *Middlemarch*. Bertie died in South Africa in 1875, during the time Eliot was writing *Daniel Deronda*. Echoing Bodenheimer, Henry suggests that the male characters of *Middlemarch* and *Deronda* offered a way for Eliot to rewrite her stepsons' failures. Both Thornie and Bertie proved unsuccessful in the careers available to them as English emigrants, while, as Henry points out, Will Ladislaw and *Deronda*'s Rex and Warham Gascoigne "look to the empire—in all but the last case fancifully—as a career."[37] In contrast to Thornie and Bertie, Will Ladislaw and Rex Gascoigne support the empire from the inside, so to speak, and are successful in their endeavors. In the letter to François d'Albert-Durade about Thornie's sudden enthusiasm for Poland, Eliot describes her stepson as "at once amiable and troublesome," which fits Ladislaw's character, and she concludes that "he may possibly [turn] out to be something useful and remarkable,"[38] which is the ending she writes for Ladislaw. Returning to the notion of a "reign of Slavs," it is a truly amazing aspect of *Middlemarch* that Eliot grants a happy, successful ending to the Polish outsider. I elaborate on this notion below, when discussing the influence of nineteenth-century science on *Middlemarch*, a novel that was originally intended to be about Tertius Lydgate, an English physician with all the advantages but one who gets eclipsed by Will Ladislaw.

The German Role in the Fashioning of Will Ladislaw

Though David L. Smith's connection of Ladislaw with specifically Polish romanticism is a stretch, he is correct in his choice of genre. Ladislaw undoubtedly belongs to romanticism—as Dorothea does to the epic, specified so in the Prelude—but this feature is explicitly linked to Germany, a culture Eliot not only knew very well but also greatly admired. It is not insignificant that German unification, achieved in January 1871 and greeted warmly by Eliot, converged with the writing of *Middlemarch*. While the good-natured Mr. Brooke compares Ladislaw to the English romantic poets from his own country, Byron and Shelley, the narrator herself places him in the following context:

> Romanticism, which has helped to fill some dull blanks with love and knowledge, had not yet penetrated the times with its leaven and entered into everybody's food; it was fermenting still as a distinguishable vigorous enthusiasm in certain long-haired German artists at Rome, and the youth of other nations who worked or idled near them were sometimes caught in the spreading movement. (176)

The German artist in Rome is identified as Will's friend Naumann later in the same chapter, while Will himself is obviously the youth of another nation who works—or, in Will's case, rather, idles—near him. In informing Dorothea of her husband's scholarly shortcomings, Will advocates for Germany:

"the Germans have taken the lead in historical inquiries" he says, adding that "if Mr Casaubon read German he would save himself a great deal of trouble" (194). It is also, notably, a German artifact that precipitates Will and Dorothea's union at the end of the novel. First it brings about Dorothea's self-awareness of her love for Will when, at a visit to Mr. Farebrother's in chapter 80, she has occasion to see a German box Will gave Mr. Farebrother's aunt, Miss Noble. Three chapters later Miss Noble appears in Dorothea's home and shows her the same box as a signal of her mission to ask on Will's behalf that Dorothea meet with him.

Ladislaw's brief homage to German scholarship recalls the idea from George Eliot's 1865 essay, "A Word for the Germans." The preposition in the essay's title implies an argument *on behalf of* (instead of *to*) the Germans and admonishes John Bull to acknowledge Germany as "the source of pre-eminently important contributions to the sum of our mental wealth."[39] This view is echoed several years later in judgment of Casaubon, whose limitations can be extended to the nation at large when Ladislaw laments how much of English scholarship is wasted "for want of knowing what is being done by the rest of the world" (194). Rosemary Ashton, who offers the most comprehensive study of the role of German letters in Eliot's life, suggests that "it is almost as if she felt that Britain was intellectually in a more primitive stage . . . than Germany."[40] Ashton also reminds us that Eliot's first major publication was her 1846 translation of David Friedrich Strauss's *The Life of Jesus* (1835), through which she "took her place in the introduction of German thought to England."[41]

If English scholarship suffers on account of its provincialism, the less educated English public can only be so much the worse and, in a paragraph comparable to a section of "A Word for the Germans," the narrator puts the following judgment in the "defiant" mind of Ladislaw:

> He was not sorry to have this occasion for appearing in public before the Middlemarch tribes of Toller, Hackbutt, and the rest, who looked down on him as an adventurer, and were in a state of brutal ignorance about Dante—who sneered at his Polish blood, and were themselves of a breed very much in need of crossing. (567)

A milder pronouncement of this judgment is Eliot's assertion in "A Word for the Germans":

> The human race has not been educated on a plan of uniformity, and it is precisely that partition of mankind into races and nations, resulting in various national points of view or varieties of national genius, which has been the means of enriching and rendering more and more complete man's knowledge of the inner and outer world.[42]

The last statement anticipates "the Middlemarch tribes" as an embodiment of "a plan of uniformity," while their "brutal ignorance about Dante" is only a small instance of the general English ignorance of "various national points of view," which explains their sneering at Will's Polish "variet[y] of national genius." Finally, Ladislaw's comment regarding the Middlemarchers as a "breed very much in need of crossing" echoes "the means of enriching" from Eliot's essay and is discussed, in the next section, in relation to nineteenth-century scientific thinking.

A German-educated quarter Pole, who was, it is important to note, "otherwise English in his equipment" (176), is just different enough—but not *too* different—to satisfy the soul-hungry heroine, provide some necessary crossbreeding to insular English society, and succeed in "working well in those times when reforms were begun" (782). In describing Dorothea's "soul-hunger" (27), the narrator offers her own rendition of a German term—*Seelehunger*—and the lack of an original English equivalent effectively mirrors the lack of a suitable English match for Dorothea. If in her essay "A Word for the Germans" Eliot wishes that the English "would conceive the typical German under some more average aspect than that of 'the cloudy metaphysician,'"[43] then she balances this view with Ladislaw's rebellious Polish heritage. Because of nineteenth-century Polish insurrections against Russia, as David Malcolm informs us, "Polishness came to be associated in Western European consciousness with rebellion and resistance to oppressive, conservative rule."[44] This is precisely the role Ladislaw plays to his frustrated older cousin and former benefactor, Casaubon; it is the role he further assumes as Mr. Brooke's secretary, working against the oppressive, conservative rule of "ante-reform times" (25); and it suits Dorothea's resistance to the kind of marital union expected of her, described so insightfully in the beginning of the novel as "merely canine affection" (8).

The Role of Nineteenth-Century Science

In her introduction to *George Eliot's Selected Critical Writings*, which contains "A Word for the Germans," Rosemary Ashton explains that the author was "so well versed . . . in contemporary scientific thinking . . . that its language came easily to her."[45] Gillian Beer opens her chapter on *Middlemarch* in *Darwin's Plots* by stating that "George Eliot was often taken to task by contemporary reviewers of her works for the persistent scientific allusions in her works."[46] Will's idea of cross-breeding in his rant about "Middlemarch tribes" is most closely related to Darwin's concept of *variation*, which, as Beer explains, "within each species . . . is the key to evolutionary development."[47] Beer notes the presence of this concept in the very beginning of *Middlemarch*, in the Prelude, which maintains that among the female species "the limits of variation are really much wider than anyone would imagine."[48] The statement refers to Dorothea, whose "variation" must be domesticated to fit the Victorian mold and is achieved, as elaborated later, in a symbiotic union with the embodiment of "variation" in Middlemarch, Will Ladislaw.

Ladislaw as the developmentally necessary "variation" for Dorothea, Middlemarch, and, ultimately, England is most conspicuously highlighted in contrast to Casaubon, whom we might identify as the gatekeeper of "this aged nation of ours" (383), to use Eliot's description of England at one point in the novel. When he returns from his scholarly labors to find Ladislaw visiting with Dorothea in their Roman honeymoon residence,

> Mr Casaubon felt a surprise which was quite unmixed with pleasure, but he did not swerve from his usual politeness of greeting, when Will rose and explained his presence. Mr Casaubon was less happy than usual, and this perhaps made him look all the dimmer and more faded; else, the effect might easily have been produced by the contrast of his young cousin's appearance. The first impression on seeing Will was one of sunny brightness, which added to the uncertainty of his changing expression. Surely, his very features changed their form; his jaw looked sometimes large and sometimes small; and the little ripple in his nose was a preparation for metamorphosis. When he turned his head quickly his hair seemed to shake out light, and some persons thought they saw decided genius in this coruscation. Mr Casaubon, on the contrary, stood rayless. (196)

The traditional connotation of light is knowledge, and the connection between the two in the above passage is confirmed in the preceding scene, the conversation that Casaubon interrupts when he walks in on his wife and cousin. It is in that conversation that Will informs Dorothea of Casaubon's scholarly limitations; he "shakes out light"—to borrow the wording of the passage—for her as he makes her wonder for the first time whether "the labour of her husband's life might be void" (195).

The rest of the word choice of the above passage only accentuates the explicit contrast offered by the narrator in terms of darkness and light, stiffness and mobility. Casaubon's portrayal consists of "unmixed," "did not swerve," and a double use of "usual," while the word used doubly to describe Will is "change," enforced by "uncertainty" and the changing contours of his jaw. The jaw was the facial feature most commonly employed in the making of racial distinctions, with an inverse correlation between jaw and brain size being considered a mark of superiority. George Eliot's knowledge of science and her close friendship with Herbert Spencer, the scientist best known for his phrase "survival of the fittest," adds further significance to this passage. In his *Principles of Biology*, which contains the famous phrase and was published in 1864, Spencer describes the "diminution of the jaws and teeth which characterizes the civilized races, as contrasted with the savage races."[49] He footnotes this statement with a report on the skull measurements he took at the Museum of the College of Surgeons, where he found that "the under jaws of Australians and Negroes, when placed side by side with those of Englishmen, were visibly larger."[50]

In such an intellectual climate, the alteration in Will's jaw size between large and small draws attention to his racial ambiguity, to his semiwhiteness, so to speak, to his muddled status between Englishman and colonial subject. To amend the term used by Herbert Spencer and employ one mentioned in the introduction as encountered in Larry Wolff's research, Will's changing jaw size brands him a demi-savage. It is, in fact, specifically his jaw that distinguishes him from his English side. Dorothea first encounters Will on her tour of Casaubon's estate, where she notices the miniature of Casaubon's aunt and Ladislaw's grandmother, who made the *mésalliance* with Ladislaw's Polish grandfather. Dorothea comments on her "deep grey eyes rather near together—and the delicate irregular nose with a sort of ripple in it" (70). When she meets Ladislaw in the garden shortly thereafter, his features are described almost verbatim—"Dorothea could see a pair of grey eyes rather near together, a delicate irregular nose with a little ripple in it"—until our attention is drawn to what distinguishes him from her: "but there was a mouth and chin of a more prominent, threatening aspect than belonged to the type of the grandmother's miniature" (73).

Eastern Europeans were, indeed, a "threatening aspect" to the West, a stance Eliot would have come across in her extensive reading of the famous German philosophers who wrote about the semicivilized and racially ambiguous Slavic peoples. Johannes Gottfried Herder, for example, saw among them "so many little wild peoples" and G. W. F. Hegel commented on their "barbaric remnants"; Johann Gottlieb Fichte, who traveled through Poland, described it as "wild and neglected" and, even more significant for the confusion that has surrounded Ladislaw's origins, "full of Jews."[51] The most damning document to circulate the continent was a 1780 French pamphlet, whose authorship was popularly attributed to Prussia's Frederick the Great, titled "The Orangutan of Europe, or the Pole such as he is."[52] As Wolff explains in his recounting of the kind of Eastern Europe imagined by the West, "precisely because Poland was so geographically accessible to Germans, in some respects even intimately related to Germany, it was interpreted as alien and backward with all the more intellectual energy."[53] As we shall see in the next chapter, Effi Briest's Polish lover is portrayed very differently than Ladislaw—the opposite, in fact—and comes to a very different end, thus offering literary testimony to the veracity of Wolff's observation. In the case of *Middlemarch*, the double-sided intimacy and animosity between Poland

and Germany sheds some light on how easily Eliot could fashion a German romantic of Polish roots who would challenge English insularity.

We might infer that in this novel, where race, class, religion, and gender all interact so well, reform is to politics what variation is to science. Eliot returns to the issue of Ladislaw's "dangerously mixed blood" after she recounts his success in politics in the Finale, thus reinforcing the relationship between miscegenation and reform. First, in depicting the imperfect reconciliation between the two brothers-in-law, she comments that "Will always preferred to have Sir James's company mixed with another kind" (784), a statement that recalls Will's earlier judgment of Middlemarch as a place in need of cross-breeding; this is followed by the information that "there came gradually a small row of cousins at Freshitt who enjoyed playing with the two cousins visiting Tipton as much as if the blood of these cousins had been less dubiously mixed" (784), which announces full assimilation in the next generation; and finally, in wrapping up Dorothea's "home epic" (779), Eliot describes it as "the mixed result of young and noble impulse struggling amidst the conditions of an imperfect social state" (784) and so assures us that, even though the Victorian age cannot support a "new Theresa," it can be invigorated by new blood.

In her book on Eliot's engagement with aspects of Spencerian "science," Nancy L. Paxton shows that *Middlemarch* contradicts "Spencer's arguments exalting the power of nature over nurture and asserting women's innate mental and moral inferiority."[54] The novel does so by highlighting Casaubon's intellectual failure and making Lydgate, in my view, a downright victim of Spencerian ideology when he completely misreads Rosamond, who, as Paxton astutely points out, "according to the most advanced scientific principles of evolutionary theory in the 1870s, is the perfect mate."[55] To Paxton's gendered reading I wish to add an ethnic angle and propose that *Middlemarch* goes a step further than showcasing the failure of men in general by portraying its unsuccessful characters as Englishmen. Both Casaubon and Lydgate are eclipsed by Ladislaw. Since the latter's intellectual superiority over his cousin and greater suitability for Dorothea have already been discussed, it is to Lydgate that we now turn.

Tertius Lydgate is the main male character of a work that was initially intended to focus solely on him. Chapter 15, which introduces him, was the original opening of the novel, when it was still envisioned as a separate work from "Miss Brooke," the latter eventually becoming part 1 of *Middlemarch*.[56] Lydgate, like Ladislaw, is a newcomer in town, but he is a gentleman with notable family connections. Therefore, unlike Ladislaw, he is received as "not altogether a common country doctor," an impression that "was significant of great things being expected from him" (133). The chapter ends with the notion that "Middlemarch, in fact, counted on swallowing Lydgate and assimilating him very comfortably" (144). However, in a trajectory exactly opposite of Ladislaw's, Lydgate demonstrates the greatest potential in the beginning of the novel but ends in banishment. Like Ladislaw, Lydgate is a promoter of reform, though medical in his case, but unlike Ladislaw in the political sphere, he fails in his endeavor. From the point of view of the Woman Question in the novel, Lydgate's downfall occurs because, unlike Ladislaw, he has the wrong conception of women and chooses the vain and small-minded Rosamond for a wife. When he first meets Dorothea, she talks to him about improving the state of the tenants' cottages and that of the hospital where he has just assumed a position. Lydgate comes away from the conversation thinking that "it is troublesome to talk to such women" (86) and that his interlocutor "did not look at things from the proper feminine angle" (88). The author punishes him quite severely for these prejudices, and Middlemarch is, in the end, forced to "swallow" and "assimilate" Ladislaw—though not "very comfortably"—instead. The Finale of the novel, which informs us that "Will became an ardent public man[,] . . . getting at last returned to Parliament by a constituency who paid his expenses" (782–83), tells us of Lydgate that, although he eventually "gained an excellent practice, alternating, according to the season, between London and a Continental bathing-place," and even published a treatise on gout, "he always regarded himself as a failure: he had not done what he once meant to" (781). The two young men symbolically exchange places earlier in the novel when in their last meeting, Ladislaw, out of compassion for his friend, "shrank from saying that he had rejected Bulstrode's money, in the moment when he was learning that it was Lydgate's misfortune to have accepted it" (736). So the person who was originally meant to be the hero of his own novel undergoes the classic (Oedipal or Arthurian) downfall and is eclipsed by an outsider, who has neither finances nor family lineage, neither proper Englishness nor a friendly neighborhood reception going in his favor. Returning to the analogy between variation in science and reform in politics, *Middlemarch* does not necessarily contradict Spencer's notions of race as it does his notions of gender, but it utilizes the principles of evolutionary biology to show that English political stagnation is due to the nation's insularity and that both can be cured by making the boundaries separating insider and outsider a little more porous.

Writing the novel at a time when English Polonophilia was at its height and after the 1867 passage of the Second Reform Bill had rectified the shortcomings of the first one from 1832, Eliot had no reason to expect that her Polish reformer would be so poorly received by the public. The lessons of *Middlemarch*, sadly, seem lost on its readers and critics, who would be loath to recognize themselves in such characters as Mr. Hawley or Mrs. Cadwallader, yet may be subject to the same criticism. The 1870s readers of this novel set in the early 1830s would have been of the same generation as that "small row of cousins at Freshitt who enjoyed playing with the two cousins visiting Tipton as much as if the blood of these cousins had been less dubiously mixed." Yet this authorial glimpse into the future remained fictional, demonstrated acutely in the warning by the famous review in the *Saturday Review*:

> If our young ladies, repelled by the faint and 'neutral' virtues of Celia on the one hand, and the powerfully drawn worldly Rosamond on the other, take to be Dorotheas, with a vow to dress differently from other women, and to regulate their own conduct on the system of a general disapproval of the state of things into which they are born, the world will be a less comfortable world without being a better one.[57]

The very last line of this statement especially demonstrates the extent of the lack of appreciation for a novel in which the direct result of the heroine's (second) marital choice is, in fact, a better world.

The Jewish Role

Fichte's description of Poland as "full of Jews," though intended as a bigoted remark on his part, as it belonged to his negative experience of Poland, was not a wholly inaccurate observation. The country's capital, Warsaw, was the Eastern European city with the largest Jewish population at the time, and this played a role in the general perception of Poles all the way through the twentieth century.[58] One cannot help but wonder whether this might have influenced Jerome Beaty's argument that Ladislaw was originally conceived of as Jewish. Beaty bases his conclusion on the gossip that goes around town after Bulstrode's first wife is revealed to have been Ladislaw's maternal grandmother, and he gives special credence to the otherwise good-natured Mr. Farebrother's pronouncement that in Ladislaw's "queer genealogy" he "should never have suspected a grafting of the Jew pawnbroker" (676). But Ladislaw's maternal ancestry is never identified as Jewish, and the conflation of "Jew" and "pawnbroker" merely reveals a pervasive stereotype. Beaty contends that Eliot neglected to remove the Jewish references once she developed the character of Will Ladislaw into something different. This reading was debunked twice only a couple of years after it was published by critics emphasizing Eliot's meticulousness and her desire to demonstrate the destructive power of gossip; as was rightly noted, when Mrs. Cadwallader dubbed Will "an Italian with white mice" (460) nobody suspected him of actually being Italian.[59] I propose that the key to understanding Beaty's mistake lies in the fact that he reads Ladislaw as an earlier version of Daniel Deronda, the protagonist who forms close ties, in the process of discovering his own forgotten past, with Eastern European Jewish immigrants in the novel.

In response to Beaty, Thomas Pinney argues that Esther Lyon of *Felix Holt* "is closer to Deronda than Will is in mistaking an adoptive father for her real one."[60] I argue, in a search for later incarnations of Ladislaw, that Herr Klesmer of *Daniel Deronda* has much more in common with him than with the eponymous hero. This novel, which of all Eliot's works is the most explicitly concerned with dispossessed peoples and national belonging, replicates the Dorothea-Ladislaw romance through two of its minor characters. Herr Julius Klesmer, identified by Mr. Bult as "a Pole, or a Czech, or something of that fermenting sort, in a state of political refugeeism,"[61] marries the wealthy Miss Catherine Arrowpoint, much to the chagrin of her parents. Like Ladislaw, Herr Klesmer "has cosmopolitan ideas," as Miss Arrowpoint asserts in his defense when she notices that Mr. Bult, who is another contender for her hand, finds Klesmer's "buffoonery rather offensive and Polish" (242). Miss Arrowpoint concludes her defense of Herr Klesmer by adding that "he looks forward to a fusion of races," which recalls Ladislaw's comment on the Middlemarchers as "a breed very much in need of crossing" (567). Further, while Ladislaw enlightens Dorothea as to the narrowness of Casaubon's scholarship, Klesmer informs the heroine of *Deronda*, Gwendolen Harleth, that the music she sings "expresses a puerile state of culture[,] . . . the passion and thought of people without any breadth of horizon," and that what it lacks is a "sense of the universal" (49).

There is one specific description of Herr Klesmer, however, voiced by the narrator herself, that can serve as an interpretive tool for Eliot's conception of Eastern Europe in general and shed further light on Will Ladislaw in particular. Klesmer is first introduced in the novel in chapter 5 as "a felicitous combination of the German, the Sclave, and the Semite" (47). This is what makes him such pleasant company, the specific ethnic formula being used by the narrator for an explanation as to why Klesmer's conversation with Gwendolen "was agreeable on both sides" (47). The "felicitous combination" of ethnicities, starting with the last one listed and progressing to the first, consists of the following: his name Klesmer, which is the Yiddish word for "musician," in addition to his comparison with the famous Jewish composers Franz Liszt and Felix Mendelssohn,[62] as well as his self-designation as "the Wandering Jew" (242); Mr. Bult's surmise that he is "a Pole, or a Czech," as well as, politically, "a Panslavist" (242), the former confirmed by Klesmer's own recollection, inspired by his acquaintance with Mirah, of "a home . . . on the outskirts of Bohemia" (482); finally, his education, which—like that of Ladislaw—is German and his title Herr, the German word for "Mister," which suggests that he moved to England from Germany. Regarding the German-Sclave combination, one can also not help but notice the similarity between the names Julius Klesmer and Julian Klaczko, the Pole whom Eliot met in Vienna in 1870.

Since the time of this meeting coincided with Eliot's writing of *Middlemarch*, it is likely that Julian Klaczko played a role in the fashioning of her two most prominent Eastern European characters, Will Ladislaw and Julius Klesmer. Regarding the former, if we take into account the prejudices of both his provincial neighbors—who dub him, after his relation to Bulstrode is discovered, "the grandson of a thieving Jew pawnbroker" (727)—and that of his real-life literary critics—mainly Beaty but also David R. Carroll and Reva Stump[63]—then this Heidelberg-educated and German romanticism-influenced quarter Pole (on his paternal grandfather's side) is, also, "a felicitous combination of the German, the Sclave, and the Semite." The "felicitous" feature of this combination, it bears repeating, is present only in the mind of the author—who was, to Henry James's great dismay, "evidently very fond of him"[64]—and in the mind of her protagonist, Dorothea.

Mirah Lapidoth belongs to the list of Eliot's minor characters in whom "the German, the Sclave, and the Semite" dovetail. She is a "Jewess" who returns to England from Prague and has "forefathers in Poland" (215). As she unravels her background for the Meyrick family, who take her in, she speaks of having lived in Hamburg and Vienna the longest while moving around with her father. She also says that before moving to those cities she "knew German quite well—some German plays almost by heart" and that her father "spoke it better than he spoke English" (215). Another *Deronda* character who belongs on that list is the philosopher Salomon Maimon, whose "wonderful bit of autobiography, the life of the Polish Jew" (385), Daniel discovers in a secondhand bookshop. The bit about the Polish Jew that remains unsaid—although one might deduce it from the reference to the title of his work, *Lebensgeschichte* (387)—is the fact that he moved to Germany as a young man and spent his life there.

With the exception of Prague, which is one of the cities she traveled to on her way from Munich to Dresden with Lewes in 1858,[65] Eliot had no direct experience of Eastern Europe. Her experience of the people of Eastern Europe, however, as already noted with Julian Klaczko, occurred in Germanic lands. Franz Liszt was another notable Eastern European Jew whom Eliot met in Germany.[66] He served as an inspiration for the creation of Herr Klesmer and his name, tellingly, constitutes the ending of Eliot's essay "Three Months in Weimar."[67] Back in London Eliot also met Sofia Kovalevskaya, the notable Russian female mathematician and author of the novel, among several others, *Nigilistika* (Nihilist Girl), when she visited England in 1869.[68] Important for Eliot's impression of Slavs is the fact that Kovalevskaya was a student at Heidelberg during the time of her London visit. Given the proximity of Kovalevskaya's visit to the writing of *Middlemarch*—begun in August of the same year, two months before the visit—it is likely that the choice for Ladislaw's educational background was inspired by that of the young Russian scholar.

Russia makes an appearance in *Deronda* through another minor character—even minuscule in terms of the number of pages she occupies in the novel—Daniel's mother, who lives there because of her second marriage to "a Russian noble" (639). The country choice is somewhat puzzling, as Catherine Brown explores in her essay, "Why Does Daniel Deronda's Mother Live in Russia?," because Russia was "the most anti-semitic country in Europe" at the time and a Russian prince's marriage to a Jewish woman "would have been considered a mésalliance far more scandalous than that of Catherine Arrowpoint and Klesmer."[69] Brown suggests that Russia's appearance in *Deronda* reflects that "for Eliot, as for many of her English readers, Russia was a contradictory cipher of barbarism, decadence, and cultural vigour."[70] The "cultural" aspect is evident in Herr Klesmer's announcement, "I must go off to St Petersburg,"[71] as well as in Daniel's mother's former singing career in Russia. The designation "contradictory cipher" can be applied to Western European notions of Eastern Europe on the whole, as already elaborated in the beginning of this chapter. Ladislaw, in his initial artistic pursuits and aimless wandering around Europe, as well as in his settling down in Middlemarch, where he gets into the habit of stretching out on the floor in Lydgate's living room and having a bunch of local children follow him around town, certainly fits Brown's description. But Russia specifically and specifically for Eliot, I would argue, through the figure of Daniel's emotionally and physically distant mother in *Deronda* and the figure of the Russian Empire that turns other Slavs into refugees in both *Deronda* and *Middlemarch*, appears as something ominous and unfathomable. The Eastern European countries Eliot chooses to focus on and portray favorably—even beneficially, for England—testify to what Nancy Henry has called "English sympathy for national liberation movements."[72] Further, one should not underestimate English hostility to Russia or overlook the effect of the Crimean War that was waged between the two countries in the mid-1850s. "Mother Russia" turns out to be nothing but a source of suffering for both Deronda and her Polish subjects. On the other hand, Polish outsiders get to marry English ladies and, in the case of Mirah Lapidoth, an English gentleman.

While Beaty's mistake regarding Ladislaw's ethnicity lies in taking a character's off-handed assessment of the outsider as authorial intent, Ladislaw can more generally be considered a precursor of Deronda as far as he represents Eliot's first novelistic foray—"The Spanish Gypsy" is a poem—into discussing dispossessed peoples. A further look into the conversation between Mr. Farebrother and Mr. Hawley that spawned Beaty's erroneous inference reveals that lack of a homeland is what nineteenth-century Poles and Jews had in common. To Mr. Farebrother's remark about "a grafting of the Jew pawnbroker," Mr. Hawley responds: "It's just what I should have expected. . . . Any cursed alien blood, Jew, Corsican, or Gypsy" (676). The seemingly haphazard listing of the ethnicities itself signifies that Mr. Hawley doesn't care so much whether Ladislaw is Jewish as he does about having "any . . . alien blood" in the neighborhood. The examples of "alien blood" in his list, however, reveal that what he means by "alien" is not just foreign, but, more specifically, homeless. The conflation of Ladislaw's already known Polish ancestry with three other ethnic groups is telling of the state of Poland at the time, its nonstate, that is. Ever since the third and final partition, the Poles had been stateless, like Jews and Gypsies, and stirred up fears that they would, as Ladislaw did, settle among the English. Corsica's history as the in-between state of France and Italy mirrored Poland's position between Russia and Germany, between one old and long-established empire (France and Russia) and another recently unified and newly emerging one (Italy and Germany).

Mr. Hawley's conflation aside, in *Gypsies in the British Imagination*, Nord shows that Gypsies were generally perceived as romantic in the British imagination, that due to their mysterious lineage and nomadic lifestyle they "play[ed] a role in bohemian mythmaking and in dreams of escaping from stifling respectability."[73] While the provincial Mr. Hawley makes no distinction between 'any cursed alien blood," Ladislaw is twice more identified as a Gypsy in an affectionate manner, which Nord employs to substantiate her argument. When Rosamond wonders whether Ladislaw's vexation at being seen in her house by Dorothea is related to matters of class, Lydgate reassures her: "No, no; it must be something else if he were really vexed. Ladislaw is a sort of gypsy; he thinks nothing of leather and prunella" (410); while the narrator herself repeats three chapters later that, "as Lydgate had said of him, he was sort of a gypsy, rather enjoying the sense of belonging to no class" (434). Regarding both groups of dispossessed peoples, Nord explains that "like many others in the nineteenth century, Eliot paired these two 'others within,' Gypsy and Jew, in her thinking about seemingly cohesive but stateless nations," though she "ultimately saw the Jews as a people tied fortuitously to history and text and, therefore, as worthy creators of a modern state."[74] I would personally offer a slightly more generous reading of Eliot than Nord does when she employs the notion of worthiness and suggest instead that Eliot's political and literary realism led her to focus, in the end, on ethnic groups more *likely* to achieve the goal of a state. With Jews and Gypsies on opposing ends of that continuum, the Poles fell somewhere in between, as a people historically tied to a land but without the accompanying sacred text. However, in the wake of the second Polish insurrection of 1863 and another, this time more brutal Russian quashing of it, Poland did not have much hope for statehood when Eliot was writing *Middlemarch*. Zionism, on the other hand, was a budding movement, and groups of European Jews, like the fictional Daniel Deronda and Mirah, were emigrating to Palestine.

Eliot's assessment of Klesmer as "a felicitous combination of the German, the Sclave, and the Semite," in addition to illuminating her fashioning of Ladislaw and her imagining of Eastern Europe in general, provides us with an accurate trajectory of her international sympathies. Her admiration for Germany begins early in her writing career, with two translations of theological works—David Friedrich Strauss's *The Life of Jesus* in 1846 and Ludwig Feuerbach's *The Essence of Christianity* in 1854—and is further expressed in essays such as "The Natural History of German Life" (1856) and "A Word for the Germans" (1865). It spills over into *Middlemarch*, where elements of German culture infuse her new interest in disinherited Slavic nations, while Jewishness is present only in the form of false rumors and is yet to be foregrounded in her final novel. Eliot's concern for the Jewish state continues after *Deronda* and culminates in the last essay of the last work she wrote, "The Modern Hep! Hep! Hep!" in *Impressions of Theophrastus Such*. Thanks to Henry's scholarship this previously neglected essay has replaced *Deronda* as Eliot's final word on nationalism, but it has also been discussed with a backward glance only as far as *Deronda*. I want to argue that its roots can be detected in *Middlemarch* based on a single line: Theophrastus expresses hope that among the Jewish race "there may arise some men of instruction and ardent public spirit, some new Ezras,"[75] a hope that was obviously embodied previously in the figure of Deronda, a product of Eton and Cambridge, who receives further instruction from the Jewish elders and ardently pursues his mission to the East. Like Ezra centuries before him, Deronda returns to Jerusalem from Babylon, the superpower in the region at the time and, in that sense, comparable to England. Ladislaw also comes from an exiled family and, although he does not repatriate with a group of Poles, to compare ancient Israel and Babylon with nineteenth-century Poland and Russia would be merely to reiterate a sentiment that was prevalent among Polish patriots at the time, as discussed in the last chapter of this book. Most significantly, though, Eliot uses (a slightly altered variation of) the phrase "an ardent public spirit" only one time previously in her entire oeuvre and this is in *Middlemarch*, when she informs us in the Finale that "Will became an ardent public man, working well in those times when reforms were begun" (782). The major difference between Will and Daniel is that the former, inspired by the novel's heroine, channels his ardor into improving "the aged nation" (383), whereas the latter leaves both heroine and nation behind. The continued presence in *Deronda*, though minimized, of the Eastern European who assimilates into an English family shows that, rather than abandoning one cause for another, the author merely expands her well-known project of sympathy. Further proof of this can be found in "Hep!," whose focus on England's Jews does not prevent Theophrastus from criticizing capricious opinions on the Eastern Question that are based on one's "preference or dislike of Russians, Serbians, or Greeks, consequent, perhaps, on hotel adventures."[76] If the eighteenth-century philosophes imagined Eastern Europe as "a domain of political play, the lands of opportunity and experiment,"[77] then George Eliot employed the region a century later as a literary testing ground for English sympathies. What her experiment shows is that self-gratifying moral outrage at Russia's brutality does not necessarily translate into accepting one (of the progeny) of its victims as a suitable match for the national literary heroine.

The Catholic Role

The speculation regarding Will Ladislaw's Jewish heritage has perhaps been given more than its due in literary criticism. As Malcolm and Smith have shown, it is his Polish heritage that ought to be the focus of our attention since, as the grandson of a Polish "refugee" and "patriot," he fits well into the context of early 1830s England. This is not the case solely because of England's international policy on Polish insurrections and Polish connections to English reform, however, but also because of one more, as yet unexplored connection between England and Poland—the Catholic Emancipation Act of 1829. The act provided English Catholics with the same religious and political freedoms that had been granted to Protestant dissenters a year earlier, and it is brought up in the very first pages of the novel as the Brooke sisters embark on their new life among "provincial families, still discussing Mr Peel's late conduct on the Catholic Question" (9). Sir Robert Peel, in the role of Home Secretary at the time, was initially against Catholic emancipation. However, when Daniel O'Connel was elected a member of Parliament but was legally prohibited from taking his seat and Irish rebellion seemed imminent, Peel and Wellington, prime minister at the time, pushed the act through. O'Connel is also significant, together with other Irish nationalists, for supporting his Polish Catholic brethren in their first insurrection against Russia. He publicly and passionately denounced the Russian tsar in his speeches, while other Irish nationalists organized a protest in Birmingham when in 1839 the Russian grand duke Aleksandr visited England.[78]

Through his Polish heritage Ladislaw is the grandson of the largest and most conspicuously Catholic Slavic nation. Polish Catholicism and, more generally, the conflation of religious and national identity in Eastern Europe—manifested most recently and brutally in the wars of succession of the former Yugoslavia—are not to be underestimated. The Counter-Reformation movement in Poland was so successful that by 1688 the Polish Diet made conversion from Catholicism punishable by death and confiscation of property.[79] Ladislaw is directly linked to Catholicism in chapter 46, which describes how "Mrs Bulstrode felt that his mode of talking about Catholic countries, as if there were any truce with Antichrist, illustrated the usual tendency to unsoundness in intellectual men" (435).

Dorothea is also linked to Catholicism through the many comparisons drawn in the novel between her and the Virgin Mary, whose role in Catholicism is immeasurably greater than in Protestantism. The comparison begins in the opening of the first chapter, whose second sentence depicts Dorothea's "hand and wrist" as "so finely formed that she could wear sleeves not less bare of style than those in which the Blessed Virgin appeared to Italian painters" (7). When a German painter, Will's friend Naumann, encounters her in Italy, he identifies her as "the most perfect Madonna I ever saw" (178). Toward the end of the novel Dorothea gets to act out the role, in addition to looking the part, when she stands up for Lydgate in his embroilment with Bulstrode and even embarks on a saving mission to Rosamond after she is misled to believe that Rosamond is involved with Will. After being encouraged by Dorothea to pursue the work at the New Hospital under her patronage, Lydgate thinks to himself, in quite the contrast to his initial impression of Dorothea: "This young creature has a heart large enough for the Virgin Mary. She evidently thinks nothing of her own future, and would pledge away half her income at once, as if she wanted nothing for herself but a chair to sit in from which she can look down with those clear eyes at the poor mortals who pray to her" (723). Correspondingly, Dorothea's disappointment in Will, when she misinterprets his relationship with Rosamond, takes on a nonsexual, maternal form: "There were two images—two living forms that tore her heart in two, as if it had been the heart of a mother who seems to see her child divided by the sword, and presses one bleeding half to her breast while her gaze goes forth in agony towards the half which is carried by the lying woman that has never known the mother's pang" (739). The following morning her servant Tantripp notices that her face "in spite of bathing had the pale cheeks and pink eyelids of a *mater dolorosa*" (742). Dorothea embarks that day on her "second attempt to see and save Rosamond" (742), whose hand she clasps in greeting "with gentle motherliness" (745).

Dorothea's comparison to the Virgin might explain why no earthly man seems suitable for her. This was encapsulated best by another one of the early reviewers of *Middlemarch*, Edith Simcox, who wrote in the *Academy* that "for a perfect woman, any marriage is a *mésalliance*."[80] But Ladislaw's union with her allows the heroine to live out her martyr fantasies—which, in their evocations of the lives of St. Theresa and St. Barbara (3, 80, 81), are explicitly Catholic fantasies—on a smaller scale by giving up Casaubon's money. On a larger scale, Ladislaw's "changing expression," his alternating jaw size, and even "the little ripple in his nose [which] was a preparation for metamorphosis" are phenotypic signifiers of his national origins that link him to the two great reform acts—Catholic Emancipation and the First Reform Bill—taking place during the three years covered by the novel. While chapter 83 of the novel ends with Dorothea renouncing her wealth for Ladislaw's sake, the next chapter opens with the Lords throwing out the Reform Bill, thus creating a contiguous link between foreign influence and the need for reform.

The Disinherited Individual and the Disinherited Nation

I suggested earlier in this chapter that Henry James and other dissatisfied critics described Ladislaw in the same vocabulary as has traditionally been used to characterize the liminal identity of Eastern Europe: vague, transitional, and so on. In James's case, I would also suggest that his distrust of Ladislaw's masculinity ("a woman's man") betrays a conflation of racial with sexual ambiguity, since it is only the former that Eliot explicitly imparts to Ladislaw in the novel. Nord's reading of Ladislaw as a transitional figure in George Eliot's progression "from disinherited individual to disinherited nation" proves useful to my argument if it is expanded into a reading of the novel as a whole. Between Eliot's earliest novels, such as *Adam Bede* and *Silas Marner*, and her last one, *Daniel Deronda*, *Middlemarch* is the transitional work in which the disinherited individual and the disinherited nation meet in the figures of Dorothea and Will. Dorothea—the later-born Theresa who is "enamoured of intensity and greatness" and "likely to seek martyrdom" (8)—certainly qualifies as an outsider, not just in Middlemarch or England, but in the Victorian novel as a genre. Further, by the end of the novel Dorothea is more literally, financially disinherited when her marriage to Ladislaw divests her of Casaubon's income, as stipulated in the codicil to his will.

The idea of a genre outsider—or "genre expatriate," as Gary Saul Morson refers to the eponymous heroine of *Anna Karenina*[81]—is worth exploring further with reference to Sarah Gates's article on the topic. Gates reads *Middlemarch* as "an interesting example of Bakhtin's definition of the novel as a collection of 'discourses' in 'dialogue' with one another,"[82] and she examines how these discourses intersect with the sexual norms of the period that produced the novel. The task of the realist novel, as Gates sees it, and one that *Middlemarch* accomplishes, is the harnessing of its heroine's "unrealistic" energies, which belong to the novel's predecessors, such as the drama and the epic, in order to assimilate her into "Victorian domesticity."[83] Dorothea's "saintly potentials" are, in the end, "sacrificed to, or appropriated for, the coherent 'safe' resting place of realistic closure."[84]

Although I agree with Gates's method of reading the novel as a mixture of genres, my ultimate conclusion about *Middlemarch* in particular is more optimistic than hers. After all, as mentioned in the beginning of this chapter, the mere fact that Dorothea survives the end of the novel, not to mention that she manages to survive it happily remarried, makes her a unique case among her fictional contemporaries from other parts of Europe. Anna Karenina incurs capital punishment, so to speak, for stepping out of the bounds of her genre, whereas Dorothea, according to my reading, finds an outlet precisely in her marriage to Will Ladislaw. Gates's conclusion that *Middlemarch* demonstrates "the tragic cost to feminine potential of masculine heroic enterprise"[85] would be more appropriate if the phrase "masculine heroic enterprise" were applied—ironically, of course—to Edward Casaubon and his overly ambitious book project, *The Key to All Mythologies*, instead of to Will Ladislaw, as Gates intends it. If Dorothea had obeyed her first husband's wish that she should collect his notes and publish his book after his death, even though she saw clearly—and partly with Ladislaw's help—that the work was hardly worth the effort, her feminine potential would have indeed been sacrificed to a (meaningless) masculine enterprise. And while the claim in the Finale that "Dorothea could have liked nothing better, since wrongs existed, than that her husband should be in the thick of a struggle against them, and that she should give him wifely help" (783) might grate on our modern-day feminist ears, it is difficult to imagine what other kind of a more meaningful life Dorothea could have had in her time. In fact, the narrator says as much further on in the Finale—"no one stated exactly what else that was in her power she ought rather to have done" (783)—and this pronouncement is as applicable to modern-day readers as it was to Dorothea's own fictional neighbors.

An important aspect of *Middlemarch* that Gates misses is that Ladislaw's unrealistic energies are harnessed in his marriage to Dorothea just as much as Dorothea's are in her marriage to him. As mentioned previously regarding his connections to Germany, Ladislaw belongs to the romantic genre. His notions about his own future, a source of frustration for his older cousin Casaubon, lie fully within the romantic tradition:

> Genius, he held, is necessarily intolerant of fetters: on the one hand it must have the utmost play for its spontaneity; on the other, it may confidently await those messages from the universe which summon it to its peculiar work, only placing itself in an attitude of receptivity towards all sublime chances. . . . The superadded circumstance which would evolve the genius had not yet come; the universe had not yet beckoned. Even Cæsar's fortune at one time was but a grand presentiment. (76, 77)

Victorian domestication for Will involves shrinking the beckoning universe to England's borders and Cæsar's career to that of a Parliament representative. His union with Dorothea turns out to be symbiotic as both of them give up their unrealistic fantasies but find their fulfillment on a smaller scale through each other.

One last point that should be added to Gates's argument is that it is precisely because of their respective genres that Dorothea and Ladislaw prove to be an excellent match. It was the romantics who rediscovered the Middle Ages, the time of the epic and of St. Theresa. Along with the Middle Ages, they also rediscovered Catholicism, Novalis—the first German romantic and one often mentioned in George Eliot's writings—being the prime example with his essay "Die Christenheit oder Europa" (Christianity or Europe). Ladislaw's longing for Dorothea, therefore, is a perfect analogy for the romantics' longing to return to the Middle Ages.

In terms of Ladislaw's Polish heritage, which is the more pressing problem of the novel, why a man of "foreign extraction" (336) is perfectly suited for Dorothea and, more important for the purposes of this book, how the two of them as a couple model a nation's successful absorption of its others, is illuminated by an Eastern European critic writing in the West, Julia Kristeva.[86] Her work *Strangers to Ourselves*, while not addressing *Middlemarch* directly, explains the attraction between, to use Nord's language, "figurative strangeness" and "foreign origins."[87] In a classic psychoanalytic turn, Kristeva proposes that our fear of the foreigner comes from our deeper fear of facing our own inner foreignness. Her explanation that "the foreigner's friends, aside from bleeding hearts who feel obliged to do good, could only be those who feel foreign to themselves"[88] not only elucidates Dorothea and Will's compatibility in a way that has escaped most of George Eliot's readers and scholars, but the aside regarding "bleeding hearts" fits Mr. Brooke perfectly, specifically his engagement in politics and his apprenticeship of Ladislaw for those purposes. A Kristevan reading suggests that Dorothea's "sense of strangeness is a mainspring for [her] identification with the other,"[89] which is why she recognizes Will Ladislaw as her own homelessness.

Dorothea's desire "to lead a grand life here—now—in England" (27) is equally unfeasible for her as a Victorian woman and for Ladislaw as a foreigner. Yet their attachment to each other results in their successful employment in the service of the empire, as Will gains a seat in Parliament and Dorothea bears progeny. If it were not for Dorothea, Ladislaw would have continued his life of a gallivanting artist while waiting for the universe to beckon. Kristeva's differentiation between the first and later generations of foreigners, in fact, encapsulates Casaubon's initial gripe with Ladislaw: "As a defiance of industrious parents, or an inevitably excessive aping of native behavior, the children of foreigners are often and from the very start within the code of *dolce vita*, slovenliness, and even delinquency."[90] Ladislaw certainly enjoys the *dolce vita* in Rome and his "slovenliness"—a term linguistically and historically related, along with its other derivatives, such as *slavish*, to the ethnic designation *Slav*[91]—represents an "aping of native behavior." Will's Polish grandfather "gave lessons for his bread" (343), and Casaubon rightfully wishes that his cousin would "choose a profession" (74).

The preparation for metamorphosis evident in Will's facial features and suggestive of England's need for reform is an attribute Kristeva imparts to the foreigner in general, as one who, being "free of ties with his own people," is "ready for the absolute."[92] Ladislaw's absolute turns out to be Dorothea, for whose sake he moves into the hostile environment of a provincial English town and works with her uncle on behalf of reform. He thus confirms Kristeva's claim that "the flame that betrays his latent fanaticism shows only when he becomes attached—to a cause, to a job, to a person."[93] Ladislaw attaches to all three, but in the reverse order of importance: his desire to stay near Dorothea is the reason he accepts her uncle's job offer, which puts him to work on behalf of *the* cause of early 1830s English politics—the First Reform Bill. The narrator spares no details in elucidating the exact order of Will's attachments, as she describes him, in chapter 39, as "low in the depths of boredom . . . obliged to help Mr Brooke in arranging 'documents' about hanging sheep-stealers . . . while there flitted through all these steadier images a tickling vision of a sheep-stealing epic written in Homeric particularity" until Dorothea is announced and he "start[s] up as from an electric shock" (363), experiencing her entrance as "the freshness of morning" (364). By chapter 46, however, Will "was beginning thoroughly to like the work of which when he began he had said to himself rather languidly, 'Why not?'—and he studied the political situation with as ardent an interest as he had ever given to poetic metres of mediaevalism." Further:

> It is undeniable that but for the desire to be where Dorothea was, and perhaps the want of knowing what else to do, Will would not at this time have been meditating on the needs of the English people or criticising English statesmanship: he would probably have been rambling in Italy sketching plans for several dramas, trying prose and finding it too jejune, trying verse and finding it too artificial. (433)

Not only does he genuinely begin to care for what Brooke cares for, but he even convinces the never-too-sure Brooke to stand up as a liberal rather than as an independent.

What *Middlemarch* offers us in the end, beyond Eliot's general sympathy for "varieties of national genius," as expressed in "A Word for the Germans," is a prescription on how to employ that otherness for the benefit of the empire. Interpretations of Eliot's attitude toward British colonialism have ranged from imperialist to, more recently, subversive, with Nancy Henry in the middle, balancing Eliot's fiction with her financial and familial investments in British colonies.[94] Both *Middlemarch* and *Daniel Deronda* tacitly engage in imperial competition with Russia, while in their absorption of Will Ladislaw and Julius Klesmer they exhibit, to use Henry's phrasing again, the "sympathy for national liberation movements" that has been part of the English tradition. In addition, *Middlemarch* manages to hit two birds with one stone: it offers a solution to the Woman Question by improving the political life of England through Ladislaw's marriage to the heroine. In his book *George Eliot and the Politics of National Inheritance* Bernard Semmel sees in *Middlemarch* Eliot's defense of England's politics of compromise and the parliamentary state, with Will Ladislaw as the spokesperson. I have attempted to show that Will's Polish background plays a heretofore ignored role in this defense of Eliot's and to emphasize Dorothea's role in attracting him to it. Although she never gets to take a missionary trip to the "country of the Moors" (3), Dorothea does draw a rebellious Pole from the artistic centers of continental Europe to the English Midlands and converts possibly wasted and certainly overlooked masculine potential into a political figure who serves the needs of England.

Chapter 2

✦

Effi Briest

German Realism and the Young Empire

The introduction to *A Companion to German Realism* opens thus: "German Realism of the nineteenth century has a bad reputation."[1] A review of a book about German realism describes the movement as "relegated to an insignificant episode of European literature that can be in good conscience ignored."[2] The truth of the matter is that nineteenth-century Germany simply did not experience the kind of flourishing of realism as a literary movement that was seen in France, England, and Russia. What Helen Chambers has dubbed the "black hole between Goethe and Thomas Mann in the discussion of German fiction by non-Germanists" is evident in introductions to English translations of Theodor Fontane, which typically describe him as the greatest German novelist between Goethe and Mann, thereby acknowledging his lack of recognizability compared to the two iconic German authors between whom he is couched.[3] The time gap between Goethe's death in 1832, which is typically used as a marker for the end of romanticism, and Mann's novelistic debut with *Buddenbrooks* in 1901 comprises more than two-thirds of the nineteenth century during which Flaubert, George Eliot, and Tolstoy were defining realism.

Some Fontane scholars, such as Alan Bance, have identified the German literary milieu of the second half of the nineteenth century as "not receptive" to realism's favorite medium, the novel, exhibiting instead "a backward-looking preference for other, traditional genres" such as the ballad and drama.[4] Fontane himself spent the three decades that saw the publication of *Madame Bovary* (1856), *War and Peace* (1865–69), and *Middlemarch* (1871–72) writing journalistic pieces, travelogues, theater reviews, and poetry. It took the author the better part of his career to turn to the novel, publishing his first one in 1878, at the age of fifty-nine. Once he did, though, he went on to become the representative figure of German realism. As Henry Garland points out, "Perhaps even more remarkable" than Fontane's late onset of novelistic expression "is the fact that [his first] novel, *Vor dem Sturm*, was followed . . . by fifteen more novels."[5] Eleven of those, including *Vor dem Sturm* (Before the Storm), fit the category typically identified as Fontane's Berlin novels and have earned the author the title of the city's most faithful chronicler.[6] Commenting on Fontane's belated novelistic flourishing, Thomas Mann saw fit to describe "die ersten sechs Jahrzehnte seines Lebens" (the first six decades of his life) as "nur eine Vorbereitung auf die zwei späten" (just a preparation for the later two).[7] The aforementioned inaugural Berlin novel, as well as two more, *L'Adultera* and *Cécile*, are discussed below for their treatment of Poland or the topic of adultery, leading up to *Effi Briest*, where the heroine's stepping outside of marital boundaries is combined with the crossing of national lines.

Bance attributes the "backward-looking" artistic preference of nineteenth-century Germany for drama and the ballad to "social backwardness,"[8] a sentiment that was acutely felt by the Germans of the time in comparison to their French and especially their English contemporaries. This feeling of "social backwardness" was closely tied to Germany's belated ascent to the status of empire, achieved by its unification under Bismarck's Prussia in 1871—the single most important event that occurred between the years of Goethe and Mann—and the subsequent scramble for colonies. Consequently, the fact that Fontane's Berlin novels flourished in the last two decades of the century also makes him the representative author of the newly unified Germany and its capital. Otto Ludwig, a German dramatist, novelist, and critic who died in 1865, before Bismarck united Germany and the new empire acquired its first overseas colonies, lamented thus regarding his homeland's political situation: "Wir haben kein London, keinen Verkehr mit Kolonien in allen Weltteilen, kein so großes politisches Leben; wir haben keine Flotten" (We have no London, no traffic with colonies in every part of the world, not much of a political life; we don't have any fleets).[9] Fontane, himself a great admirer of England and English politics, placed Berlin on the literary map.

The conclusion regarding German realism, then, is that its primary representative is Theodor Fontane and that if we were to seek out the German novel of adultery, it would be Fontane's *Effi Briest*, the most successful of his Berlin society novels, published in book form in 1896. The work that might come to mind first as the German novel of adultery is more likely Goethe's *Wahlverwandtschaften* (Elective Affinities), which was mentioned briefly in the introduction in the context of Tony Tanner's study and was without doubt influential in Fontane's work. However, its publication in 1809 predates the Woman Question that is typically associated with the novel of adultery, in addition to the general concern with the unfaithful wife as a subject of novelistic investigation. Furthermore, it predates the national concerns my argument raises in relation to the trope of adultery as the cosmopolitan Goethe, who coined the term *Weltliteratur*, could not have foreseen the kind of national tensions that could be explored through that trope in the second half of the nineteenth century. This is evident in the way that *Wahlverwandtschaften* presents us with a love quadrangle rather than a triangle. The husband and wife each become attracted to their houseguests, but the human version of the chemical process after which the novel is named fails: the original couple draws farther apart, neither finds happiness with his and her other love interest, and both die in the end. In Tanner's assessment, *Wahlverwandtschaften* is obsessed with order and thus relies on a chemical process as a paradigm for quadrangular human relations precisely in order to avoid the chaos that "the introduction of a third may precipitate."[10] It is Fontane, at the other end of the nineteenth century, who offers us a German view of the problem already explored in its French and Russian incarnations.

Barbara Everett claims that the difference between *Effi Briest* and its European predecessors cannot "be explained in merely nationalistic terms,"[11] as she points out that Effi Briest has more in common—her innocence and youth especially but also the time of the novel's publication—with the heroines of later English writers, such as Thomas Hardy's and Henry James's, than with Emma Bovary or Anna Karenina. After all, as more of a child than a woman, Effi does resemble Hardy's eponymous Tess of the D'Urbervilles (published in 1891) or James's Nanda Brookenham in *The Awkward Age* (1899). Dorothea Brooke of *Middlemarch* is not only three years older than Effi—she is "not yet twenty" (8) in the opening of the novel—but her life experiences of being orphaned and raised in a posh Swiss boarding school also make her a lot more independent. It is her independence, in fact, that gives her the strength to marry Casaubon against her family's better judgment. Deprived of an education, she believes that "the really delightful marriage must be that where your husband was a sort of father, and could teach you even Hebrew, if you wished it" (10), while the particular choice this fantasy inspires constitutes her act of rebellion. Her bold attitude is the exact opposite of Effi's ignorant acquiescence to marrying a more closely associated father figure, the man whom her own mother had refused twenty years earlier. Tolstoy's Anna Karenina, based on her son's age, is about a decade older than Effi and a polished society woman, one who could never be accused of being "zu prätentiös" (too pretentious), as happens to young Effi when she is abruptly thrust from her sheltered parental home into the role of a provincial governor's wife.[12]

Despite her youth, however, and the novel's belatedness, Effi's life trajectory follows the story lines of the earlier but older heroines much more closely than those fashioned by Hardy or James. Like Dorothea and Anna, Effi "burst[s] upon the reader as young, attractive, blooming, and physically active,"[13] only to be sacrificed in a marriage to a much older and unfulfilling man, which is why she is frequently grouped in the critical literature with her French, English, and Russian predecessors.[14] Also, in what is probably the most authoritative study of Fontane to date, Gordon A. Craig describes

Effi Briest as "a novel that, in the incisiveness of its social analysis and its psychological insight into the predicament of women in the nineteenth century, bears comparison with *Madame Bovary* and *Anna Karenina*."[15] Rather than disqualify *Effi* from their ranks, I argue that the heroine's youth and the literary belatedness of her story reflect the youth of the German Empire compared to those inhabited by the other heroines. For this reason, it is important to investigate Effi precisely—though by no means "merely"—in "nationalistic terms." Such a reading allows for connections to be made between Germany's Johnny-come-lately status on the world scene and its belated novel of adultery.

Theodor Fontane and the Slavic World

Like George Eliot, Theodor Fontane had exhibited an interest in Poland since his first writings. He was a month shy of his eleventh birthday when the first Polish insurrection broke out in late November 1830. During this first insurrection, the liberal segment of the Prussian and wider German public was sympathetic to the Russian Poles and joined the rest of Western Europe in denouncing the tsar for his cruel policies. The following decade, in fact, saw a flourishing of a new subgenre of German poetry that has variously been called *Polengedichte*, *Polenpoesie*, *Polenlieder*, and *Polenlyrik*—the plethora of labels itself attesting to the proliferation of pro-Polish sentiment—and to which several of the younger Fontane's ballads also belong. The fervor was strongest in the two years immediately following the insurrection, during which over three hundred poems supporting the suffering Poles were published.[16] Another famous German who, perhaps surprisingly, expressed sympathy with the Poles was Richard Wagner. During his young student days in Leipzig he was purportedly inspired by a night of drinking with some Polish refugees, in 1832, to compose an overture he named "Polonia." However, as his early years were fraught with disappointments and failed operas, the piece was not performed until 1881, when the manuscript accidentally fell back into his hands.[17]

Fontane confesses in his autobiographical work, *Meine Kinderjahre* (My Childhood), "Kein anderer Krieg, unsere eigenen nicht ausgeschlossen, hat von meiner Phantasie je wieder so Besitz genommen wie diese Polenkämpfe, und die Gedichte, die an jene Zeit anknüpfen" (No other war, our own wars not excluded, has ever again taken possession of my fantasy as much as these Polish struggles and the poetry that started up at the time) (*SW* 14:115). His observation several lines down that "Freiheitskämpfe haben einen eigenen Zauber" (struggles for freedom have a special charm) (*SW* 14:115) sums up perfectly that "sympathy for national liberation movements" that Nancy Henry is cited attributing to the English in the previous chapter, though I would amend that statement into "sympathy for *small, distant, and non-threatening* national liberation movements." As chapter 3 shows, Russia, while being the great villain to the Poles, supported the national liberation movements of other smaller Slavic nations that posed no territorial threat to its borders. About a decade after quashing the second Polish uprising, Russia not only sympathized with but also waged and won a war on behalf of the South Slavic provinces rebelling against Ottoman rule. The nature of such a pick-and-choose attitude is perfectly encapsulated in a line from *Middlemarch* that was not discussed in the previous chapter. The liberal and well-meaning yet incompetent Mr. Brooke is criticized by his conservative competitor as "a philanthropist who cannot bear one rogue to be hanged, but does not mind five honest tenants half-starved," and this quote precedes the following insightful definition of a philanthropist: "a man whose charity increases directly as the square of the distance" (360). Such was certainly the case on a national level in Russian policies on the Poles in contrast to the South Slavs as well as in English sympathies for the Poles in contrast to their treatment of the Irish. It also turned out to be the case for Prussia, whose *Polenfreundschaft* of the early 1830s did not last very long. Even the *Polenbegeisterung* (Polish enthusiasm) of those few years, as Kristin Kopp notes, was particularly evident among "those hailing from the southwestern German states,"[18] in other words, those Germans whose "square of distance" from Poland was greater than that of their compatriots residing in the northeasternmost state of Prussia. Nevertheless, Prussia's most successful novelist of the late nineteenth century remained sympathetic to the Poles and their plight throughout his literary career, even when he embraced, as we shall see with *Effi Briest*, some of the Prussian prejudices of his time.

In the several decades following the first Polish insurrection, Prussian policies on Poland changed drastically. This was due mostly to the fears spurred by imagining what such an uprising on the home turf might mean for the dominant Prussian culture, and it was later solidified with the 1871 election of Otto von Bismarck to the post of chancellor. Bismarck's attitude to Poland resembled that of the Russian tsars. When the second insurrection broke out on January 22, 1863, he declared that "the restoration of an independent Polish state . . . would constitute a threat to Prussia,"[19] and on February 8 he signed an agreement with Russia that offered logistical assistance to tsarist troops pursuing Polish rebels along Prussia's borders.[20] This tactic was beneficial for Prussia for one more reason beyond attempting to frighten its own potential Polish rebels, as aiding Russia secured the tsar's support for German unification, an event that was perceived as a threat by England and certainly not welcomed by France. The 1871 unification of Germany was followed by a vehement pursuit of internal enemies, who were defined in Bismarck's *Kulturkampf*—literally "culture struggle," officially launched in 1873—as Germany's Catholics and especially the Poles. "The era of sympathy for the separate Polish identity," as Agnieszka Nance notes, "culminat[ed] in a law of 1876 which affirmed German the only permitted language in all of Prussia."[21]

Fontane's first Berlin novel, *Vor dem Sturm*, is commonly referred to as his Polish novel and, published in 1878, appeared at the height of Bismarck's anti-Polish *Kulturkampf*. It is also significant that Fontane first began working on this novel during the winter of 1863–64, which was the time of the second Polish insurrection, but he took a long, twelve-year break from the work, "not from any lack of interest," according to Garland, "but simply because it was crowded out by other work."[22] Subtitled *Roman aus dem Winter 1812 auf 13* (Novel from the Winter of 1812 to '13), *Vor dem Sturm* describes Prussia's experience with the Napoleonic wars and is, for that reason, also often compared to Tolstoy's *War and Peace*. This comparison must be qualified, however, with the observation that Fontane's novel did not enjoy great success, not when it was first published and, except for a brief rediscovery after World War II, not since. As Craig notes, "By the critics *Vor dem Sturm* tends to be disregarded, and it is virtually unknown abroad."[23] Nonetheless, plot-wise, like *War and Peace*, *Vor dem Sturm* looks at the lives of two families during the time of Napoleon's downfall. The contrast lies in the sense of national belonging of the families in the two novels; whereas Tolstoy's Bolkonskys and Rostovs represent old Russia and are contrasted favorably to the westernized, materially and sexually promiscuous Kuragins, Fontane depicts a Prussian and a Polish family, both representative of pre-Bismarck *Altpreußen*, whose progeny fail to intermarry.

Fontane was himself a "Tolstojschwärmer" (Tolstoy enthusiast), which is a designation he assigns to the protagonist of his final novel, *Der Stechlin*. The young Woldemar von Stechlin hails the decline of "Sentimentalitäten," as he declares, "Wir stehen jetzt im Zeichen von Tolstoj und der *Kreutzersonate*" (We stand now under the sign of Tolstoy and the *Kreutzer Sonata*), and, when contradicted, "wollte für den russischen Grafen eine Lanze brechen" (wanted to break a lance for the Russian count) (*SW* 8:119). Tolstoy's novella *The Death of Ivan Il'ich* belonged to Fontane's list of "Meisterstücke" (masterpieces), and he wrote a glowing review of Tolstoy's play *The Power of Darkness* after it premiered on the German stage on January 26, 1890. But these three references to Tolstoy's works in Fontane's oeuvre indicate that he saw the great Russian author primarily in terms of his later and shorter works, those of the 1880s to be specific, since *The Death of Ivan Il'ich* and *The Power of Darkness* were published in Russia in 1886 and *The Kreutzer Sonata* in 1889. His omission of Tolstoy's two defining works that share more common ground with his own account of the Napoleonic wars and the story of an unhappily married woman who commits adultery might be indicative of the general German distaste for large novels during the period preceding Thomas Mann. *Vor dem Sturm* is by no means a short work, but its 600 pages or so still comprise less than half the length of *War and Peace*, and the length of the rest of Fontane's novels rarely exceeds 200 pages, indicating thus a strong preference for brevity on the author's part.

Although *Vor dem Sturm* is considered Fontane's *War and Peace*—as we might consider *Effi Briest* his *Anna Karenina*—critics speculate that it is unlikely that he had read the Russian masterpiece when preparing the Prussian version.[24] He might have even resented the comparison, since he described his writing of the novel to Wilhelm Hertz, his publisher, thus: "Ich habe . . . vorgenommen, *die Arbeit ganz nach mir selbst*, nach meiner Neigung und Individualität zu machen, ohne jegliches bestimmte Vorbild" (I have . . . set myself to do this work *absolutely in my own way*, in accordance with my own inclination and personality, without any definite model).[25] If it is unlikely that Fontane had read *War and Peace*, it would have been impossible for him to have read *Anna Karenina* prior to writing his first novel, since both were published in 1878. This makes his choice for the names of two of the protagonists of *Vor dem Sturm*—Lewin and Kathinka—an utterly remarkable coincidence and one worth mentioning despite the lack of influence.

Levin and Kitty of *Anna Karenina*, as elaborated in the following chapter, are the ideal(ized) couple, descendants of two of the oldest Moscow families who almost fail to merge because of Vronsky, who briefly courts Kitty without any intention to marry her until he meets and falls in love with Anna. Lewin and Kathinka of *Vor dem Sturm* come from a Prussian and Polish family, respectively, and are supposed to marry until Kathinka elopes with a Polish patriot, Count Bninski, who had fought on the French side in Spain and before that, while still a boy, in an earlier Polish uprising against Russia, led by the famed Tadeusz Kościuszko in 1794. Each character from the initial love pair also has a sibling of the opposite sex—Renate is Lewin's sister and Tubal is Kathinka's brother—who are expected to marry, but Tubal dies at the hands of the French and Renate eventually joins a Protestant convent. The way in which the couples pair off and the way in which Tubal meets his end, I argue, is telling of the deterioration of Prusso-Polish relations that occurred in the few decades preceding the novel's publication. Thus, while describing the short period of events between December 1812 and May 1813, the novel casts light on the political tensions of the 1860s and 1870s.

The novel is also one of generational differences—not an uncommon theme for Fontane, who returns to it in subsequent works, such as *Frau Jenny Treibel* (1892) and the previously mentioned *Der Stechlin* (1898)—and is, in that sense, comparable to another Russian masterpiece, Ivan Turgenev's *Fathers and Children* (1862).[26] The most significant generational difference in *Vor dem Sturm* is evident in the Polish family, whose patriarch, *Geheimrat* (Councilor) Alexander von Ladalinski, was born in what became Russian Poland and, like his future son-in-law, participated in Kościuszko's uprising of 1794. That was a year before the final partition that wiped Poland off the map and Ladalinski, anticipating Russia's victory, expatriated himself to Prussia. The narrator informs us that "in dem alten Ladalinski sich polnisches Blut und preußische Doktrin wie Feuer und Wasser befehdeten" (in the old Ladalinski the Polish blood and Prussian doctrine feuded with each other like fire and water) (*SW* 1:324). This inner feud results in a strong sensitivity to his Polish background, which is only aggravated by his children's national awakening and Kathinka's final marital choice. Neither does it help the matter that Kathinka's fiancé perceives old Ladalinski as a sellout. While she worries about breaking her promise to her father "nichts zu tun, das seine Stellung untergraben oder seine Zugehörigkeit zu diesem Lande neuen Verdächtigungen aussetzen könnte" (to do nothing that could undermine his position or release new suspicions regarding his belonging to this land), Bninski evaluates his future father-in-law and his chosen homeland in the following manner: "er ist Pole vom Wirbel bis zur Zeh'. Er täuscht mich nicht mit seiner loyalen Preußenmiene. Preußen! Warum gerade Preußen, das uns zuerst um dreißig Silberlinge verschacherte" (he is a Pole from head to toe. He doesn't fool me with his loyal Prussian demeanor. Prussia! Why must it be Prussia, which would trade us for thirty pieces of silver given the first opportunity) (*SW* 1:424). This reference to Judas is the most damning of Bninski's pronouncements against Prussia, and it must have sounded all the more jarring to its original readers in the political context of the 1870s.

Kathinka's jilted fiancé, Lewin von Vitzewitz, ends up marrying a commoner named Marie, the biological daughter of traveling entertainers and the adopted daughter of a neighboring nonaristocratic family. Lewin marries Marie with his father's blessing, thus signifying an attenuation of class differences. Garland reads this ending as "rearrangement, not overthrow and replacement," pointing to "a new order, an order of conciliation and harmony."[27] I prefer to turn the focus on the national "rearrangement" that is present in the plot's unfolding, as it points away from "conciliation and harmony" and reflects the *Kulturkampf* of the 1870s. If the novel appears to endorse a merging of classes, the optimistic ending it offers obscures the significance of national separation that, in fact, enables the class merger. Prussians marry other Prussians and Poles marry other Poles. Moreover, Prussians stay in Prussia, while Poles leave, as do Kathinka and Bninski when they elope in Paris, the seat of Prussia's greatest enemy at the time.

The other Prusso-Polish couple is also doomed, as Tubal's marriage to Renate is prevented by the former's death, occasioned by his successful rescue of Lewin, who has been captured by the French. Therefore, this Pole is not only eliminated, but he is symbolically sacrificed for the sake of a Prussian Junker. The tragic event effects a change in old Ladalinski's relationship to his origins, as he decides to honor his son's wish to return to the motherland by burying him in Poland and moving there in the process. Nance insightfully observes that "with Ladalinski's return to Poland, the storyline of *Vor dem Sturm* comes full circle: the once patriotic and active independence fighter who afterward became a 'gehorsam' [obedient] Prussian citizen . . . will be returning to his homeland and his Polish culture," yet she fails to problematize Fontane's "solidarity with the Polish nation."[28] While the novel does offer several invectives against Prussia and this seems courageous for a work published in the late 1870s, those invectives are sufficiently weakened by being placed in the mouth of a Pole and thus merely reflect a successful execution of the realist aesthetic that dominated the second half of the century.

Having a Prussian character voice Bninski's criticisms would have been more effective but also more dangerous at the height of Bismarck's power. Craig observes that "most of the people in Fontane's novels who talk about Bismarck are critical of him (the exception is Instettin in *Effi Briest*, who works for him and admires him), and his figure seems to invite historical comparison with tyrants and violent men."[29] The reference to people who *talk* about Bismarck is significant because conversation is the most frequently praised feature of Fontane's novels. One particular conversation, the one between Effi's cuckolded husband and his best friend about the necessity of a duel, is considered the best conversation in German literature.[30] Garland points out in his chapter on *L'Adultera* that "conversation occupies approximately 40 per cent of the text, a figure which also applies, with moderate variation to a large number of Fontane novels."[31] Such heavy reliance on conversation makes it easy for the author to place all criticisms of Prussia in his historical novels, and of Bismarck in his contemporary society novels, in the mouths of his characters and thus remain ambiguous regarding his own views. As Craig notes, Fontane's views on these issues are also glaringly absent from his letters, which yield no more information than his novels do.[32] Regarding the exception of Innstetten, it is important to remember that the love of Bismarck by this, one of fiction's cruelest husbands is portrayed in a novel that first began to be serialized in 1894, that is, four years after the chancellor's rule ended.

A final note on *Vor dem Sturm* is that its replacement of internation marriage with interclass marriage mirrors the shift in anxieties that the rise of nationalism produced in the nineteenth century. Kathinka's choice of Bninski over Lewin and the aristocratic society's acceptance of Lewin's subsequent choice of Marie illustrate a shift in the definitions of insiders and outsiders. If, as the popular saying goes, birds of a feather flock together, then the feathers begin to be differentiated by the colors of the national flag instead of one's status on the socioeconomic scale. It is the more conservative Tolstoy who reaffirms both class and national boundaries when he successfully unites his Levin—an autobiographical character who expresses a disgust for the merging of classes[33]—and Kitty in a blissful union.

The Woman Taken in Adultery

Although more than one of Fontane's Berlin novels addresses adultery as a central topic, *Effi Briest* is typically singled out because it is considered the author's crowning masterpiece, in addition to the already mentioned fact that it follows the typical trajectory of *Madame Bovary* and *Anna Karenina*, ending with the death of the transgressing heroine. *L'Adultera*, published in 1882, and *Cécile*, published in 1887, are two more examples.[34] Fontane's first novel to be set in contemporary Berlin, *L'Adultera* also happens to be his first novel of adultery.[35] The author was aware of the tradition of naming novels of adultery after the transgressing heroine, evident in his almost naming the novel *Melanie van der Straaten*,[36] after the young woman married, in typical fashion for the genre, to a boorish man over twenty years her senior. *L'Adultera*, however, is not the typical novel of adultery, since it has a happy ending; not because, as in *Middlemarch*, the oppressive older husband conveniently dies, but because Melanie's husband offers forgiveness and accepts his former wife's new life with her new husband. The novel's ultimate title, after Tintoretto's painting of the New Testament story about the woman taken in adultery—famous for Jesus's pronouncement that he who is without sin should cast the first stone—more appropriately suits its content.

The famous Italian painting is unveiled and discussed in chapter 2, also titled "L'Adultera," and is obviously meant to foreshadow further developments in the plot. Melanie exclaims to her husband after recognizing the painting, "Aber daβ du gerade *das* wählen musstest! Es ist eigentlich ein gefährliches Bild, fast so gefährlich wie der Spruch . . . Wie heiβt es doch?" (But that you just had to choose *that one*! It is really a dangerous picture, almost as dangerous as the saying . . . How does it go?) (*SW* 4:12). After her husband recites the saying—"Wer unter euch ohne Sünde ist . . ." (Who among you is without sin . . .)—Melanie continues, "Richtig. Und ich kann mir nicht helfen, es liegt so was Ermutigendes darin . . . Es ist so viel Unschuld in ihrer Schuld . . . Und alles wie vorherbestimmt" (That's right. And I cannot help myself, there is something encouraging in there . . . There is so much innocence in her guilt . . . And all as if predestined) (*SW* 4:12–13). The German word play with innocence and guilt is lost in the English translation, since "innocence" in German is literally "nonguilt": *Schuld—Unschuld*. Melanie is, thus, unguilting the guilty woman, and the rest of her speech about encouragement and predestination functions as an absolution of her own wrongdoing, or at least of the responsibility for it, before she even commits it. As will become obvious in my further discussions of *Cécile* and *Effi Briest*, Fontane continues with the tendency to portray his heroines thus, which has earned them the collective label *femme fragile* instead of *femme fatale*.[37]

The original version of the story depicted in Tintoretto's painting appears in the Gospel of John. The story was and still is viewed with suspicion, and, like Fontane's novel centuries later, had trouble making it into the canon. While Fontane's novels typically appeared in book form shortly after serialization, within a year or less, *L'Adultera* was serialized in the summer of 1880, but it took the author two years to find a book publisher for it. Contemporary printings of the New Testament bracket off the eleven verses of the story of the woman taken in adultery (John 8:1–11) with a footnote that "this episode is not found in the most authoritative manuscripts."[38] If, as St. Augustine surmised, the verses were taken out of some Gospel versions for fear that they would grant women license to commit adultery, then Fontane's censors had reason to be concerned that the modern German version of the story would compel husbands to do what Tolstoy's obtuse Karenin could not be persuaded to do: grant his unfaithful wife a divorce and part amicably. In the Gospel of John, Jesus spares the adulterous woman's life by challenging those in the crowd who have never sinned to throw the first stone. The part of the story that gets left out of most discussions, however, the very end, is not so liberating. After everybody disperses, Jesus tells the woman, "Neither do I condemn you," but he adds one more sentence, which constitutes the final line of the story: "Go your way, and from now on do not sin again."[39] Jesus does, in fact, condemn the woman when he names the behavior in which she has been caught and for which she was about to be stoned "sin." Since he condemns her behavior, the phrase "Neither do I condemn you" must imply "to death." Further, "do not sin again" can only mean forsaking her lover and returning to her husband. This, incidentally, was the same argument Augustine used for keeping the story in John's Gospel:

> This proceeding, however, shocks the minds of some weak believers, or rather unbelievers and enemies of the Christian faith: inasmuch that, after (I suppose) of its giving their wives impunity of sinning, they struck out from their copies of the Gospel this that our Lord did in pardoning the woman taken in adultery: as if He granted leave of sinning, Who said, *Go and sin no more*![40]

The lesson for the crowd eager to witness Jesus's reaction does not include a condoning of adultery but a strong statement that their sins, sexual or not, are no different. Fontane takes forgiveness a big step further when he allows his heroine to leave her husband and marry her lover.

The circumstance employed to bring about the adultery is a live-in guest, which is a reproduction of Germany's most famous novel of adultery prior to *Effi Briest*, the already mentioned *Wahlverwandtschaften*. Fontane even employs the very term "Wahlverwandtschaften" (*SW* 4:122) in the last chapter of the novel, which informs us of the reconciliation between all three parties and the eventual reintegration of the new couple into society, among which a number of "Esoterischer" (esoteric ones) attribute the whole affair to elective affinities. The third chapter of *L'Adultera* is titled "Logierbesuch" (A Live-In Guest) and, as it immediately follows the "L'Adultera" chapter, suggests a sequential connection between adultery and a live-in-guest. The cuckolded husband is *Kommerzienrat* (Commercial Councilor) Ezechiel van der Straaten, a converted Jew who is affectionately known as Ezel. This nickname sounds a lot like *Esel*, the German word for "donkey," and is illustrative of his uncouth behavior. After unveiling Tintoretto's painting in chapter 2, he shocks his wife again in chapter 3 with news of the imminent arrival of his friend's son Ebenezer Rubehn. The wife, Melanie—affectionately Lanni—protests the very idea of a male live-in guest, all the more vehemently for the sound of his name. The lengthy conversation she has with her husband on this topic is worth citing in full:

> "Ebenezer Rubehn," wiederholte Melanie langsam und jede Silbe betonend. "Ich bekenne dir offen, daβ mir etwas Christlich-Germanisches lieber gewesen wäre. Viel lieber. Als ob wir an deinem Ezechiel nicht schon gerade genug hätten! Und nun Ebenezer. Ebenezer Rubehn! Ich bitte dich, was soll dieser Accent grave, dieser Ton auf der letzten Silbe? Suspekt, im höchsten Grade suspekt!"
>
> "Du musst wissen, er schreibt sich mit einem *h*."
>
> "Mit einem *h*! Du wirst doch nicht verlangen, daβ ich dies *h* für echt und ursprünglich nehmen soll? Einschiebsel, versuchte Leugnung des Tatsächlichen, absichtliche Verschleierung, hinter der ich nichtsdestoweniger alle zwölf Söhne Jakobs stehen sehe. Und er selber als Flügelmann."
>
> "Und doch irrst du, Lanni. Wie stand es denn mit Rubens? Ich meine mit dem großen Peter Paul? Nur, der hatte freilich ein *s*. Aber was dem *s* recht ist, ist dem *h* billig. Und kurz und gut, er ist getauft. Ob durch ein Bischof, stehe dahin; ich weiß es nicht und wünsch es nicht, denn ich möcht etwas vor ihm voraushaben. Aber allen Ernstes, du tust ihm unrecht. Er ist nicht bloß christlich, er ist auch protestantisch, so gut wie du und ich. Und wenn du noch zweifelst, so lasse dich durch den Augenschein überzeugen."

> "Ebenezer Rubehn," Melanie repeated slowly and emphasizing every syllable. "I openly confess to you that something Christian-Germanic would have been more to my liking. Much more. As though with your being Ezechiel we haven't already had enough! And now Ebenezer. Ebenezer Rubehn! I beg you, what is that *accent grave* supposed [to mean], that emphasis on the last syllable? Suspect, in the highest degree suspect."
>
> "You should know, he spells it with an *h*."
>
> "With an *h*! You don't expect me to take this *h* as original and authentic? An interpolation, an attempt to deny the factual, a de-

> liberate disguise, behind which I can nonetheless see Jacob's twelve sons standing. And himself on the flank."
>
> "And yet you're wrong, Lanni. How is it with Rubens then? I mean with the great Peter Paul? Now, he admittedly had an *s*. But an *h* is as good as an *s*. And anyway, he's been christened. Whether by a bishop is neither here nor there; I don't know and I wish he wasn't, because then I could have an advantage over him. But seriously, you're doing him an injustice. He's not only Christian, he's also Protestant, as good as you and I. And if you're still doubting, then let your eyes convince you." (*SW* 4:18)

The spelling of last names is of particular concern in the novel's plot. The first chapter, titled "Kommerzienrat van der Straaten," discusses Ezechiel's, namely, the question of his near or distant relation to Manasse Vanderstraaten, a Jewish character in Karl Gutzkow's 1864 play, *Uriel Acosta*. Ezechiel is fully assimilated, as evidenced by his repeatedly mentioned "spezifisch lokalen Stempel" (typically local manner), "echtberlinische[n] Hange" (truly Berlin tendency), and general "Berlinismen" (Berlinisms), as well as his own tripartite answer to the above question: his last name is spelled not as one word but three; he was baptized by none less than a Lutheran bishop; and, finally, he "seit längerer Zeit des Vorzugs genieße, die Honneurs seines Hauses nicht durch eine Judith, sondern durch eine Melanie machen lassen zu können" (for some time now has enjoyed the advantage of having as mistress of his house not a Judith but a Melanie) (*SW* 4:8).

This introduction to Ezechiel's ethnic origins is mentioned as if in passing, since the main concern of family friends, who "ermangelten selbstverständlich nicht, allerhand Trübes zu prophezeien" (were naturally not lacking in gloomy prophecies) (*SW* 4:9), is not that the husband is a (former) Jew but that he is so much older than his wife—he married the seventeen-year-old Melanie when he was forty-two—and embarrassingly unsophisticated. Ezechiel is the opposite of the popular trope, employed also in Gutzkow's play, of the "wandering Jew," since his uncouth nature is attributed to the fact that, except for a few short trips to Paris and Italy, "er zu wenig 'draußen' gewesen war" (he had been too little in the outside [world]) (*SW* 4:7). As far as ethnic origins are concerned, it is actually the bride's Swiss French that comes into question regarding the potential success of the marriage, since Ezechiel wonders whether "alle Vorzüge französischen Wesens" (all the advantages of [her] French being) may also come with potential "Schwächen" (weaknesses) (*SW* 4:8).

The reference to the potential weaknesses of Melanie's "French being" might be an allusion to the literary aftermath of Gustave Flaubert's *Madame Bovary*, and there is at least one study that assesses Fontane's novel as an answer to the depressing outcomes depicted by his French and Russian predecessors. In her excellent work *The Changing Image of Theodor Fontane*,

Helen Chambers takes on the task of reviewing the author's reception from his own time to our contemporary period. She briefly discusses Hanni Mittelmann's *Die Utopie des weiblichen Glücks in den Romanen Theodor Fontanes* (The Utopia of Female Happiness in the Novels of Theodor Fontane), which points to novels such as *L'Adultera* as progressive antidotes to Flaubert and Tolstoy. In her comparison, Mittelmann does not go into detail, which would reveal a number of resemblances, as well as one very noteworthy contrast, between *L'Adultera* and *Anna Karenina*, and would thus significantly strengthen her argument. To begin with the similarities, the adulterous couples in both novels travel to Italy to escape the scandal at home and, on returning, both heroines are shocked at the degree to which society ostracizes them. Another similarity is that Melanie's husband, although still hoping to persuade her to stay with him, promises to accept the child with whom she is pregnant by Rubehn "als ob es mein eigen wäre" (as if it were my own) (*SW* 4:89). This is what Karenin initially does with Anna's baby by Vronsky, which is discussed in more detail in the following chapter. The noteworthy contrast between the two novels, aside from the obvious difference in their endings, is the way in which those endings are predicted with the framing of each story. If the very title of *L'Adultera* evokes the New Testament tale and its theme of forgiveness, then the ominous epigraph of *Anna Karenina*—"Vengeance is mine and I will repay"—conjures up the image of the angry Old Testament God, who is typically contrasted to the gentler Jesus. In this regard, it is worthwhile to observe that the forgiving husband is, like Jesus, a Jew. Fontane's Prussian officers in his subsequent novels of adultery, such as *Cécile* and *Effi Briest*, prove incapable of forgiveness.

Fontane's decision to make both husband and lover converted Jews has been deemed "puzzling." Craig suggests, following Peter Demetz's assessment, that the author "lacked the confidence to describe the working out of his love triangle in autochthonous society and was trying to ease his problem by marginalizing his characters."[41] Craig concludes that this weakens the novel as a critique of German society, but I wish to suggest that, if examined within Fontane's larger oeuvre, it actually puts the highly placed Prussian husbands of his later novels to shame. Neither *Cécile* nor *Effi Briest* ends with a reconciliation, and their tragic endings have always been understood as a critique of Prussian society. Mittelmann's conclusion regarding the later novels is that, in Chambers's words, "an unhappy end makes a greater appeal to the reader's sense of discomfort and so calls forth a stronger conviction that change is necessary."[42] To look at the other gender as well, we might add that Fontane seems unable to portray a fickle-hearted Prussian heroine, making the adulterous woman of *L'Adultera* Swiss French and the eponymous heroine of *Cécile* Slavic. *Effi Briest*, of course, is the great exception, but as we shall see, Effi is a victim, plucked right out of her childhood, and she demonstrates no more passion for her conniving lover than she does for her husband's "etwas müden Zärtlichkeiten" (somewhat tired caresses) (*SW* 7:256).

Before moving on to the novel in which the adulterous heroine is Slavic, it must be acknowledged that the Slavic element is not lacking from Fontane's Jewish novel either. It appears through the figure of Melanie's brother-in-law, her younger sister's Polish husband, Major von Gryczinski. In contrast to *Vor dem Sturm*'s respectable old Ladalinski who returns to his Polish and Catholic roots, Gryczinski is portrayed as a careerist intent on dismissing anything that could stand in the way of his climb to the top. This not only includes his Polish nationality and Catholic religion, but also his fallen sister-in-law, with whom he prohibits his wife from communicating. Thus, not only Fontane's future Prussian husbands but this Polish husband also pale in comparison to the magnanimous Ezechiel van der Straaten. To be fair, though, the difference between Ladalinski and Gryczinski can also be explained in terms of the different political situation the Prussian Poles faced in the earlier part of the nineteenth century versus the later, Bismarckian part. Gryczinski has no other way of climbing to the top in the 1870s than by disavowing his Polish heritage and any connections with people committing morally objectionable actions. Whether in accurate reflection of the political exigencies or due to an inability to resist the prejudices of his day, Fontane's male Polish characters following the Ladalinskis sink into moral turpitude, with the worst of them being represented by Effi's corrupter, Major Crampas. The depiction of female Polish characters, however, is entirely different, as both *Cécile* and *Effi Briest*—the final two novels under consideration—show.

A Tragic Polish Heroine

Cécile is Fontane's first novel in which the Polish element and the trope of adultery are intertwined, and, as such, it provides a useful segue to *Effi Briest*. It also provides—together with *Effi Briest*, but for slightly different reasons—a meaningful comparison with *Middlemarch*, as outlined further below. If *L'Adultera* is Fontane's first novel of adultery, then *Cécile* is his first typical novel of adultery, with a typical ending, and thus appropriately named after the transgressing heroine.[43] Young Cécile is unsatisfied in her marriage to Colonel Pierre St. Arnaud, an "ältere Herr, ein starker Fünfziger" (elderly man, well into his fifties) (*SW* 4:129), as he is described in the opening of the novel, and she falls in love with a dashing cosmopolitan Scottish émigré to England. This lover, named Leslie-Gordon, is portrayed as more reflective than the typical home wrecker of the nineteenth-century novel, based on his first assessment of Cécile's marriage—"Dahinter steckt ein Roman. Er ist über zwanzig Jahre älter als sie" (There is a novel in this.

He is more than twenty years older than she) (*SW* 4:136)—and a later, more cynical conclusion:

> Was bleibt übrig? Ich glaube jetzt klar zu sehen. Sie war sehr schön und sehr verwöhnt, und als der Prinz, auf den mit Sicherheit gerechnet wurde, nicht kommen wollte, nahm sie den Obersten. Und ein Jahr später was sie nervös, und zwei Jahre später war sie melancholisch. Natürlich, ein alter Oberst ist immer zum Melancholisch werden. Aber das ist auch alles. Und schließlich haben wir nichts als eine Frau, die, wie tausend andre, nicht glücklich und auch nicht unglücklich ist.
>
> What more is there? I believe I see things clearly now. She was very beautiful and very indulged, and when the prince on whom she had reckoned with certainty did not come, she took the colonel. And a year later she had trouble with her nerves, and two years later she was melancholic. Naturally, an old colonel is always enough to make one melancholic. But that is all there is to it. And in the end we have nothing but a woman who, like a thousand others, is not happy and also not unhappy. (*SW* 4:236)

As is repeated subsequently in *Effi Briest*, the cuckolded husband shoots the lover in a duel and Cécile, assuming more agency than Effi, commits suicide after reading about the duel in the newspapers. Unlike in *Effi Briest*, however, it is Cécile, the adulterous heroine, who is of Slavic origins, not her lover, and this swap between ethnicity and gender is tied to a further difference between these two Fontane novels. Effi's half Polish lover is entirely devoid of charm, and the heroine is never even described as attracted to him. By contrast, it is Gordon's English sheen, in addition to his youth, that gives him the advantage over Cécile's husband, who, despite his obviously French name, is never identified as anything but Prussian. When examined in conjunction with *Middlemarch*, this ethnic configuration becomes a continued metaphor of Anglo-Polish affinities but one shown from the German side, whose cuckolded colonel must exact his revenge. German political attitudes toward England and Poland could not have been further apart; England was held in high esteem, an empire to be aspired to, whereas Poland was the primitive neighbor to be brought into submission and, as historians and literary scholars of Germany have argued—about which more later—the country's ersatz colonial space. This difference explains why the English lover is so attractive in *Cécile* and the Polish one decidedly not in *Effi Briest*. Related to *Middlemarch*, Cécile's cheating on an oppressive German husband with an Englishman reflects quite nicely the national situation of (part of) Poland's inferior position under Germany's thumb and the English desire to liberate it.

The presence of an English character in a leading role in this novel justifies an interlude for a discussion of the author's own strong affinity for England. George Eliot's great love of German intellectual thought that was discussed in the previous chapter was reciprocated by Fontane's fascination with England. He had less flattering things to say about the celebrated English author, though, as revealed in the one instance of his writings that mention her. Gerlinde Röder-Bolton notes in her book *George Eliot in Germany* that Eliot was introduced to the German poet Paul Heyse in Munich in1858.[44] It was from Heyse, as Fontane's letter from April 26, 1870, reveals, that he received the rather unfavorable impression of the English "genius":

> George Elliot ist in der That die Frau von Mr. Lewis. Einige sagen, sie seien nicht getraut. Was aber, bei der Richtung beider, ganz gleich ist; sie gerieren sich als Mann und Frau. Es sind zwei Genies; *sie* vielleicht noch mehr als er. Dabei beide hässlich, *er*, glaub ich, kakerlakig, und beide gleich selbstbewusst und unausstehlich. Sie waren 'mal in München und Paul Heyse hat sie mir vor 6 oder 8 Jahren in dieser Weise beschrieben. Obs zutrifft, weiß ich nicht genau.
>
> George Elliot [*sic*] is indeed the wife of Mr. Lewis [*sic*]. Some say they are not married. This, however, is of no consequence considering the leanings of the two; they conduct themselves as husband and wife. They are two geniuses, *she* perhaps even more so than he. At the same time, both are ugly, *he*, I believe, cockroach-like, and both equally self-assured and intolerable. They were once in Munich and Paul Heyse described them to me in this manner 6 or 8 years ago. Whether it's accurate, I don't exactly know.[45]

Fontane first visited England on holiday in 1844, followed by a six-month stay in 1852, and finally resided there for a period of a little over three years, between 1855 and 1859, while working as a newspaper correspondent. His writings on England constitute one entire volume (17) of the twenty-four-volume edition of his *Sämtliche Werke* (Collected Works) and almost another hundred pages of the following volume in the collection. His essay "England und Engländer" (England and the English) opens with this line: "Seit Jahren blickt' ich auf England wie die Juden in Ägypten auf Kanaan" (For years I have looked upon England as the Jews in Egypt upon Canaan) (*SW* 17:466). He goes on to list "die Macht des Gesetzes, die Freiheit des Individuums" (the power of the law, the freedom of the individual) (*SW* 17:467) and the fact that "die Englische Presse ist *frei*" (the English press is *free*) (emphasis Fontane's) (*SW* 17:468) as reasons for considering England the "gelobtes Land" (promised land) (*SW* 17:467). This culminates in a poetic—and somewhat obsequious—naming of other impressive things English in a series of sentences that open with the phrase "ich lobe mir das Land . . ." (I praise the land . . .) (*SW* 17:469).

The changing political climate in nineteenth-century Prussia, as Clifford Albrecht Bernd demonstrates, supported Fontane's love for England. While the emperor Friederich Wilhelm III had been, since the 1815 Congress in Vienna, indebted to Austria for Prussia's significant territorial gain along the Rhine after Napoleon's defeat, when Friederich Wilhelm IV took the throne in 1840 he attempted to win England as Prussia's new ally. The sentiment was not returned, especially as, during the following decades, England perceived Germany's unification as a threat. George Eliot had to work hard to convince her readers to acknowledge Germany as "the source of preeminently important contributions to the sum of our mental wealth,"[46] while on the continent, as Bernd observes, "fires of Anglophilia rag[ed] in Prussia."[47] Friederich IV sought to extricate himself from Austrian domination and strengthen Prussia's ties with England based on a common Protestant heritage, which was important to emphasize also as a common difference from Catholic Austria, since Germans and Austrians were geographically closer and spoke the same language. The anti-Catholic sentiment later fanned the flames against other nations standing in the way of Prussia's rise, such as France and Poland.

The English Protestant and the Polish (former) Catholic meet in an illicit liaison in *Cécile*, and Gordon suspects from the beginning that Cécile has Slavic origins. Upon first seeing her he says that "wirkt sie katholisch" (she gives the impression of being Catholic), and after a couple more guesses as to her geographic roots he feels convinced: "Jetzt hab ich es: Polin oder wenigstens polnisches Halbblut" (Now I've got it: a Pole or at least half Polish) (*SW* 4:136). He reveals the ultimate standard of superiority, however, when he "gestand sich, selten eine schönere Frau gesehen zu haben, kaum in England, kaum in den 'States'" (confessed to himself that he had rarely seen a more beautiful woman, even in England, even in the States) (*SW* 4:140). In a letter to his sister, where he confesses his "Neugier" (curiosity) about Cécile, Gordon writes, "Ich finde, sie schlesiert ein wenig" (I find a bit of Silesia in her) (*SW* 4:169), and his conjecture is confirmed a few chapters later when Cécile tells him of "der kleinen oberschlesischen Stadt, darin ich geboren und großgezogen war" (the little Upper Silesian town where I was born and brought up) (*SW* 4:190).

The little Upper Silesian town is where St. Arnaud first encountered his future wife, in the house of her mother, who had once herself been a "berühmte Schönheit" (famous beauty) (*SW* 4:251). Recounting this family history in another letter, this time to his friend Roby, Gordon describes Cécile's childhood home as the house "der verwitweten Frau von Zacha, richtiger Woronesch von Zacha, in deren bloßem Namen schon, wie Dir nicht entgehen wird, eine ganze slawische Welt harmonisch zusammenklingt" (of the widowed Frau von Zacha, more precisely Woronesch von Zacha, in the sound of whose very name, as will not have escaped you, a whole Slavic world harmoniously rings) (*SW* 4:251).

As has already been shown with *L'Adultera*, the sound of names plays an important role in Fontane's Berlin society novels. This is particularly—though not exclusively, as we have seen—the case with Polish-sounding names. In *Frau Jenny Treibel*, for example, published between *Cécile* and *Effi Briest*, Jenny's husband makes a parenthetical remark while discussing the whereabouts of one his dinner guests, who has just departed: "Den Sommer über ist sie jetzt regelmäßig bei den Kraczinski's, in der Zossener Gegend; weiß der Teufel, wo seit Kurzem all die polnischen Namen herkommen" (During the summer she's now regularly at the Kraczinskis', in the Zossen area; the devil knows where all the Polish names have been coming from recently) (*SW* 7:37). A Kraczinski also makes an appearance in *Cécile*, at a lunch hosted by the St. Arnauds, where he is identified as "Kriegsministerialoberst und polnisch-katholisch" (a colonel in the war ministry and a Polish Catholic) (*SW* 4:239). His Polish background is further highlighted by the way in which his family had fragmented along the same lines as the partitioned nation: this Prussian colonel "zwei Brüder in der russischen und einen dritten in der österreichischen Armee hatte" (had two brothers in the Russian and a third one in the Austrian army) (*SW* 4:245). The trend continues to Fontane's last novel, *Der Stechlin*, whose patriarch, Dubslav, begrudges his father for giving him a Pomeranian name—in honor of his Pomeranian wife, Dubslav's mother—instead of one more appropriate for someone who hails from Brandenburg, such as Joachim or Woldemar, the latter being the name Dubslav gave his son. Like Will Ladislaw's name in *Middlemarch*, the end of Dubslav's also contains his (partial) ethnicity. Pomerania had a large Slavic population, which presents a much greater problem, as will be shown, in *Effi Briest*, and when Dubslav ruminates over his name, what he really means by Pomeranian is Slavic. His son Woldemar himself acknowledges in his journal that "es bleibt mit den Namen doch eine eigne Sache" (there really is something special about names after all) (*SW* 8:107). Fontane's sensitivity to this must have had something to do with his own Germanized French last name. The author's Huguenot family settled in Germany in 1694, following Friedrich Wilhelm I's invitation to French Protestants after Louis XIV revoked the Edict of Nantes and drove them from France. Fontane's grandfather was the one to officially drop the *i* from Fontaine, and the author himself hardly ever used his inherited first name, Henri.[48]

Henry Garland identifies *Cécile* among Fontane's Berlin novels as one that commences a trend in which "the Roman Catholic Church appears to be more prominent than the Lutheran." In *Cécile*, particularly, "it plays an important role in the closing stages."[49] Cécile's husband, victorious in the duel against Gordon, sends his wife a letter in which he summons her to him, only to find out in a reply from the court chaplain that, on reading the news and the result of the duel in the paper, Cécile fell ill, refused treatment, and was found with "ein Batisttuch über Kinn und Mund" (a cambric cloth over [her] chin and mouth) (*SW* 4:283). "Es war mich nicht zweifelhaft" (I was in no doubt), the chaplain continues in his written report to the husband, "auf welch Weise sie sich den Tod gegeben; ihre Linke hielt das kleine Kreuz mit dem Christuskopf, das sie beständig trug" (as to the manner in which she took her life; her left hand held the small cross with Christ's head that she always wore) (*SW* 4:283). In her farewell note, Cécile bequeaths this cross to the chaplain, who visited her often during the last weeks of her life, with the following words: "Ihre hundertfach erprobte Milde wird nicht Anstoß daran nehmen, dass es ein katholisches Kreuz ist, und auch daran nicht, dass ich, eine Konvertitin, meine letzten Gebete an eben dies Kreuz und aus einem katholischen Herzen heraus gerichtet habe" (Your charity, put to the test a hundred times, will not take offense at it being a Catholic cross, nor at the fact that I, a convert, directed my last prayers to this very cross and from a Catholic heart) (*SW* 4:284).

Like the Polish family in *Vor dem Sturm*, who return to Poland, this Polish heroine comes full circle, by returning in the last moments of her life to the faith from which she converted. The moral of this story seems to be that you can take the girl out of the Slavic world—which Gordon, we recall, hears harmoniously ringing in the sound of her mother's name—but you cannot take the Slavic world out of the girl. Fontane's treatment of the Polish heroine here, like his treatment of the Polish family in *Vor dem Sturm*, is overtly sympathetic, though I would argue that the sympathy is attenuated somewhat through Gordon's remark, quoted above, that Cécile, in her unhappy marriage, is "nothing but a woman . . . like a thousand others." Effi Briest would, in Gordon's estimation, belong in that category, but the author never gives us a sense that her situation is not unique. Effi as the most pitiable of the many heroines—not only Fontane's—that is sacrificed to a loveless marriage in nineteenth-century fiction was most strongly articulated, in a line often quoted in relation to the novel, by Samuel Beckett's Krapp: "Scalded the eyes out of me reading *Effie* [*sic*] again, a page a day, with tears again."[50] Fontane's sympathy for the Poles, as will become clear with the exposition on *Effi Briest* below, pales in comparison to his sympathy for the young Prussian heroine who comes to ruin at the hands of one of them. Furthermore, if Fontane's sympathy for his Polish as opposed to his Prussian heroine is a matter of gradation, then his treatment of the Polish heroine as opposed to the Polish home wrecker displays a set of national prejudices that are rarely attributed to the otherwise liberal author. I argue that this latter disparity is an issue of gender difference and the way in which the two genders represent the nation differently. When Poland is embodied in an unhappy wife of a Prussian colonel, she is the object of pity for her subservient position within the empire that he helps to manage. However, when Poland is cast in the mold of an undesirable "national character"—to use Hobsbawm's term for male images of the nation—who takes advantage of the embodiment of Prussia or, by extension, the young and fledgling German empire, then he becomes the most unappealing lover figure to inhabit the genre of the novel of adultery.

Effi Briest

As mentioned in the beginning of the chapter, Effi is younger than the other heroines that share her lot, not just in age, but also in spirit, "a young sixteen," as Garland describes her.[51] When Geert von Innstetten, her own mother's former suitor, comes to try his luck with the next generation, he actually interrupts her in her play with friends. A foreboding moment in that play, at the close of the first chapter, is when the friends dispose of the gooseberry skins from their snack by placing them in a paper bag together with a stone and letting them sink in the garden pond. As they do this, Effi comments that "so vom Boot aus sollen früher auch arme unglückliche Frauen versenkt worden sein, natürlich wegen Untreue" (that is also how poor unfortunate women used to be drowned, from boats like this, for infidelity of course). To calm her friend's protest—"Aber doch nicht hier" (But surely not here)—Effi laughingly reassures her: "Hier kommt so was nicht vor. Aber in Konstantinopel . . ." (that kind of thing does not happen here. But in Constantinople . . .) (*SW* 7:177). When in the last chapter of the book, played out over a decade later, the exhausted and defeated Effi dies of consumption, a natural death perhaps the most comparable to drowning, the reader is left with the feeling that high Prussian society has little reason to consider itself superior to the Turkish one.

The same can be said of Effi's arranged marriage. When her mother, in a moment of concern that the pair might be ill matched, seeks reassurance from Effi that the bride-to-be loves her betrothed, she receives an answer that is heartbreaking in its revelation of Effi's childlike innocence. The girl cannot distinguish the attachment she feels for her three childhood friends, her beloved pastor, or her parents from the one she is supposed to feel for her husband-to-be:

> Warum soll ich ihn nicht lieben? Ich liebe Hulda, und ich liebe Bertha, und ich liebe Hertha. Und ich liebe auch den alten Niemeyer. Und dass ich euch liebe, davon spreche ich gar nicht erst. Ich liebe alle, die's gut mit mir meinen und gütig gegen mich sind und mich verwöhnen. Und Geert wird mich auch wohl verwöhnen.

> Why shouldn't I love him? I love Hulda, and I love Bertha, and I love Hertha. And I also love old Niemeyer. And that I love the two of you, I don't need to say. I love everybody who is good to me, and kind to me, and who spoils me. And Geert will surely spoil me too. (*SW* 7:194)

Effi's youth and lack of experience, as well as the previously discussed topical belatedness of this novel of adultery, reflect Germany's status in the late nineteenth century as a new European empire. What Russell Berman identifies as "Germany's own liminal situation—never quite a full fledged European nation-state, never indisputably part of the modern West"[52]—can be seen in Effi's liminal location between child and woman—never quite a full-fledged wife (or a full-fledged mistress, for that matter), never indisputably part of the adult world.

This most successful of Fontane's novels is also the one that lends itself most easily to a postcolonial reading; it speaks to both Prussia's national fears and Germany's imperial desires as embodied in the young heroine. National fears were inspired by Polish proximity, while imperial desires officially took hold in 1884, with Bismarck's embarkation on the pursuit of overseas colonies. The two—Poland's proximity and the pursuit of overseas colonies—were intertwined in the German case, since the new empire's dearth of colonies resulted, as mentioned briefly in the section on *Cécile*, in the treatment of Poland as an ersatz colonial space. In his well-known study of German history, *The Long Nineteenth Century*, David Blackbourn makes the claim that "Germany's real colonial sphere was central and southeastern Europe."[53] In a more recent work, *Germany's Wild East*, Kristin Kopp slightly alters the argument by making a distinction between Germany's "inner" and "outer" colonies, with the "inner" encompassing the country's contiguous territory to the east and the "outer" the overseas acquisitions in Africa and the Pacific. Both Blackbourn's reference to the "real colonial sphere" and Kopp's designation "inner" for Germany's Polish territories are ways of dealing with the oddity that Maria Todorova has labeled, we recall from the introduction, "semicolonialism." As Kopp demonstrates in her discussion of Paul Langhans's 1893 *Deutscher Kolonial-Atlas*, Germany's dearth of "outer" colonies made the importance of the "inner" or semicolonies all the more important. Kopp notes how Langhans's "inclusion of adjacent continental space broke with the conventional European image of 'colony.'"[54] In doing this, the cartographer achieved a twofold objective: he endowed Germany with a far greater amount of colonial space than its overseas territories alone would have allowed for, and, given the long history of German involvement with Poland, he depicted the country as a much older colonial force than it had been in the mere nine years that transpired between the beginning of Bismarck's overseas endeavors and the publication of the atlas. As shown below, Effi's expectations from and experiences in her marriage to a provincial governor reveal both "inner" and "outer" colonial fears and fantasies.

Before analyzing those fears and fantasies in the novel's text, however, it is important to pose the question of the author's own complicity in them. First of all, because of his self-conception as well as the setting of his novels, Fontane has always been understood as more Prussian than German. Since Prussia was the leading state of the German federation, however, and Fontane was writing from within and about its capital city in the decades immediately following the unification, his proximity to German imperialism is undeniable. The question of his own complicity with it, as previously mentioned in regard to *Vor dem Sturm*, is difficult to answer. While George Eliot is well known for her "doctrine of sympathy" and Tolstoy, as the next chapter shows, for his invectives against imperialism, Fontane scholars continue to rely on the term "ambivalent" in describing his relationship to political power and nationalism.[55] His extensive use of conversation, as we have already seen, is his primary modus operandi for distancing himself from any strong opinions, though in *Effi Briest* he does prefigure one xenophobic character's view in the narrator's voice, which enters into my discussion below. The discussion does not resolve the decades of quandary regarding Fontane's political views, but it examines the novel's heroine as the embodiment of the nation without being able to rely much on the aid of the author himself. This section proceeds by analyzing the novel's allusions to colonial powers greater than Germany, specifically Russia and England, and ends with a reading of Effi's affair with the half Polish Major Crampas as a seduction of a ruler's wife by a colonized "native."

Not only Effi's affair but also her betrothal and the beginning of her marriage can be read as a colonial adventure in miniature. Effi herself certainly experiences it as such, articulated most notably in her expectation that in her new life as the wife of a provincial governor she will discover "Eine ganz neue Welt . . . vielleicht einen Neger oder einen Türken oder vielleicht sogar einen Chinesen" (A whole new world . . . maybe a Negro or a Turk or maybe even a Chinaman) (*SW* 7:204–5). After Innstetten makes his proposal, Effi's mother encourages her to accept him by pointing out the benefit of marrying a man old enough to be her father: "stehst du mit zwanzig Jahren da, wo andere mit vierzig stehen" (you will find yourself at twenty where others get at forty) (*SW* 7:180). The mother herself had refused Innstetten two decades earlier because at that time he did not hold a position that was considered worthy of her. Now that he has risen to the post of governor, Effi's mother sees the advantage in it for her daughter, who will not have to wait twenty years to be able to call herself a governor's wife, as the mother would have had to if she had accepted Innstetten's proposal. The mother's statement about skipping ahead a couple of decades in gaining status, combined with Effi's expectation of encountering "exotic" peoples, invites a reading that focuses on Germany's sense of belatedness in colonial acquisitions. A more detailed analysis of all that Effi expects of her marriage and how she experiences the first encounter with her new home invites further comparisons of the same kind.

Germany's overseas territories were meager in comparison to those of France and especially England, as the latter possessed almost a quarter of the globe by the time *Effi Briest* was published. Yet hemmed in as it was in Mitteleuropa and longing for England's ocean fleets—as expressed in the quote by Otto Ludwig earlier in the chapter—Germany also had reason to envy the vast Russian expanse and could relate to Russia as another empire with contiguous colonies, Russia's in Central Asia. Poland was the contiguous semicolony that the two empires shared but with the difference in the sense that Poland did not cramp Russian space. The desire for Russian-like vastness in *Effi Briest* is featured in the young bride's naive preparations for her marriage. The groom's governmental position at the time is that of *Landrat* (prefect) of an eastern Pomeranian province, where he makes his home in the small town of Kessin, on the Baltic coast. Yet Effi amuses herself by thinking of her future home "als einen halbsibirischen Ort . . . wo Eis und Schnee nie recht aufhörten" (as a half Siberian place . . . where ice and snow never really end) (*SW* 7:189) and, consequently, requests from her mother a fur coat as part of her newlywed wardrobe. The groom himself reminds her a short while later, as they travel from their Italian honeymoon toward his residence, that she is not moving too far away from her hometown: "Wir sind hier fünfzehn Meilen nördlicher als Hohen-Cremmen und eh' der erste Eisbär kommt, musst du noch eine Weile warten" (We're seventy miles further north than Hohen-Cremmen here and you'll have to wait a while for the first polar bear) (*SW* 7: 207). In her conversation with her mother, however, Effi insists, "Aber da mir's nun mal bestimmt ist, so hoch nördlich zu kommen . . . ich bemerke, dass ich nichts dagegen habe, im Gegenteil, ich freue mich darauf, auf die Nordlichter und auf den helleren Glanz der Sterne" (But since it seems I am destined to come so far north . . . and I must say I have nothing against it, on the contrary I'm looking forward to the northern lights and the bright gleam of the stars) (*SW* 7:189). When her mother offers a dose of reality—"Aber Effi, Kind, das ist doch alles bloß leere Torheit. Du kommst ja nicht nach Petersburg oder nach Archangel" (But Effi, child, that is all plain empty folly. It's not as if you're going to Petersburg or Archangel) (*SW* 7:189)—Effi responds in a way that signals German political ambitions: "Nein, aber ich bin doch auf dem Wege dahin" (No, but I'm on the way there) (*SW* 7:189). The mother's primary concern is to ground her whimsical daughter, but in the end, perhaps reminded of her own appeal to a twenty-year advantage that is to be gained from the marriage, she is forced to acquiesce: "Gewiss, Kind. Auf dem Wege dahin bist du. . . . [W]enn du's wünscht, so sollst du einen Pelz haben" (Sure, child. You are on the way there. . . . [I]f that's what you wish, a fur coat you will have) (*SW* 7:189). The mother's initial response, in which she names the Russian capital, serves not only to remind Effi of the geographic distance between Pomerania and Russia; it also reminds the reader of the discrepancy in power between Berlin—where Effi and her mother have traveled to purchase the wedding trousseau—and Petersburg. The geographic distance is the most salient aid in depicting the disparity in the territorial possessions of the two empires, and the mother's agreement that the Pomeranian province is "on the way" to Russia signals an agreement with the inferred colonial aspirations. The fact that the population of this eastern province is mostly Polish, that is, its inhabitants are Germany's primary colonial subjects, strengthens the link between the naive bride-to-be and the fledgling young empire with few overseas territories.

Shortly after the exchange about the fur coat, the mother attempts once again to curb her daughter's imagination by warning her, "Es kommt dir vor wie ein Märchen, und du möchtest eine Prinzessin sein" (It seems to you like a fairy tale and you want to be a princess), to which Effi simply responds: "Ja, Mama, so bin ich" (Yes, mama, that's how I am) (*SW* 7:191). At face value, Effi's proclamations reveal her to be too much of a child to get married, and a spoiled child at that, one who uses the occasion to get an expensive and unnecessary piece of winter apparel. However, a different reading of these passages depicting a German "princess" and her imaginary move to Russia, a reading with a view toward empire, conjures up the image of a real German princess who did move to Russia and ruled over it for close to three and a half decades (1762–96)—Catherine the Great. The similarities with Effi or, rather, with her fantasies and the themes of *Effi Briest* continue. Catherine was not only a very young German princess—sixteen at the time of her marriage to Peter III—she was from Prussia, and within Prussia she came from Pomerania, from the town of Stettin. Her most famous portraits depict her draped in fur. She was also an adulterous woman, though, unlike Effi, a victorious one. Together with one of her lovers she organized a coup d'état, had her husband assassinated, and assumed rule that would propel the Russian Empire into its golden age. During her reign, Russia expanded significantly in territory, especially to the west, as Catherine presided over all three partitions of Poland. No doubt this reading of Effi as a miniature Catherine goes beyond anything Fontane could have imagined for his novel. Nevertheless, the connections between a nineteenth-century Prussian wannabe princess, whose move to a nearby Polish province assumes for her the grandeur of a move to Russia, and the real eighteenth-century Prussian princess who came to rule Russia and subjugate Poland are too close to remain unacknowledged.

The move to Kessin does not, initially, kill the fantasy for Effi but rather alters it according to the new environment of the Baltic coast. Coastal proximity engenders English fantasies of overseas colonies, as Effi's reaction to her new house reveals that she imagines herself there in the position of a princess ruling over India:

> Ich finde immer wieder, es hat alles so was Fremdländisches hier, und ich habe noch nichts gehört und gesehen, was mich nicht in eine gewisse Verwunderung gesetzt hätte, gleich gestern abend das merkwürdige Schiff draußen im Flur und dahinter der Haifisch und das Krokodil, und hier dein eigenes Zimmer. Alles so orientalisch, und ich muss es wiederholen, alles wie bei einem indischen Fürsten.
>
> I find over and over again that everything here is so foreign, and I have not yet heard or seen anything that did not positively astonish me, starting yesterday afternoon with the strange ship out in the hall and the shark behind and the crocodile, and your own room here. Everything so oriental, and I have to repeat it, everything as for an Indian prince. (*SW* 7:216)

Innstetten's house decorations betray his bourgeois pretention but also his own fantasies, concomitant with his position of, to use the appropriate water analogy, a big fish in a small pond. As a *Landrat*, he is in charge of a *Kreis*, the smallest administrative district in Prussia, which makes him the lowest-ranking official in terms of the amount of space under his control. Unbeknownst to her in her childish innocence, Effi flatters Inntetten with her fantastical grandeur, which he enjoys and decides to play along with. To her observations quoted above, he responds, "Meinetwegen. Ich gratuliere, Fürstin" (If you like. I congratulate you, princess) (*SW* 7:216), and thus designates the two of them as rulers of his "oriental" colony of eastern Pomerania.

Effi's encounter with her new residence occurs precisely in the way that Edward Said describes English and French encounters with their colonies, maintaining that, above all else, orientalism is a discourse. Said shows that European experiences of "the Orient" were colored by the exotic adventure tales that possessed the imaginations of those involved in the overseas explorations and conquests. Effi realizes quickly, on her arrival, that Kessin is nowhere near Siberia, but as Innstetten tells her the town's stories while driving through it on the way to his house, she exclaims, "Das ist ja wie sechs Romane" (That is like six novels) (*SW* 7:206). After touring the house with its seaside paraphernalia, she reveals where her Indian fantasy comes from: "Ich habe mal ein Bilderbuch gehabt, wo ein persischer oder indischer Fürst—denn er trug einen Turban—mit untergeschlagenen Beinen auf einem roten Seidenkissen saß . . . Und sieh, ganz so sieht es hier bei dir aus" (I once had a picture book where a Persian or Indian prince—because he wore a turban—sat with crossed legs on a red silk pillow . . . And look, that is just what it looks like here) (*SW* 7:214). If the English experienced their overseas colonies based on fiction, then the young Effi experiences the Polish part of Prussia based on a picture book that is likely of English origins—or at least inspired by English pursuits—revealing thereby the doubly derivative nature of her experience. This scene, like the previous debate over the fur coat, is meant to emphasize Effi's childishness, but it also points out the contrast between those empires with overseas colonies and Germany's unexotic, undesirable neighbor. Unlike the English with India, Germans did not have to *imagine* Poland, which was next door, or, conversely, they had to imagine it all the harder. Effi demonstrates this conundrum by viewing Germany's "inner" colony, to use the language of Kopp's study, with the exoticism typically reserved for the "outer" colonies.

Effi's tragic end occurs because she commits the gravest mistake that a ruling princess can commit, which is an affair with a "native." Her fall is foreshadowed by a ghost story she hears from Innstetten on the way to his house. Prompted by her expectations of "a Negro or a Turk or maybe even a Chinaman," Innstetten begins telling her of the Chinese ghost that haunts his residence, but Effi stops him because, she says, "[ich] möchte doch nicht, wenn ich diese Nacht hoffentlich gut schlafe, gleich einen Chinesen an mein Bett treten sehen" ([I] don't want to see a Chinaman approaching my bed tonight, when I hope I will be sleeping soundly) (*SW* 7:205). Her response evokes the typical colonial fear, discussed briefly in the introduction, of a white woman from the ruling class being raped by a subjugated native. Despite halting the story, Effi does have trouble sleeping. Inspired by another picture, this one discovered in Innstetten's house, of a Chinese man in national dress, Effi develops a real fear of the ghost and misinterprets the nightly sound of curtains swishing over the floor by the open window as his moving around the house.

Effi eventually learns that the house was previously inhabited by a Captain Thomsen, who settled there together with his granddaughter and a Chinese servant after being "viele Jahre lang ein sogenannter Chinafahrer, immer mit Reisfracht zwischen Shanghai und Singapur" (for many years on the so-called China run, always with freights of rice between Shanghai and Singapore) (*SW* 7:239). The ship, the shark, and the crocodile that so fascinate Effi are his leftovers. Old Captain Thomsen, as Effi learns, chose another captain as bridegroom for his granddaughter or niece—the relation is unclear—and threw her a wedding, at the end of which she disappeared. Two weeks later, the Chinese servant, who was the last to dance with her at the wedding, was found dead, so the presumption, although "niemand weiß, was da vorgefallen" (nobody knows what happened there) (*SW* 7:241), is that the Thomsen granddaughter/niece and the Chinese servant had some sort of liaison.

If Henry James considered George Eliot's Will Ladislaw the "only eminent failure in the book," then the German literary scholar J. P. M. Stern pronounced Fontane's Chinese ghost the novel's "only blemish."[56] The two criticisms have additional overlap, with Stern's "obscure imagery" echoing James's assessment that Ladislaw "lacks sharpness of outline and color" and "remains vague and impalpable." Writing in 1957, Stern was of the opinion that the ghost was "a piece of bric-à-brac left over by poetic realism" and merely mentioned him in a footnote, but the advent of postcolonial theory has caused subsequent scholars to take the Chinese ghost a lot more seriously. The author himself considered him of paramount importance, though he realized that was not the case with most readers when he wrote to Josef Victor Widmann in November 1895—eight months after the last installment of the novel was published in the *Deutsche Rundschau* but before it came out as a book (1896)—in a now well-known excerpt: "Sie sind der erste, der auf das Spukhaus und den Chinesen hinweist; ich begreife nicht, wie man daran vorbeisehen kann, denn erstlich ist dieser Spuk, so bilde ich mir wenigstens ein, an und für sich interessant, und zweitens, wie Sie hervorgehoben haben, steht die Sache nicht zum Spaß da, sondern ist ein Drehpunkt für die ganze Geschichte" (You are the first to allude to the haunted house and the Chinese man; I don't understand how one can overlook it because first, the ghost, at least as I imagine it, is interesting in and of itself, and second, as you have suggested, the matter is not there for fun, but is the turning point for the entire story).[57] More recent scholars frequently reference Germany's interest in China at the time the novel was written when discussing the role of the ghost in *Effi Briest.* As Kopp notes, "Plans for territorial seizures in China and the Pacific were already well under way" in the mid-1890s; and, as Judith Ryan points out, these plans culminated in the German overtaking of the Kiao-Chau bay in 1897, three years after the novel's serialization began.[58] The Chinese ghost is also typically associated with repressed sexual desire, which seems the most obvious explanation given his role in the novel of foreshadowing Effi's affair.[59] Kopp cleverly points out that "with the introduction of Crampas, the Chinese apparition ceases to haunt Effi" and suggests that "this sudden disappearance occurs because, in the moment of his seduction, Crampas usurps the function of the Chinese as repository for repressed libidinal excess."[60]

What interests me most about the Chinese ghost is that he is another instance of the conflation of "inner" and "outer" colonialism, matching Effi's experience of Pomerania as India. The use of another site of German colonial ambition to foreshadow Effi's affair with a half-Polish Pomeranian resident adds further impetus to reading *Effi Briest* as a novel of empire and the heroine's downfall as more than a problem of the Woman Question. When Effi hears the Chinese ghost story in its entirety she imagines Captain Thomsen to be "einen Dänen oder Engländer" (a Dane or an Englishman) (*SW* 7:240), and Innstetten confirms, without specifying which one. The inclusion of those possible nationalities of the captain, however, is noteworthy. While England was the empire that Germany wished it could be, Denmark, "the Baltic Sea Empire" of the Middle Ages, was a recently vanquished competitor, as Prussia's overtaking of Denmark's province of Schleswig-Holstein in 1864 was the first of the three victories that secured Germany's unification.

The foreshadowing of Effi's marital infidelity through the Chinese ghost story elevates Innstetten to the position of a captain of a powerful seafaring empire while distancing and exoticizing Crampas as "oriental." The story of Captain Thomsen alludes to Germany's English aspirations, which were undoubtedly bolstered by Prussia's victory over Denmark, as it also reminds us that Innstetten occupies a home whose former resident had traveled and conquered farther than this provincial governor ever will.

Two more instances in the novel suggest that Crampas is the flesh-and-blood version of the Chinese ghost, which consequently designates the Poles as "semioriental" in the German imagination, or at least in the imagination of its best-known novel of adultery. The first instance involves the development of the story of the Chinese ghost and the second involves two overlapping descriptions of the town's male Polish residents. The story of the ghost is brought up again after Innstetten has discovered the illicit love letters, over six years after the affair had ended, at the time that the Innstettens moved to Berlin, and he drives back to Kessin with his friend Wüllersdorf in order to engage Crampas in a duel. As the two friends pass the house where Effi and Innstetten used to live, Wüllersdorf inquires about the tales of the house being haunted, and Innstetten responds, "Ach, dummes Zeug: alter Schiffskapitän mit Enkelin oder Nichte, die eines schönes Tages verschwand, und dann ein Chinese, der vielleicht ein Liebhaber war" (Ah, nonsense: an old ship captain with a granddaughter or a niece, who disappeared one fine day, and then a Chinaman, who was maybe a lover) (*SW* 7:378). Innstetten's retelling of this story to his friend differs in one major respect from the way in which he previously told it to his wife; Effi learned only that "nobody knows what happened," whereas Wüllersdorf receives the version with the word *lover* in it. Innstetten may claim that it is all "nonsense," but his use of the word *lover* for the apparition that once bothered his wife, as well as his use of it on the way to a duel, shows that Crampas and the "oriental" ghost are conflated in the cuckolded husband's subconscious, as they are in the novel as a whole.

The second instance of orientalizing the novel's Poles occurs in the portrayal of Crampas and that of another half Pole before Effi's affair commences. Effi encounters her first Kessin "native" on her initial tour of the town, and Innstetten describes him to her thus:

> Er ist nämlich ein halber Pole, heißt Golchowski, und wenn wir hier Wahl haben, oder eine Jagd, dann ist er oben auf. Eigentlich ein ganz unsicherer Passagier, dem ich nicht über den Weg traue, und der wohl viel auf dem Gewissen hat. Er spielt sich aber auf den Loyalen hin aus, und wenn die Varziner Herrschaften hier vorüber kommen, möcht er sich am liebsten vor den Weg werfen. Ich weiß, dass er dem Fürsten auch zuwider ist.

> He is a half-Pole, to be exact, named Golchowski, and when we have an election here or a hunting party, then he is in his element. Actually a completely dubious character whom I wouldn't trust out of my sight and who probably has a lot on his conscience. But he pretends to be a loyal subject, and when the gentry from Varzin pass by, he all but throws himself in front of their path. I know that he is also repugnant to Prince Bismarck. (*SW* 7:203–4)

The description of a dubious, untrustworthy, yet obsequious character recalls the trope of the "sneaky Oriental," and, as it is also applied to Crampas, the other half Pole in the novel, we can conclude that all Polish males are characterized as such in *Effi Briest*. Innstetten's warning to Effi about Crampas is similar to the one he issues about Golchowski: "Aber er ist so'n halber Pole, kein rechter Verlass, eigentlich in nichts, am wenigstens mit Frauen. Ein Spielernatur. Er Spielt nicht am Spieltisch, aber er hazardiert im Leben in einem fort, und man muss ihm auf die Finger sehen" (But he's one of those half Poles, not very reliable, not in anything, actually, least of all with women. He is a gambler. He doesn't gamble at the game table, but he hazards his way through life, and one has to keep an eye on him) (*SW* 7:295). The description of both men opens with their ethnicity, which is then connected to their particular character flaws, mainly untrustworthiness: Crampas's lack of reliability—"not in anything"—echoes Golchowski's "completely dubious character," while Innstetten's need to "keep an eye on" Crampas echoes his not trusting Golchowski "out of [his] sight."

In the only known instance of Fontane the narrator affirming one of his negative character's prejudices, instead of leaving them consigned to conversation, Instetten's view of Crampas is prefigured in the following way:

> So rücksichtlos er im Punkte chevaleresker Liebensabenteuer war, so sehr war er auch wieder guter Kamerad. Natürlich, alles ganz oberflächlich. Einem Freude helfen, und fünf Minuten später ich betrügen, waren Dinge, die sich mit seinem Ehrbegriffe sehr wohl vertrugen. Er tat das eine und das andere mit unglaublicher Bonhomie.

> As careless as he was regarding chivalrous romantic adventure, he could be a good comrade to the same degree. Naturally, all of it completely superficial. To help a friend and to cheat him five minutes later were things that his sense of honor tolerated very well. He did the one and the other with unbelievable bonhomie. (*SW* 7:284)

As Kopp notes, "Crampas's character is thus confirmed at the meta-narrative level of the text."[61] To this I would add, again, the trope of the "sneaky Oriental," evident in every single sentence of the quote above. It is important to observe that a significant difference between the narrator and Innstetten is that the former does not overtly link Crampas's "dangerously mixed blood"—to recall a memorable *Middlemarch* phrase—with his character flaws. Nevertheless, his general portrayal of the novel's Polish males, while instructive of Prussian prejudices, also shows that this author, who is otherwise considered liberal and sometimes contrasted to the conservative Gustav Freytag as a Polish sympathizer, was not immune to those prejudices when the purity of the Prussian heroine came into question.[62] Fontane does condemn Prussian society in his novel, but he condemns the aristocracy's strict and outdated code of honor, which propels Innstetten into a duel long after the affair has ended, and not its anti-Polish prejudices, at least as far as Polish men are concerned. He could have chosen a character of a different ethnicity for Effi's seducer, or just another Prussian, or a German from another state, which would have been indicative of a different set of anxieties relating to unification. He could have, also, granted her forgiveness, as he did with Melanie van der Straaten, but his selection of a half Pole from *Hinterpomern* as the instigator of the heroine's death reveals his own susceptibility to Prussian national anxieties.

The use of a Chinese ghost to foreshadow the Prussian heroine's affair with a Polish member of society, the casting of the novel's Polish males in the mold of the "sneaky Oriental," and the general conflation of "outer" and "inner" colonialisms that has been expounded so far all point to the usefulness of the term "semicolonial" in discussing Poland's relationship to Germany. In the case of *Effi Briest*, the derivative term "semioriental" is especially meaningful. The Germans of Fontane's day had their own version of those terms, since Eastern Europe was, as Kopp points out, frequently described as "Halb-Asien" (Half-Asia) thanks to Karl Emil Franzos, who, starting in 1876, wrote a series of stories with that term in the title. Although Franzos had the Eastern European Jews in mind, Kopp notes that the designation "came to be mapped onto all non-German space in the East, including Polish regions,"[63] and the quote she offers by Franzos recalls Balzac's description, used by Larry Wolff and quoted in the previous chapter, of Eastern Europe as "the geographic frontier between Europe and Asia" and "the philosophical frontier between civilization and barbarism": "In the political and social relations of these lands, we find a singular intersection of European *Bildung* and Asian barbarism, of European drive towards progress and Asian indolence."[64] Exactly thirty years separate Balzac's *La Cousine Bette*, published in 1846, and the appearance of Franzo's first story, which shows that the view of Eastern Europe as half Asia was well established across Western Europe in the nineteenth century, and Wolff has demonstrated that it dates to the eighteenth. In this context the Chinese ghost represents much more than "obscure imagery" and his initially odd-seeming conflation with Effi's Polish lover actually makes a lot of sense. Rather than "a piece of bric-à-brac left over by poetic realism," he is a powerful signifier of German attitudes toward its Polish semicolony.

Fontane could not even bring himself to depict Crampas as attractive. Whereas Dorothea and Anna have a difficult time suppressing their desires for Ladislaw and Vronsky, Effi is never depicted as attracted to Crampas but gives herself over to him with the same resignation with which she obeys her parents' advice to marry Innstetten. She thus has no *Wahl* (choice)—to use the language of Goethe's novel—in either of her *Verwandtschaften* (relations). As Christiane Seiler rightly observes when she compares Effi to Emma Bovary and Anna Karenina, the Prussian heroine pays "too high a price for a lapse which didn't even involve love."[65] Unlike the lovers of the English and Russian novels, Crampas is, in addition, not younger than Effi's husband and hence not more suitable for her in age. When she writes home to her parents of the people she has met in her new surroundings, she mentions that Crampas's wife "ein Jahr älter als er, also sagen wir fünfundvierzig" (is a year older than he, so say forty-five) (*SW* 7:257), revealing that Crampas is actually older than Innstetten, who is thirty-eight at the time of their wedding. Crampas's marital status also differentiates him from the lovers in the English and Russian novels, which makes him all the more morally abhorrent. His enlightening of Effi as to her husband's shortcomings, unlike Ladislaw's of Dorothea, is also morally abhorrent. Another "sneaky" gesture on his part, when he reveals to Effi that Innstetten, "der geborene Pädagog" (the born pedagogue) (*SW* 7:282), is using the concept of the haunted house as a disciplinary measure over his young wife, he merely uses this truth to seduce a bored and frightened teenager. Finally, Crampas is not even endowed with a first name but appears only as Major Crampas when identified fully; he is, so to speak, semi-named. This lack of a first name puts even more emphasis on the last, which evokes the sound of the German word for "cramp"—*Krampf*—as in muscle spasm or paralysis, thus connoting this lover as a cramp in the Prussian nation's body. Fontane's national anxiety, then, does not come in the form of a dashing young lover who might steal the heroine's heart but in the form of an old—he is Casaubon's age, after all—and morally decrepit neighbor.

The reason I have taken care to emphasize that the anti-Polish prejudice in *Effi Briest* is directed at the novel's men is because of the important role played by Effi's sympathetic maid, Roswitha, who is really the heroine's Polish doppelgänger. Her name, as Julian Preece insightfully observes, "combining red and white, must refer to the Polish national colours,"[66] casting her thereby in the image of the nation. Roswitha and Crampas both enter the novel at the same time, perhaps significantly, in chapter 13. Effi finds Roswitha in a desperate state, after her mistress has just been buried and she has nowhere to go. As Roswitha relates her woes, she adds, "Und das kommt auch noch dazu, dass ich eine Kattolsche bin" (And I'm papish too, that's another thing) (*SW* 7:263). Her presence in *Effi* is part of that trend Garland perceives as commencing with *Cécile*, where the Catholic Church plays a greater role in Fontane's Berlin novels than the Protestant Church does. Roswitha goes on to describe the disadvantages of being a Catholic in Prussia and uses the pejorative term she has internalized—*Kattolsche*: "Und das Kattolsche, das macht es einem immer noch schwerer und saurer. Viele wollen keine Kattolsche, weil sie so viel in die Kirche rennen" (And bein' papish makes things even more difficult and 'ard to take. A lot of people don't want papish maids, because they're always runnin' off to church) (*SW* 7:264).[67] In the last part of her comment Roswitha captures what Prussian intellectuals and administrators saw as the Catholic impediment to the creation of a liberal German state. Helmut Walser Smith explains in *German Nationalism and Religious Conflict* that "to the Protestant mind, the hierarchical structure of the church assured Catholics that they would be spared the onerous burdens of independent reasoning, the prerequisite to true tolerance."[68] Smith points out that the founder of the Protestant League, Willibald Beyschlag, viewed all elements of the fantastic in Catholicism, such as exorcism and apparitions, as unnecessary relics of a medieval worldview that were harmful to the German future. However, it is precisely the fantastic element in Catholicism that draws the "fest protestantisch erzogen" (staunchly raised Protestant) (*SW* 7:267) Effi to Roswitha. In addition to genuine pity for the newly homeless maid, Effi trusts that "der Katholizismus uns gegen solche Dinge 'wie da oben' besser schütze" (Catholicism protects us better against some things 'like those upstairs') (*SW* 7:267), the thing upstairs referring, of course, to the Chinese ghost.

Effi even takes Roswitha into her own bedroom, while moving Innstetten out, and is relieved to find that her new maid can sleep soundly in the haunted house. When they move to Berlin and she discovers that the other maid—the Protestant Johanna, long established in the Innstetten household—has brought the picture of the Chinese man along, she decides to ask Roswitha to buy an image of a saint. Innstetten, who guesses Effi's intention, responds thus: "Nun, tu was du willst. Aber sag es niemandem" (Well, do what you like. But don't tell anyone about it) (*SW* 7:349). His reaction to Roswitha from the beginning is the exact opposite of his attitude toward the two Polish men in town. While he deems Golchowski and Crampas untrustworthy, when Effi first suggests Roswitha as an employee, he agrees to "nehmen wir sie auf ihre gutes Gesicht hin" (take her on the strength of her good face) (*SW* 7:266). In Roswitha's case, as opposed to Crampas's, Fontane paints a sympathetic picture through conversation as well as narration. The narrator describes her as "ganz selbstsuchtslose" (utterly selfless) (*SW* 7:347) and informs us that in Berlin "war doch Roswitha die einzige, mit der sie von all dem Zurückliegenden, von Kessin und Crampas, von dem Chinesen und Kapitän Thomsens Nichte frei und unbefangen reden konnte" (indeed Roswitha was the only person [Effi] could talk to freely and without restraint about all that lay behind them, Kessin and Crampas, the Chinaman and Captain Thomsen's niece) (*SW* 7:363). If he corroborates Instetten's negative view of Crampas, then he also corroborates Effi's positive view of Roswitha, prefiguring the mistress's "meine gute Roswitha" (my good Roswitha) (*SW* 7:397) at the metanarrative level with his own "die gute Roswitha" (the good Roswitha) (*SW* 7:369).

Roswitha functions as Effi's Polish doppelgänger in the novel because of her own sexually sullied past. When Effi warns her about flirting with the married coachman Kruse—another foreshadowing of what is, ironically, about to happen to Effi—Roswitha assures her that she learned her lesson "das erste Mal" (the first time) (*SW* 7:321). She tells her mistress how she got pregnant out of wedlock, presumably with a married man, and her father came "mit einer Stange auf mich los, die er eben aus dem Feuer genommen hatte, und wollte mich umbringen" (at me with an iron 'e'd just taken out of the fire and was goin' to kill me) (*SW* 7:322). Roswitha relates that her baby was taken away from her, which is what happens to Effi's child, Annie, who remains with her father after the affair is discovered. After she ends her story, Roswitha exclaims, "Ach, gnädigste Frau, die heil'ge Mutter Gottes bewahre Sie vor solchem Elend" (Oh my lady, may Mary Mother of God preserve you from misery like that) (*SW* 7:322), but this wish, expressed in a typical Catholic way, does not come true. Kicked out by her husband and disowned (temporarily) by her parents, Effi moves into a cheap boardinghouse where her window, perhaps in a nod to *Anna Karenina*, looks out on the train tracks. The only person who shows her compassion is Roswitha, who moves in with her, claiming, "Für Roswitha ist alles gut, was sie mit der gnädigen Frau teilen muss, und am liebsten, wenn es was Trauriges ist" (Anythin' Roswitha has to share with her mistress is fine, especially if it's somethin' sad) (*SW* 7:399). Thus Fontane employs a poor Polish Catholic maid to show up heartless Prussian high society, just as he employed a kindhearted Jew in *L'Adultera* for the same purpose.

If the Poles of *Vor dem Sturm* are killed and exiled while Cécile's misfortune is no more special than that of a thousand other women, then Fontane's ambivalence regarding the Slavic world is nowhere more evident than in this novel that paints Roswitha so sympathetically at the same time that it treats Crampas (and Golchowski) so harshly. The harsh treatment of Crampas, it bears repeating, lies not so much in his elimination via the duel, which is the standard in the novel of adultery—Karenin contemplates it and Vronsky expects it, but the former is too cowardly—as it does in his utterly unattractive depiction, which is a departure from the standard. Roswitha, by contrast, is meant to elicit the reader's compassion, as she is first offered compassion by the heroine and later returns the favor. The ambivalence stems from the interaction between the categories of gender and national minority, which in *Effi Briest* and Fontane's oeuvre at large demonstrates the potency of the image of the gendered nation. Casting the nation in the female mold, whether it be a young Prussia as embodied by Effi or a subservient Poland as embodied by Cécile and Roswitha, makes her the object of a protective impulse and allows the author to demonstrate compassion while at the same time relying on his male characters to set the standard of national purity and eliminate those who challenge it.

Chapter 3

✦

Anna Karenina

The Slavonic Question and the Dismembered Adulteress

Tolstoy's transition from *War and Peace* in the 1860s to *Anna Karenina* in the 1870s has typically been read as a transition from an emphasis on the nation to an emphasis on the family. The famous opening line of the latter novel supports this view—"Все счастливые семьи похожи друг на друга, каждая несчастливая семья несчастлива по-своему" (All happy families resemble one another, each unhappy family is unhappy in its own way) (*PSS* 18:3)—as does the oft-quoted statement of Tolstoy's, recorded by his wife: "Чтоб произведение было хорошо, надо любить в нем главную, основную мысль. Так, в *Анне Карениной* я люблю мысль *семейнную*, в *Войне и мире* любил мысль *народную*, вслествие войны 12-го года" (For a work to be good, one must love the main, basic idea in it. So, in *Anna Karenina* I love the *family* idea, in *War and Peace* I loved the *national* idea, because of the war of [18]12).[1] Consequently, studies of *Anna Karenina* have treated the novel as a work that participates in, subverts, or fuses the English and French strands of the nineteenth-century novelistic tradition. Boris Eikhenbaum's classic study, for example, discusses *Anna Karenina* as "a combination of the English family novel and the French 'adultery' novel."[2] In more recent examinations, Amy Mandelker makes the claim that Tolstoy's novel subverts the paradigms of the English and French traditions, while Judith Armstrong's psychoanalytic reading, with its emphasis on Tolstoy's idealized image of his dead mother, also privileges the family as the analytical subject of the novel.[3] Studies that have engaged the "national idea" in Tolstoy's fiction other than *War and Peace* tend to rely on texts that make an obvious fit with Edward Said's conception of orientalism or allow for its easy transposition into the Russian realm, such as *The Cossacks* and *Hadji Murat*.[4]

The reopening of the Eastern Crisis or the Slavonic Question, which took place during the novel's serialization (1875–77) and even affected its publication, invites a reading of *Anna Karenina* through the lens of "the national idea." The Soviet critic Eduard Grigor'evich Babaev was the first to read the family as symbolic of the nation in *Anna Karenina*'s opening line when he noted its similarity with the French saying, "Happy nations have no history," which is also alluded to in the second epilogue of *War and Peace*.[5] In discussing the movement of history and the development of nations, Tolstoy claims that all theories fail "как только являются революции, завоевания, междоусобия, как только начинается история" (as soon as revolutions, conquests, civil wars occur, as soon as history begins) (*PSS* 12:313). The French saying regarding happy nations did make it into the first draft of *Anna Karenina*, its first chapter no less, thus creating an even stronger link with the end of *War and Peace*. Like *War and Peace*, the first draft of *Anna Karenina*—titled at the time *Molodets–baba*, which in English would best be rendered as "You Go, Girl"—opens with an evening party scene. The guests in attendance search for topics of conversation and settle on malicious gossip, eventually leading to Anna's affair, because "счастливые народы не имеют истории" (happy people have no history) (*PSS* 20:16). The same conversation includes another saying relevant to the woman-nation analogy and evocative of Ernest Gellner's comparison, quoted in the introduction, between every nation having its own state and every woman having her own husband: "Как говорят, народы имеют то правительство, которого они заслуживают, так и жены имеют именно тех мужей, которых они заслуживают" (As they say, people have that government which they deserve, so wives have exactly those husbands which they deserve) (*PSS* 20:16). Important to note in regard to Tolstoy's use of the phrase is the multivalence of the Russian word *narod*, which can mean "nation," "people," or "peasants," depending on the context. George Eliot, whom Tolstoy not only read, but greatly admired, was the first to apply the saying about people or nations in general to their female half when, in describing the troubles of Maggie Tullivers's youth in *The Mill on the Floss* (1860), she observed that "the happiest women, like the happiest nations, have no history."[6]

The present chapter draws parallels between the story of Tolstoy's unhappy heroine and his misgivings about the course of Russia's history. Olga Matich notes that, in contrast to *War and Peace*, *Anna Karenina* is a novel "in which war and its dismembering consequences loom outside the text and only at the end," while "the battle site is the body of Anna."[7] I attempt to show how, through the framework of gendered nations, Anna's dismembered body becomes symbolic of Tolstoy's indictment of the war that occupies the end of the novel. Engaging his polemic with the Slavonic Question, I read the foregrounded "family idea" as national allegory and compare the breaking of family boundaries through the act of adultery with the breaking of national boundaries through the act of war. Both result in death. Unlike George Eliot, who wrote *Middlemarch* after the two Polish insurrections, and Theodor Fontane, who wrote *Effi Briest* after the reign of Otto von Bismarck and his anti-Polish *Kulturkampf* had passed, Tolstoy began writing his novel of adultery before the commencement of the Eastern Crisis. As the crisis progressed during the novel's serialization, however, and came to be addressed in its last few sections, it opened up the possibility of reading the story of adultery as a fitting backdrop for the author's political denunciation.

Another difference between *Anna Karenina* and the novels covered in the previous chapters is that the heroine's lover is not the national outsider to the degree that Will Ladislaw and Major Crampas are. A Serbian or Turkish lover would have been more suitable for my reading of the novel against the political backdrop of the Eastern Crisis; a Serbian would have made for a better comparison with *Middlemarch*, since the "Polish fever" in England resembled Russia's resolve to save the South Slavs, and a Turkish one with *Effi Briest*, if Prussia's *Kulturkampf* might be likened to Russia's Islamophobia. Russia stands out among the other two empires, however, in that it colonized itself with French and English culture, which the author's mouthpiece, Levin, identifies as "ненормально привитая России внешняя цивилизация" (an alien civilization abnormally grafted on to Russia) (*PSS* 19:52), while Vronsky is continually othered on that account. When Vronsky begins his "заманиванье" (decoying) of Kitty "без намерения жениться" (without the intention to marry) (*PSS* 18:61), Kitty's father sees right through him and upbraids his wife for favoring Vronsky over Levin: "Левин в тысячу раз лучше человек. А это франтик петербургский, их на машине делают, они все на одну стать, и все дрянь" (Levin is a thousand times the better man. Whereas this one is a little Petersburg fop, they are machine-made, all to one pattern, and all rubbish) (*PSS* 18:60). Levin's authentic Russianness, by contrast, is illustrated by the fact that he feels "какую-то кровную любовь к мужику, всосанную им, как он сам говорил, вероятно с молоком бабы-кормилицы" (a sort of blood-love for the peasants, which he had sucked in, as he himself said, probably with the milk of his peasant nurse) (*PSS* 18:251–52). Concomitantly, when observing the upbringing of his friend Oblonsky's children, Levin equates "выучить по-французски" (teaching French) with "отучить от искренности" (unteaching sincerity) (*PSS* 18:286). After Kitty initially rejects him and Oblonsky attempts to comfort him by saying that Kitty and her mother were only charmed by the polished Vronsky's "совершенный аристократизм" (perfect aristocratism), Levin strongly protests the term:

> Ты считаешь Вронского аристократом, но я нет. Человек, отец которого вылез из ничего пронырством, мать которого Бог знает с кем не была в связи . . . Нет, уж извини, но я считаю аристократом себя и людей, подобных мне, которые в прошедшем могут указать на три-четыре честные поколения семей, находившихся на высшей степени образованиа (дарованье и ум—это другое дело), и которые никогда ни пред кем не подличали, никогда ни в ком не нуждались, как жили мой отец, мой дед.
>
> You consider Vronsky an aristocrat, but I don't. A man whose father crawled up from nothing by cunning, whose mother has had liasons

> with God knows whom . . . No, excuse me, but I consider myself an aristocrat and people like myself, who can point to three or four honest family generations in their past, who had a high degree of education (talent and intelligence—that's another thing), who have never lowered themselves before anyone, never depended on anyone, as my father lived, and my grandfather. (*PSS* 18:181–82)

The importance of the family lineage reemerges in a happier setting, after Levin and Kitty have wed, and he watches her sitting "на том самом кожаном старинном диване, который стоял всегда в кабинете у деда и отца Левина" (on that same old leather couch that had always stood in the study of Levin's grandfather and father) (*PSS* 19:51–52). By contrast, as Levin's previous bitter assessment indicates, Vronsky is not only inauthentically Russian but also inauthentically aristocratic. He is what we would today call nouveau riche, and this becomes most obvious when he sets up his new home with Anna. When Dolly, ever the faithful friend, comes to visit, "всё производило в ней впечатление изобилия и щегольства и той новой европейской роскоши, про которые она читала только в английских романах, но никогда не видала еще в России" (everything produced in her the impression of opulence and display and that new European luxury she had only read about in English novels, but had never yet seen in Russia) (*PSS* 19:191), and the bedroom Anna sets her up in "напомнила ей лчшие гостиницы за границей" (reminded her of the best hotels abroad) (*PSS* 19:190). The reference to hotels especially speaks to the inauthenticity of the home, pointing thereby also to the inauthenticity of the family residing in it. If Levin is the embodiment of a true Russian (with the long lineage and the right kind of breast milk to boot), who eventually becomes the model husband to Kitty and father to their children, then Vronsky is merely—to employ and amend Maria Todorova's theoretically productive phrase—a semi-Russian, as he is a semihusband to Anna once they move in together and a semifather to their daughter who legally bears Karenin's last name. The same doubt is cast, as we shall see below, on Russia's magnanimous feelings toward her brother Slavs living under Ottoman rule. Just as Vronsky seduces Anna into an inauthentic relationship, so the passionate Slavophiles seduce Russia into war.

The national and family ideas are intertwined in Tolstoy's oeuvre as a whole, manifested by his simultaneously growing disregard for both. Starting with *War and Peace* in the 1860s and ending with *Resurrection* in the last years of the nineteenth century, Tolstoy's heroines become increasingly more promiscuous as his view of Russia rapidly declines. *War and Peace* idealizes both Russia—in contrast to France—and the woman—in the figure of Natasha Rostova. Russia's victory over France is cast in terms of *moral* superiority,[8] and Natasha is saved from eloping with Anatole Kuragin, becoming instead the perfect wife and mother in the first epilogue. By contrast, *Resurrection* casts a hardened prostitute in the leading female role and exposes Russia as a perpetrator of crimes against women and other minorities. Moreover, *Resurrection* was much more closely engaged in battling state policies than merely decrying them in its pages, although the vitriol against the Orthodox Church expressed in those pages proved to be the last straw that led to Tolstoy's excommunication in 1901. The novel was written long after Tolstoy had already abandoned, even renounced, the genre and for the sole purpose of financing the emigration of a Christian sect called Dukhobortsy (literally, "spirit fighters"), who were being persecuted by the state church. The Dukhobortsy rejected church ritual and ascribed to other beliefs that would have found an amenable ear in the older Tolstoy, such as pacifism, vegetarianism, and teetotalism. Since they rejected church sacraments, including the sacrament of marriage, their own marriages were deemed illegal and so, in addition to exile, their punishment involved the breaking up of their families by exiling their members to different parts of the empire. The freeing of a religious sect from a corrupt nation by means of a story about a corrupt(ed) woman thus completes the downward trajectory that began with an ideal woman and a morally superior nation. *Anna Karenina* occupies the middle ground between the two extremes as a novel that features an adulteress and criticizes Russia's military involvement on behalf of other Orthodox Slavs.

War and Peace

Natasha Rostova is the only ideal woman Tolstoy ever created in his fiction, which is why she is frequently discussed in Russian studies of gendered nations, especially her role in one of the most beloved scenes of the novel, where her "неподражаемые, неизучаемые, русские" (inimitable, unteachable, Russian) dance movements make the narrator wonder, "Где, как, когда всосала в себя из того русского воздуха, которым она дышала—эта графинечка, воспитанная емигранткой-француженкой, этот дух, откуда взяла она эти приемы, которые pas de châle давно бы должны были вытеснить?" (Where, how, when had this young countess, brought up by an émigré Frenchwoman, sucked in from the Russian air she breathed that spirit, where had she gotten those manners, which the *pas de châle* should have supplanted long ago?) (*PSS* 10:267).[9] The answer, of course, is contained in the question: Natasha's Russianness comes to her as naturally as breathing, and the setting of the novel against Napoleon's invasion also makes patriotism as natural as life itself.

The national figure and even the name of the heroine in *War and Peace* is complemented by the narrator's own voice as he frequently uses the first plural possessive—*nash*—in discussing Russia's military feats: "нашей стороне" (our side) (*PSS* 9:306); "наших улан" (our Uhlans), "наша пехота" (our infantry), "наши пушки" (our cannons) (*PSS* 11:62); "нашу армию" (our army) (*PSS* 12:69); "наших полков" (our regiments) (*PSS* 12:71); and so on. Over the course of the novel, like Russia herself, Natasha comes to feel ours—*nasha Natasha*—and we feel as protective of her against the advances of Anatole Kuragin as we do of Russia against Napoleon. Both the nation and the heroine eventually experience a moral victory, and concomitant with the idea of the gendered nation, Pierre Bezukhov participates in both. He saves Natasha from eloping with Kuragin shortly before he starts making plans to assassinate Napoleon, thus hoping to save Russia.

Pierre and Natasha are the future perfect couple and the havoc that the Kuragin brother-sister pair, Anatole and Hélène, cause in their lives is representative of the havoc wreaked on Russia by the French occupation. The first chapter of the novel describes the depth of what might be called the French cultural seduction of Russia when Vasily Kuragin, Hélène and Anatole's father, speaks "на том изысканном французском языке, на котором не только говорили, но и думали наши деды" (in that refined French language, in which our grandfathers not only spoke, but also thought) (*PSS* 9:4). Anatole, as mentioned above, almost succeeds in seducing Natasha, while Hélène does succeed with Pierre—in one of the more comical as well as superbly insightful passages of the novel that is worth citing—by leaning forward at the right moment and exposing him to "жив[ая] прелесть ее плеч и шей[,] . . . тепло ее тела, запах духов и скрып ее корсета при движении" (the living charm of her shoulders and neck[,] . . . the warmth of her body, the smell of perfumes, and the creak of her corset as she moved) (*PSS* 9:251). The naive Pierre is first captured by Hélène and later on by the French. After the war and Hélène's death he feels doubly liberated, as he basks in happiness "когда ему вспоминалось, что жены и французов не больше" (when he remembered that the wife and the French were no more) (*PSS* 12:205).

The patriotism of Tolstoy the narrator of *War and Peace* was matched by Tolstoy the author in regard to the second Polish insurrection, which was occurring during the writing of the novel. Since Napoleon was a friend to the Poles, briefly establishing the Duchy of Warsaw after his defeat of Prussia in 1806, it is easy to see how the writing of *War and Peace* and the contemporaneous turmoil occurring in Poland could reinforce each other in the author's mind.

The second Polish insurrection broke out in January 1863, and in May Tolstoy wrote to his friend, the poet Afanasy Afanas'evich Fet, about joining: "Что вы думаете о польских делах? Вед дело-то плохо, не придется ли нам с вами и [Иваном Петровичем] Борисовым снимать опят меч с заржавевшего гвоздя?" (What do you think of this Polish business? You see it is bad, will you and I and Borisov have to take down the sword again from the rusty nail?) (*PSS* 61:17). Both Fet and Tolstoy were veterans of the Crimean War, while Tolstoy's additional military adventures in the Caucasus must have been on his mind at the time because of the recent reviews of his *Cossacks*, which he discussed with Fet in the same letter. By September 1863 Tolstoy's wife Sofya Andreevna, age nineteen and nursing a newborn, expressed in her diary—on the day of their first wedding anniversary, no less—grave concern that Tolstoy might be serious about joining this war: "До сих пор я думала, что шутка: вижу, что почти правда. На войну. . . . Нынче женнился, понравилось, родил детей, завтра захотелось на войну, бросил" (Up till now I thought it was a joke: now I see it is almost true. To war. . . . Today he got married, liked it, had a child, tomorrow he felt like going to war, left).[10] This rift between husband and wife is replicated in the first part of *War and Peace*, when the newly married Andrei Bolkonsky, despite the pleadings of his pregnant wife, Lise, leaves for war. Regarding the author's real life, it is interesting to consider that had Tolstoy carried through with his intentions and had George Eliot's stepson Thornie gone to Poland instead of South Africa, the two would have been fighting on opposite sides and Tolstoy would have potentially faced one of his favorite author's stepsons as an enemy.

Sofya Andreevna's diary entry is filled with painful ruminations, but it also contains a moment of remarkable insight, one Tolstoy himself would come to embrace a decade later: "Не верю я в эту любовь к отечеству, в этот enthousiasme в 35 лет. Разве дети не то же отечество, не те же русские?" (I don't believe in this love for the fatherland, in that enthusiasm at age 35. Are the children not that very same fatherland, not those very same Russians?).[11] Her double use of the term "fatherland" resonates with the literary masterpiece Tolstoy was crafting at the time, since *War and Peace* is, appropriately for its topic, sprinkled with the term, fifty-one instances of it, to be exact. One of those instances occurs in the thoughts of the old Countess Rostova as she despairs over her youngest son Petya's descision to join the war. While pondering the futility of attempting to change his mind, the countess feels as unmoved by the call of the "fatherland" as Sofya Andreevna did in her diary entry: "он скажет что-ныбуд о мужчинах, о чести, об отечестве,—что-ныбуд такое бессмысленное, мужское, упрямое, против чего нельзя возражать" (he will say something about men, honor, the fatherland—something senseless, masculine, obstinate, to which it was impossible to object) (*PSS* 11: 307).[12]

Fourteen years later, when Fet and Tolstoy exchanged letters on the Slavonic Question, their tone had more in common with that of Countess Rostova, Lise Bolkonskaya, and Tolstoy's despairing young wife than with the two authors' previous patriotic enthusiasm. Tolstoy was looking for rest "от всей этой сербской бессмыслицы" (from all that Serbian nonsense) (*PSS* 62:287), and both he and Fet expressed concern for the latter's forty-two-year old brother who had been fighting in the Balkans and was wounded. Sofya's insistence in her diary entry that her children are the Russians who need their father's most immediate attention is echoed fourteen years later in Levin's unapologetic prioritizing of his wife and newborn son over any concern for his South Slavic brothers. The epilogue of *Anna Karenina*, as shown below, depicts precisely the opposite family climate of the one that inhabited the Tolstoys' home in 1863, the knowledge of which makes for a wishful reading of Levin's attentiveness to his new family as the author's belated apology to his wife.

Donna Orwin's distinction between *War and Peace* and *Anna Karenina* on matters of life, morality, and the natural can easily be applied to the difference between the two novels in their treatment of national allegiances. *War and Peace*, Orwin observes, presents life as an answer, whereas in *Anna Karenina* it is a question to be grappled with, as the suicidal Levin finds out even after he has attained what he thought would bring him life's highest happiness—a family. When it comes to family life, according to Orwin, it is in accord with the natural in *War and Peace*, whereas the purpose of the family in *Anna Karenina*—unsuccessfully so in the case of the eponymous heroine—is to legitimize the natural.[13] Similarly, the case can be made that the idea of the nation and national belonging is natural in *War and Peace*, whereas, like the family, the figure of the woman, and life itself, Russia is problematized in *Anna Karenina*. Not only is the heroine—and by extension, the nation—more promiscuous, but the hero, Levin, does not feel at one with the nation (*narod*) in the epilogue and receives no consolation for his pressing existential questions from Slavophile writings. In *Resurrection*, to complete the trajectory, both hero and heroine find peace in exile—and, it is imperative to note in connection to the declining family idea, *not* as a couple—while the purpose of the novel itself was to help a group of people flee Russia.

"Love Is a Battlefield"

National and family ideas interact most creatively in the first two of Tolstoy's three great novels by borrowing each other's terminology: men embrace patriotism with the passion of romantic love, while women apply military tactics for arranging love. On the night she orchestrates the match between Pierre and Hélène, Anna Pavlovna Scherer finds herself "в раздраженном состоянии полководца на поле битвы" (in an excited state of a commander on the battlefield) (*PSS* 9:250) and in anticipation of Anatole Kuragin's possible proposal to her sister-in-law, Lise Bolkonskaya "как старая полковая лошадь, услыхав звук трубы . . . готовилась к привычному галопу кокетства" (like an old warhorse, having heard the sound of trumpets . . . prepared for her habitual gallop of coquetry) (*PSS* 9:277). The war similes do not remain confined to the war novel, however, but continue into the family novel, where Kitty feels like a "юноша пред битвою" (young man before battle) (*PSS* 18:51) on the night when she expects a proposal from Vronsky and refuses Levin.

Levin's feelings for Kitty are not much different from Nikolai Rostov's rapturous patriotism in *War and Peace*. During a surprise visit by the tsar to the troops, Nikolai "был счастлив, как любовник, дождавшийся ожидаемого свидания" (was as happy as a lover when the moment of the anticipated rendezvous arrives) (*PSS* 9:311). Later, on catching a glimpse of the tsar after the debilitating battle of Austerlitz, he experiences more of the same:

> как влюбленный юноша дрожит и млеет, не смея сказать того, о чем он мечтает ночи, и испуганно оглядывается, ища помощи или возможности отсрочки и бегства, когда наступила желанная минута, и он стоит наедине с ней, так и Ростов теперь, достигнув того, чего он желал больше всего на свете, не знал, как подступить к государю.
>
> As a young man in love trembles and thrills, not daring to utter what he dreams of at night, and looks about fearfully, seeking help or the possibility of delay and flight, when the desired moment arrives, and he stands alone with her, so now Rostov, having attained what he desired more than anything in the world, did not know how to approach the sovereign. (*PSS* 9:352)

Levin's experience upon meeting Kitty at the skating lake when he has come back to Moscow to propose to her is almost identical:

> Всё освещалось ею. Она была улыбка, озарявшая всё вокруг. "Неужели я могу сойти туда на лед, подойти к ней?" подумал он. Место где она была, показалось ему недоступною святыней, и была минута, что он чуть не ушел. . . . Он сошел вниз, избегая подолгу смотреть на нее, как на солнце, но он видел ее, как солнце, и не глядя.
>
> Everything was lit up by her. She was the smile that brightened everything around. "Can I really go down there on the ice, walk up to her?" he thought. The place where she was appeared to him unapproachably holy, and there was a moment when he almost left. . . . He went down, avoiding looking long at her, as at the sun, but he saw her, like the sun, even without looking. (*PSS* 18:31–32)

Not only are Levin's doubts about approaching Kitty analogous to Nikolai's vacillations about being in the tsar's presence, but his viewing of her as the sun is an act of reverence expressly reserved for emperors and one that Nikolai experiences when he first meets the tsar:

> Не смея оглядываться во фронте и не оглядиваясь, он чувствовал восторженным чутьем его приближение. И он чувствовал это не по одному звуку копыт лошадей приближавшейся кавалькады, но он чувствовал это потому, что, по мере приближения, всё светлее, радостнее и значительнее и праздничнее делалось вокруг него. Всё ближе и ближе подвигалось это солнце для Ростова, распространяя вокруг себя лучи кроткого и величественного света.
>
> Not daring to turn to look while in line and not looking, he felt with rapturous senses his approach. And he felt it not only from the sound of horses' hoofbeats of the approaching cavalcade, but he felt it because as it approached everything around him became brighter, more joyful and significant and festive. Nearer and nearer moved this sun for Rostov, spreading around itself rays of mild and majestic light. (*PSS* 9:311)

In the first chapter of a much later work, *Father Sergei* (1898), Tolstoy satirizes this intense love for the tsar when the hero, who "еще со времен корпуса страстно, именно страстно, любил Николая Павловича" (still from his time as a cadet passionately, just passionately loved Nicholas I) and "испытывал восторг влюбленного, такой же, какой он испытывал после, когда встречал предмет любви" (experienced the same rapture of a person in love that he experienced later, when he met the object of [his] love) (*PSS* 31:6), finds out that his fiancée had been the tsar's mistress. Returning to *Anna Karenina*, which occupies the midpoint between the idealization of the emperor in *War and Peace* and his disgrace in Tolstoy's later fiction, Levin's experience of Kitty as the sun is also commensurate with the fact that his family constitutes the world for him. When he returns to his estate right after his dreams of raising his own family in it with Kitty have been crushed, he is described as occupying and heating the entire large house, against his own frugal principles, because "дом этот был целый мир для Левина" (that home was the entire world for Levin) (*PSS* 18:101). His devotion to home and hearth leads him to realize, as we shall see further on, that attempting to do anything for all of Russia is pointless.

Anna Karenina and Pan-Slavism

It is somewhat strange and worth exploring how one of the world's most popular novels of adultery underwent censorship not for its sexual content but for the political sentiments expressed in its epilogue. Twenty years after the famous lawsuit against Gustave Flaubert for the "indecency" of *Madame Bovary*, the epilogue to *Anna Karenina* did not appear, as planned, in the May 1877 issue of *Russkii vestnik* (the Russian Herald). While the editor, Mikhail Nikiforovich Katkov, had objected to the "яркий реализм" (vivid realism) of the consummation of Anna and Vronsky's affair a couple of years earlier, he desisted when Tolstoy maintained that he could not change anything about that scene.[14] Levin's lack of patriotism, however, proved non-negotiable, in spite of the fact that Tolstoy rewrote the epilogue twice. His revisions involved relegating many of the narrator's criticisms to the voices of the characters, which is reminiscent of Fontane's method of remaining politically ambiguous. Unconvinced by these changes, Katkov simply summarized the end of the novel for the readers of the *Russian Herald* himself:

> В предыдущей книжке под романом *Анна Каренина* выставлено: "окончание следует". Но со смертию героини собственно роман кончился. По плану автора, следовалъ бы еще небольшой епилог, листа в два, из коего читатели могли бы узнать что Вронской, в смущении и горе после смерти Анны, отправляется добровольцем в Сербию и что все прочие живы и здоровы, а Левин остается в своей деревне и сердится на славаянские комитеты и на добровольцев. Автор быть-может разовьет ети главы к особому изданию своего романа.
>
> In the last issue under the novel *Anna Karenina* it was posted: "conclusion to follow." But for all intents and purposes the novel ends with the death of the heroine. According to the author's plans, a small epilogue was to follow, a printer's sheet or two, from which the readers could find out that Vronsky, in confusion and grief after Anna's death, leaves for Serbia as a volunteer and that all others are alive and well, but Levin remains in his village and is angry at the Slavonic committees and the volunteers. The author may develop those chapters in a special edition of his novel.[15]

The actual epilogue would have made a poor fit with the rest of the May 1877 issue, since its table of contents reads almost like a history of Russia's wars with Turkey on behalf of other Orthodox Christians, with titles such as "Россия и Европа на Востоке пред Андрианопольским миром" (Russia and Europe in the East before the Treaty of Andrianople), "Восточная война" (The Eastern War), and the contemporaneous "Воспоминания добровольца" (Memories of a Volunteer).

The plight of Orthodox Christians under Ottoman rule had been of concern to Russia since the Crimean (Eastern) War and the first Slavic Benevolent Committee—the object of much ridicule in *Anna Karenina*—was founded in Moscow in 1858.[16] However, it was not until almost two decades later that the Eastern Crisis, reopened as a result of the Balkan uprisings, became the all-consuming public issue that the epilogue describes. In early July 1875 a scant summer harvest that threatened starvation, combined with the general consciousness of the increasingly obvious decline of the Ottoman Empire, triggered the first of a wave of uprisings in Herzegovina. It might be worth considering this largely peasant rebellion that was more agragrian than nationalistic in its origins in ironic juxtaposition to the beautiful mowing scenes described in chapters 4 and 5 of part 3 of *Anna Karenina*. A span of only three months separates the two events, and the famous scenes in which Levin works harmoniously with his peasants, loses all sense of time, and experiences oneness with the universe—or, in Jane Costlow's ingenious formulation, "the zen of scything"[17]—were included in the last installment of the novel published before the uprisings began. Tolstoy himself took a break following that installment of April 1875 to tend to the harvesting of his own fields and repeated the writing interruption for the same reason the following year. Herzegovina was soon followed by Bosnia and Bulgaria, while Serbia and Montenegro, confident of Russian support, declared war on Turkey in early July 1876. Writing about the relationship of the latter two Balkan states to Russia over half a century later in her famous travelogue on Yugoslavia, Rebecca West recalls the following anecdote: "It is said that a traveller said to a Montenegrin, 'How many of your people are there?' and he answered, 'With Russia, one hundred and eighty millions.'"[18] The political crisis generated by the uprisings garnered the kind of public involvement in Russia that was compared to 1812,[19] with the added dimension of being fueled in an unprecedented manner by the press, which is also criticized in the epilogue for drowning out all other voices (*PSS* 19:390).

Pan-Slavism, which was up until that time a philosophical idea debated by a handful of intellectuals, turned into a massive grassroots movement that aided the Balkan states without any official government involvement or permission. As the epilogue itself partially describes, church services incorporated prayers for the Balkan rebels and collected monetary donations, while the volunteer movement of several thousand soldiers under the leadership of General Mikhail Grigor'evich Cherniaev, as well as groups of doctors and nurses, reinforced the Serbian troops. Ivan Sergeevich Aksakov, who presided over the Slavic Committee during the Balkan uprisings and, consequently, the committee's greatest political relevance (from 1875 to 1878), lamented in the late 1850s that "the Slavic question does not extend to the core of the people, it is alien to them."[20] The Balkan uprisings changed all that, providing a political platform for such Pan-Slavists—henceforth referred to as Slavophiles—as Aksakov, Katkov, the poet Fedor Ivanovich Tiutchev, and Tolstoy's equivalent as the other giant of Russian literature, Fedor Mikhailovich Dostoevsky. Tolstoy took his usual place as contrarian, accusing the press of sensationalism and the cause itself of providing yet another diversion for the idle wealthy classes. On April 24, 1877, caving under the immense public pressure and reneging on his policy of *recueille-*

ment, Tsar Aleksandr II officially declared war on Turkey. The plan for the contested epilogue's publication less than a month later thus proved to be of particularly bad timing.

It is an interesting coincidence that in the same month that Katkov rejected Tolstoy's epilogue for its lack of patriotic feeling for the South Slavs, the prime minister of England, William Gladstone, published an essay titled "Montenegro: A Sketch" in the May 1877 issue of the prominent London journal *The Nineteenth Century*. Gladstone's famous rivalry with Benjamin Disraeli manifested itself in the issue of the Balkans with particular intensity. While Disraeli mistrusted Russian involvement and supported Turkey as a necessary balancer of power and protector of British routes to India, Gladstone supported the independence of the Balkan states from Turkey but shared Disraeli's mistrust of Russia. This mistrust is perhaps best encapsulated by an illustration that appeared in England's satirical *Punch* magazine on June 17, 1876, just two weeks before Serbia and Montenegro declared war on Turkey. It depicts a Russian man sending the Balkan dogs of war after a Turkish man, while the Englishman—all three nationalities identifiable by their stereotypical headgear: a fur hat, a fez, and a Bobby cap—peers fearfully at the Russian and his dogs from over the fence. The dogs all have the names of the Balkan states rebelling against Turkey printed on their collars; from left to right: Herzegovina, Servia, Montenegro, Bosnia.

Gladstone's essay acquainted the English public with previously unheard-of lands, described the role of the Balkan nations as buffers between Islam and Christianity, and proclaimed that "no Russian, no Austrian eagle will build its nest in the Black Mountain."[21] The essay was prefaced by Alfred Tennyson's sonnet, also named "Montenegro" and written especially for the occasion. The message of both the poem and the article could be summarized as "the little nation that could": while Tennyson praises "the smallest of nations" for "beating back the swarm of Turkish Islam for five hundred years,"[22] Gladstone offers story after story of brave Montenegrin warriors withstanding the far more numerous Turks. "The little nation that could" was, in the end, romanticized by both England and Russia but for slightly different reasons. As the following chapter shows, Croatians living under Austrian rule had their own reasons for doing the same.

Russian involvement in the Balkans was romanticized especially by Dostoevsky, who discussed the Slavonic Question at length in his self-published *Dnevnik pisatelia* (Writer's Diary) and commented extensively on *Anna Karenina*. He defended Russia's involvement in the face of Western mistrust as "почти беспримерное в других народах по своему самоотвержению и бескорыстию, по благоговейной религиозной жажде *пострадать за правое дело*" (almost unprecedented among other nations in its self-sacrifice and disinterestedness, in its pious religious thirst *to suffer for the right deed*).[23] Russia's role in the Balkans was, for Dostoevsky, part of her mission in "единении всего славянства, так сказать, под крылом России" (uniting all

THE DOGS OF WAR.

"The Dogs of War," *Punch*, July 17, 1876

of Slavdom, so to speak, under Russia's wing) (*PSS* 23:47), and her responsibility toward her fellow Slavs was that of "покровительница их и даже, может быть, предводительница, но не владычница; мать их, а не госпожа" (their protector and even, perhaps, leader, but not ruler; their mother, and not mistress) (*PSS* 23:49). Dostoevsky's general admiration for Tolstoy, his praise for the forgiveness scene between Anna, Karenin, and Vronsky after Anna's nearly fatal childbirth experience (*PSS* 25:51–53), and his assessment of Levin as a "чистый сердцем" (pure-hearted) type of Russian nobleman "которым принадлежит будущность России" (to whom the future of Russia belongs) (*PSS* 25:57) made his disappointment in the epilogue all the greater. In a July–August 1877 entry, titled "Опять обособление. Восьмая часть *Анни Карениной*" (Isolation Again. Part Eight of *Anna Karenina*), he recaps the events surrounding the epilogue's fate with the *Russian Herald* and bemoans Levin's isolation from the people, who overwhelmingly support the volunteers.

The difference of opinion on the Slavonic Question between the two giants of Russian literature, both of whom are typically considered Slavophiles and placed in juxtaposition to the third great Russian realist and Westernizer, Ivan Turgenev, calls for a reevaluation of the political terms. Tolstoy, a vehement anti-Westernizer who once, in a letter to Turgenev, compared Paris to Sodom and begged him to get out of there,[24] could nevertheless not properly be labeled a Slavophile either, at least not in the context of the Eastern Crisis. He was no more convinced of the authenticity of the Slavophiles' grand desire to liberate their Orthodox brothers in the Balkans than he was of the Western ideals. The less inclusive designation "Russophile" might be more appropriate for the period when he was composing *Anna Karenina*—though certainly not for his later period—especially given the pronouncement of Levin's father-in-law in the censored epilogue that he and Levin belong to those "люди, интересующиеся только Россией, а не братьями славянами" (people, interested only in Russia and not in brother-Slavs) (*PSS* 19:388).

"Serbia—Vronsky's Last Love"

Anna's story, as Katkov observes in his terse summary, ends in the last part of the novel that he published in his journal, but the specter of Anna does make an appearance in the epilogue: the image of her corpse haunts her grieving lover as he boards the train for Serbia. As a volunteer, Vronsky follows a whole host of unfortunate characters whose disappointing circumstances at home inspired them to join the war abroad. The first chapter of the epilogue describes the academic failure of Levin's half brother Sergei Ivanovich Koznyshev, whose six-year book project on government in Russia and Europe merited two negative book reviews and, aside from those, overall silence. "На его счастье" (Fortunately for him), as the narrator puts it, the Slavonic Question had just come into vogue and "он посвятил всего себя на служение этому великому делу и забыл думать о своей книге" (he devoted himself completely to the service of that great work and forgot to think about his book) (*PSS* 19:352, 353). Koznyshev does not fail to notice, however, that

> при этом общем подъеме общества выскочили вперед и кричали громче других все неудавшиеся и обиженные: главнокомандующие без армий, министры без министерств, журналисты без журналов, начальники партий без партизанов.
>
> in this general upsurge of society the ones who leaped to the forefront and shouted louder than the rest were all the failures and the aggrieved: commanders in chief without armies, ministers without ministries, journalists without journals, party chiefs without partisans. (*PSS* 19:352–53)

Koznyshev himself fits the list as a scholar without book accolades, and so might Vronsky as a lover without a mistress.

In chapter 3 Koznyshev's companion Katavasov enters a second-class carriage in order to meet the volunteers and encounters a boasting drunkard, a retired officer who had been juggling various professions his entire life, and a cadet who had failed his artillery examination. Katavasov attempts to engage another, more respectable passenger in a conversation about this pitiful scene, but his interlocutor, in what seems like Tolstoy's jab at the editor and other Slavophiles, restrains himself, "по опыту зная, что при теперешнем настроении общества опасно высказать мнение, противное общему, и в особенности осуждать добровольцев" (knowing by experience that in the present mood of society it was dangerous to express an opinion contrary to the general one, and especially to condemn the volunteers) (*PSS* 19:358). In chapter 4 Koznyshev runs into Vronsky's mother at the train station and finds out that Vronsky was persuaded to join the cause by his friend Yashvin, who had lost everything at cards. Regarding Vronsky, his mother proclaims, "Это Бог нам помог–эта Сербская война. Я старый человек, ничего в этом не понимаю, но ему Бог это послал" (This is God helping us—this Serbian war. I am an old person, I don't understand anything about it, but God has sent this to him) (*PSS* 19:360). Her statement not only puts Vronsky in the same category with the other, utterly unheroic, down-and-out volunteers, but her "theology" is an even harsher affront to the Slavophiles, who preferred to see Russia as God's help to Serbia instead of Serbia as a destination for Russians who could not make themselves useful at home. Tolstoy's portrayal of the volunteers is verified by other writings, such as Gleb Ivanovich Uspensky's "Letters from Serbia," which describe the volunteers as motivated by the prospects of material gain that was unavailable to them in Russia and as largely ignorant of Pan-Slavic ideology.[25]

The first four chapters of the epilogue lead up to the description of Vronsky himself, in chapter 5, where the Pan-Slavic movement is most closely linked to adultery, since Vronsky joins the volunteers as a direct response to losing his mistress. He is too wealthy to go in pursuit of material gain and too sophisticated to be ignorant of Pan-Slavic ideology. But he makes it clear that he does not care for the latter when, in response to Koznyshev's offer to write him a letter of introduction to a couple of Montenegrin political figures, he wryly replies, "Нет, благодарю вас; для того чтоб умереть, не нужно рекомендаций. Нешто Туркам" (No, thank you; one needs no recommendations in order to die. Unless it is to the Turks) (*PSS* 19:361). Within the broader tradition of gendering nations as female, the adulterous heroine of a novel that ends with a strong political critique invites the analogy even without discussing the fate of her grieving lover. But Vronsky's trip to Serbia—his last love, as cleverly noted in an essay title by a twentieth-century Serbian author[26]—allows for the analogy to be made from within the novel itself.

The space of the train station naturally reminds Vronsky of the site of Anna's suicide:

> При взгляде на тендер и на рельсы . . . ему вдруг вспомнилась *она*, то есть то, что оставалось еще от нее, когда он, как сумасшедший, вбежал в казарму железнодорожной станции: на столе казармы бесстыдно растянутое посреди чужих окровавленное тело, еще полное недавней жизни.
>
> As he looked at the tender and the rails . . . he suddenly remembered *her*, that is, what was still left of her when, like a madman, he ran into the railway shed: on the table in the shed, shamelessly stretched out before strangers, lay the blood-stained body still filled with recent life. (*PSS* 19:362; emphasis Tolstoy's)

Attention to grammar in the Russian original reveals Anna as the subject—as opposed to the object—of Vronsky's memory, and an emphasized subject at that, with the italicized *она*. It might, therefore, be more accurate in English to say that "*she* suddenly appeared to him" instead of "he suddenly remembered *her*." Such a rendition would also emphasize the spectral aspect of Anna that I referred to above, though it misses the Russian use of memory. Vronsky's subsequent failed attempt "вспомнить ее такою, какою она была тогда, когда он в первый раз встретил ее тоже на станции" (to remember her as she was when he met her for the first time, also at a station) (*PSS* 19:362) can be read as his failed attempt to reverse those roles and become the subject, as mirrored in the grammar reversal. Anna remains the agent and haunts the epilogue in her last, most grotesque, and, to Vronsky, most unsettling, incarnation.

The unnecessary, though typically Tolstoyan reminder, that it was "also at a station" that the two lovers first met creates another link between the extramarital affair and Russia's war with Turkey. Never a fan of the railroad, when advising Turgenev to leave Paris, Tolstoy adds in his letter, "но только не по железной дороге" (but only not by railroad), and goes on to make a comparison that would reverberate in his novel about illicit sex twenty years later: "Железная дорога к путешествию, что бардель к любви" (The railroad is to travel what the brothel is to love) (*PSS* 60:170). Prior to the epilogue the train is associated almost exclusively with the adultery plot; in fact, it frames the adultery plot as its inception and its end. Other characters travel by train as well, and children play with toy trains or hope to get them for their birthday, as Anna's son does, but in no case is the train and its station actually dwelled on as it is in the three scenes associated with the affair: the one that occasions Vronsky's and Anna's first meeting as she arrives in Moscow in the same compartment with his mother, the one where Vronsky follows Anna back to Petersburg and openly confesses his intentions, and the one that leads Anna to suicide. The train, then, has two main roles in the novel: breaking family boundaries by facilitating adultery and breaking national boundaries by transporting men to war.

Madonna / Whore

Vronsky's vision of Anna's shameful, bloodstained, dismembered ("what still was left of her") body stands in gruesome contrast to the saintly, virginal, self-sacrificing female image of Russia that underpins the rhetoric of the Slavophiles and is briefly referenced in the epilogue in a speech delivered to the volunteers: "На великое дело благословляет вас матушка Москва" (For the great deed mother Moscow blesses you) (*PSS* 19:354). The Pan-Slavic movement relied, as did many a national movement steeped in the Judeo-Christian tradition, on a rhetoric of Russia's destiny to be the savior of the world, or at least of its Orthodox brothers in the East for the time being. More specifically, the Russian image of that savior had always been cast in the mold of the Virgin Mary, whose icons preceded armies into battle and were considered to be endowed with miraculous powers. One of the more famous examples is the Pochaev Icon of the Virgin, who in 1675 turned the Tatar arrows back upon the enemy and thus saved the monastery. The most often cited statement regarding the paramount role of the Virgin Mary in Russian culture is Nikolai Berdiaev's from *The Russian Idea*: "The fundamental category is motherhood. The Mother of God takes precedence over the Trinity and is almost identifed with it. The people have felt the nearness of the interceding Mother of God more vividly than that of Christ."[27] The presence of grammatical gender in the

Russian language, which marks the nation and all of its attributes as feminine, only reinforces the parallel. Dostoevsky's previously listed catalog of feminine nouns by which he defined Russia's relationship to the South Slavs gets lost in the English translation because of its lack of feminine endings: *pokrovitel'nitsa . . . predvoditel'nitsa, no ne vladychnitsa; mat' ikh, a ne gospozha.* As the protector(ess) of South Slavs, their (female) leader/not ruler, and their mother/not mistress, these images recall the role in Orthodoxy commonly assigned to the Mother of God and thus depict the nation in a way that is contradicted by Tolstoy's dismembered adulteress.

Even as a corpse, Anna's "закинутая назад уцелевшая голова" (thrown back intact head) with the "полуоткрытым румяным ртом" (half-open red mouth) (*PSS* 19:362) suggests a sexual pose, while the reference to her body being "shamelessly stretched out before strangers" recalls the shame incurred by the affair. Most significantly, her dismembered body presents the realization of the disturbing simile used in the description of her first physical union with Vronsky. In arguably one of the weirdest love scenes in nineteenth-century literature, and the one objected to by the editor for its "vivid realism," the consummation of the affair is also portrayed as dismemberment:

> Он же чувствовал то, что должен чувствовать убийца, когда видит тело, лишенное им жизни. . . . Но, не смотря на весь ужас убийцы пред телом убитого, надо резать на куски, прятать это тело, надо пользоваться тем, что убийца приобрел убийством. И с озлоблением, как будто со страстью, бросается убийца на это тело, и таищит, и режет его; так и он покрывал поцелуями ее лицо и плечи.

> He felt what a murderer must feel when he looks at the body he has deprived of life. . . . But, despite all the murderer's horror before the murdered body, this body must be cut into pieces and hidden away, and he must make use of what he has gained by the murder. And with animosity, as if with passion, as the murderer throws himself upon that body, and drags, and cuts it; so he covered her face and shoulders with kisses. (*PSS* 18:157–58)

As Olga Matich puts it, "Tolstoy completed the dismemberment of Anna in her suicide."[28] My own argument is that if the above passage likens adulterous sex to bodily dismemberment, if it foreshadows death as the consequence of marital infidelity, then the epilogue's allusion to that first love scene by the grieving lover-turned-volunteer suggests a link between foreign involvement and national dismemberment.

The link gains further relevance when considering the change that took place in that last scene at the train station between the drafts of the epilogue and its final version. In an earlier draft, Levin is the one described as viewing Anna's corpse (*PSS* 20:562). Such a turn of events, no doubt, would have strengthened those readings of the novel that privilege the author, through the autobiographical Levin, as the one wreaking the vengeance prophesied in the much puzzled over epigraph, especially since Tolstoy himself went to view the body of his neighbor's dead mistress who inspired the novel. Further, another meeting of the two protagonists in the epilogue, though posthumous for one of them, might have satisfied those critics who saw the novel as divided into the Anna story and the Levin story. Vronsky's viewing of the corpse, on the other hand, reinforces the image of Anna as *his* victim and thus confirms the hints made about his role as murderer in the consummation of the affair in chapter 11 and in his accident while riding Frou-Frou at the races in chapter 25 of part 2. Such a confirmation of an earlier simile and metaphor in the epilogue that criticizes Russia's foreign policy reinforces the parallels between an adulterous woman and an adulterous nation, as it points to Vronsky's role in being the agent of harm to both.

As is well known, Tolstoy's idea for the manner of Anna's suicide came from the act committed by his neighbor Bibikov's mistress about a year before he commenced the writing of the novel.[29] The real-life story provided the author with material for the Oblonsky as well as the Karenin marriage troubles. Anna Stepanovna Pirogova threw herself under the train on January 4, 1872, after learning that the widowed Bibikov had fallen in love with his children's German governess, the difference in the opening of the novel being that the Oblonsky governess was French and Stiva had no intention of leaving his wife for her. The fictional Anna's suicide is the result of her increaing jealousy over Vronksy's freedom and the fear of his mother's attempts to marry him off to the young Princess Sorokina. Anna Pirogova's suicide does not account, however, for the precise manner in which Tolstoy chose to foreshadow Anna's death in describing the consummation of her affair with Vronsky. That scene recalls passages from the so-called pornoprophetic sections of the Bible, in which Israel's prophets identify the nation as an adulterous woman and prophesy her destruction at the hands of her lovers. Tolstoy's depiction, as we shall see next, turns out to have more in common with the ancient texts of Isaiah, Ezekiel, and Hosea than it does with the writings on adultery by his more immediate European predecessors, such as Goethe or Flaubert. If Matich suggests that "Tolstoy's evocation of sexual violence in *Anna Karenina*" is "perhaps based on his own punitive sexual fantasy displaced by Old Testament vengeance,"[30] then I employ the Old Testament theme to explore the link between the adulterous woman and the adulterous nation.

Recalling once more, from the introduction, Tony Tanner's invitation to examine the "relationships between a specific kind of sexual act, a specific kind of society, and a specific kind of narrative," we find in several passages from the Old Testament an attempt to regulate societal conduct through allegories of sexually promiscuous women whose behavior is punished by their violent death. As Renita J. Weems articulates in the introduction to her book *Battered Love: Marriage, Sex, and Violence in the Hebrew Prophets*, "The prophets' success or failure as orators depended in the end on their ability to convince their audiences that viable connections could be drawn between the norms governing the sexual behavior of women and God's demands on Israel."[31] The typical narrative of Israel's adultery begins with God's delivery of his people into the promised land, followed by the subsequent generations' forgetting of this deed, and, as phrased in Judges 2:17, their "lust[ing] after other gods and bow[ing] down to them."[32] The prophetic books of Isaiah, Jeremiah, Ezekiel, and Hosea contain chapters that make the litigation-worthy passages from *Madame Bovary* or the "vivid realism" that Katkov objected to in *Anna Karenina* seem tame by comparison. They depict Israel's adultery in pornographic terms, which at times include images of both male and female genitalia, as well as descriptions and condemnations of the woman's enjoyment of the adulterous sex acts. To use the most striking and positively shocking of these instances as an example, verses from Ezekiel 23:19–20 read thus: "Yet she increased her whorings, remembering the days of her youth, when she played the whore in the land of Egypt and lusted after her paramours there, whose members were like those of donkeys, and whose emission was like that of stallions. Thus you longed for the lewdness of your youth, when the Egyptians fondled your bosom and caressed your young breasts."[33] Such lewd expression is, needless to say, beyond anything that even the incisive "seer of the flesh" would have ever committed to paper, though the last verse, whose indictment is by far the more common one among the prophets, does bring to mind Tolstoy's frequent condemnations of women's décolletage.[34] The porno-prophetic echoes we find in *Anna Karenina*, as shown below, are in the violent punishment that ensues. The first piece of scholarship to address such biblical passages as pornographic was T. Drorah Setel's 1985 article, "Prophets and Pornography: Female Sexual Imagery in Hosea." Setel painstakingly demonstrates, relying on the writings of Andrea Dworkin and others, that pornography is, indeed, a justifiable label for certain sections of prophetic writings. Subsequent feminist theorists, most notably Athalya Brenner and Fokkelien van Dijk-Hemmes in the 1990s, have used and popularized the term "porno-prophetics" in reference to those writings.[35] The porno-prophetic gendering of the nation, the use of adultery as a metaphor for national betrayal, and the foretelling of death as ensuing punishment provide a fruitful cultural context for analyzing *Anna Karenina* against the political backdrop of the Eastern Crisis.

The porno-prophetic motif of God's punishment of the adulterous woman/nation is perhaps best encapsulated in one particular verse from Isaiah: "Your nakedness shall be uncovered, and your shame shall be seen. I will take vengeance, and I will spare no-one."[36] Nakedness, shame, and vengeance at the hands of her own lover(s) is prophesied to both Babylon and Israel by Isaiah and to Jerusalem by Ezekiel. In chapters 16 and 23 of the latter, the adulteress is to be handed over to her lovers, who will strip her naked and hack her to pieces. The foretelling of disaster or the subsequent explanation of it based on a people's disobedience to a higher power has been termed a *jeremiad*, an obvious combination of the title *Iliad* with the name of one of the Hebrew prophets who engages in that kind of rhetoric. I wish to propose an additional use of the term as a passive participle, in the sense that what happens to a disobedient woman/nation is that she gets *jeremiad*. This is precisely what happens to Anna, metaphorically, at the hands of Vronsky, as maintained by many interpretations of the novel, including the popular association of the fate of Vronky's horse, Frou-Frou, with Anna's.[37] Nakedness, shame, and vengeance are also the images that inform the bizarre postcoital scene in part 2, chapter 11. Following the author's famous ellipsis and his almost clinical assessment in the opening line of the chapter that "это желание было удовлетворено" (that desire had been satisfied) (*PSS* 18:157), he depicts Anna lowering her "когда-то гордую веселую, теперь же постыдную голову" (once proud, happy, but now shame-stricken head) (*PSS* 18:157) and feeling oppressed by "стыд пред духовную наготою своей" (shame at her spiritual nakedness) (*PSS* 18:158). The passage is as replete with the word *shame* when describing Anna as it is with *murder* when describing Vronsky, the agent of Anna's porno-prophetic demise. Shame subsequently recurs in the epilogue through Vronsky's memory of Anna's corpse "shamelessly stretched out before strangers" as he prepares to commit murder in the Balkans. To describe Vronsky's final action in this way is not an exaggeration of the text, since Levin—the author's mouthpiece—expresses the same sentiment in the discussion of the Slavonic Question that takes place in the epilogue. While Koznyshev and Katavasov attempt to engender sympathy in him for "православных людях, страдающих под игом 'нечестивых Агарян'" (Orthodox Christians suffering under the yoke of the "infidel Hagarenes") (*PSS* 19:388), Levin protests the idea of "убивать Турок" (killing Turks) (*PSS* 19:391). In *War and Peace* Tolstoy also describes war as murder, as well as a long list of other crimes, in the opening of volume 3 (*PSS* 11:3), which is—significantly, I would argue—the midpoint, that is, the very center, of the four-volume book. According to Tolstoy's worldview, then, both adultery and war—the former demonstrated in the fates of both Hélène Bezukhova and Anna Karenina, the latter in *War and Peace* and in Levin's assessment of Russia's "rescue" of the Ottoman Slavs—are equivalent to murder.

Rhetoric of the porno-prophetic type can be detected in the writings of the Slavophiles as well, and these provide a fruitful interpretive context for *Anna Karenina*. While using the image of the Madonna when proclaiming Russia's virtues, they take up the tone of Old Testament prophets when denouncing her failings. One might even consider a view of nineteenth-century

Slavophiles as playing the role of modern-day Hebrew prophets in Russian culture, given that their appeal to their fellow citizens to resist Western influences and hold fast to their own unique traditions is analogous with the prophets' call on ancient Israelites to resist the religions of their influential neighbors. A first-generation Slavophile, one whom Levin recalls reading in the epilogue, was Aleksei Stepanovich Khomiakov. His writings enjoyed a resurgence in popularity during Russia's war with Turkey in the late 1870s, and Tolstoy, who had met him frequently in the late 1850s, read his works again in the spring of 1877, that is, as he was completing *Anna Karenina*. Khomiakov had fought the Turks in Bulgaria in 1828, he wrote a "Letter to the Serbs" to warn them against Westernization in 1860, and on the eve of the Crimean War in 1853 he composed his famous poem "Rossii" (To Russia), of which I include two memorable stanzas:

В судах черна неправдой черной
И игом рабства клеймена,
Безбожной лести, лжи тлетворной,
И лени мертвой и позорной,
И всякой мерзости полна!

О, недостойная избранья,
Ты избрана! Скорей омой
Себя водою покаянья,
Да гром двойного наказанье
Не грянет над твоей главой!

With dark injustice art thou blackened,
And branded art with slavery's yoke;
With godless flattery, noxious falsehood,
With indolence, moribound and shameful,
And every vileness art thou filled!

O thou, unworthy to be chosen,
Chosen thou art! Hasten to wash
Thyself with waters of repentance,
So that no punishment redoubled
Should break like thunder on thy head![38]

The references to slavery and chosenness, sin and shame, and the call to repentance are all suggestive of the heedings of the Hebrew prophets.

Similar invocations are present in the rhetoric of a second-generation Slavophile, the previously mentioned president of the Moscow Slavonic Benevolent Committee. Addressing the committee regarding the 1878 Congress of Berlin, where Russia was forced to make concessions to Western European powers and reduce the gains she had made for the Balkan states in the victory over Turkey, Aksakov delivered the following fiery speech:

> Ты ли это, Русь-победительница, сама добровольно разжаловавшая себя в побежденную? Ты ли на скамье подсудимых как преступница, каешься в святых поднятых тобою трудах, молишь простить тебе, твои победы? . . . Едва сдерживая веселый смех, с презрительной иронией, похваляя твою политическую мудрость, Западниыя державы, с Германией впереди, нагло срывают с тебя победный венец, преподносят тебе взамен шутовскую с гремушками шапку, а ты послушно, чуть ли с выражением чувствительнейшей

> признательности, подклоняешь под нее свою многострадальную голову.
>
> Is it you, Russia—the winner, who yourself voluntarily demotes yourself to a defeated one? Is it you who sits on the bench of the accused as a criminal, repenting of your holy efforts, asking for forgiveness for your victory? . . . Barely withholding the happy laughter, with despising irony, praising your political wisdom, the western powers, with Germany in front, impudently pluck your victory wreath and offer you instead a fool's cap with jingles, while you obediently, almost with an expression of the most heartfelt gratitude, lower your martyred head underneath it.[39]

Nineteenth-century social mores prohibited Aksakov, as they did Khomiakov, from using more vivid Old Testament images of harlotry, but the undertone is there in the accusatory pitch, in the suggestion that Russia has sold herself to Germany, and in the invoking of shame through the image of the lowered head. Tolstoy's isolationist politics—to reference Dostoevsky's musings on the epilogue to *Anna Karenina*—were in direct conflict with Slavophile imperialism, which used the image of the benevolent Mother of God to depict Russia's protective impulses toward the South Slavs. Both sides availed themselves of porno-prophetic rhetoric, however, when issuing criticism. Matich's observation that "Anna's dismemberment in the sexual sense is the direct consequence of transgressing God's law"[40] can be extended to the national sphere when considering the porno-prophetic inflection of her dismemberment and Tolstoy's own misgivings about the war. Within that framework, Vronsky's memory of Anna's mangled body on his way to the Balkans creates an implication that Russia might be punished in the same way for what, in the mind of the increasingly pacifist author, are her own transgressions of God's law.[41]

The porno-prophetic motifs in *Anna Karenina* inevitably call for yet another reexamination of the novel's epigraph, "Мне отмщение, и Аз воздам" (Vengeance is mine, and I will repay) (*PSS* 18:3). Previous research suggests that Tolstoy got the idea for it from book 4 (*Ethics*), chapter 62, of Arthur Schopenhauer's *The World as Will and Representation*, where the Bible verse is quoted.[42] Since the author is, effectively, God of the world of his novel, all the more for the omniscient narration, the most straightforward interpretation, one embraced by Eikhenbaum,[43] has been the one mentioned above in connection with the draft that has Levin viewing Anna's mangled body—that Tolstoy himself punishes Anna for her transgression. Yet Tolstoy is sympathetic to Anna and unsympathetic to the hypocritical society that surrounds her, which prompted Viktor Shklovsky to conclude that it was people, and not God, who pushed Anna under the train.[44] Since the verse about vengeance occurs both in the Old Testament—as God's threat to Israel—and in the New—as an injunction against human action—interpretations of the epigraph, such as the two examples just listed, can be grouped according to which Testament they rely on. Schopenhauer had the New Testament in mind, since he quotes the verse in support of his statement that "no person has the authority to set himself up as a moral judge,"[45] and Tolstoy's rendering of the Old Church Slavonic comes from the verse in Romans.[46] Considering the verse in relation to the political message of the epilogue, the New Testament context supports Levin's qualms about Russia's vengeance against Turkey on behalf of oppressed Orthodox Slavs, especially given his use of (a variant of) the actual word when he refuses to accept "такую мысль, которая выражается в мщении и убийстве" (such a thought, which expresses itself in revenge and murder) (*PSS* 19:392). The Old Testament is still significant, however, not only as the original source of the verse, but because the context of the verse, the so-called Song of Moses, follows the same pattern as the prophecies of Isaiah, Ezekiel, and Jeremiah, although without the gendered and pornographic elements: it starts by reviewing God's deliverance of Israel, then warns the nation of forgetting this deed and worshipping other gods, and, finally, enumerates the ensuing punishment.

God's vengeance in the "Song of Moses" takes the form of national dismemberment—by means of arrows and swords, pestilence and plague, and the scattering of the people of Israel—which is, incidentally, the fear that Levin, and Tolstoy through him, expresses for Russia when he lumps her war with Turkey together with other rebellions and conquests that presented a threat to the nation. He comments that "в восьмидесятимиллионном народе всегда найдутся не сотни, как теперь, а десятки тысяч людей, потерявших общественное положение, бесшабашных людей, которые всегда готовы—в шайку Пугачева, в Хиву, в Сербию" (among eighty million people, there are always to be found, not hundreds like now, but tens of thousands of people who have lost their social position, reckless people, who are always ready—to join Pugachev's band, to go to Khiva, to Serbia) (*PSS* 19:389). Vladimir Alexandrov claims that the epigraph, functioning as "metaphoric montage," is "clearly relevant to a novel named after an adulteress,"[47] and I have attempted to show that it should also be considered in light of Tolstoy's political concerns. If we relate the epigraph and the epilogue to each other as two bookends of the novel, then the Old Testament threat of vengeance applies to the adulterous nation as much as it does to the adulterous heroine, while the New Testament prohibition against mortals taking God's business into their own hands applies to the zealous Slavophiles.

The Cuckolded Husband-Statesman

If Vronsky dismembers Anna and overextends the empire into war, then the cuckolded Karenin engages in a vain attempt to keep both wife and empire in order. The disobedient wife and the disorderly empire appear as a pair of troubles and spill into each other for this high-ranking public official. Chapter 14 of part 3 in the novel is divided between Karenin's first decisive move regarding Anna's infidelity and his drafting of a plan for investigating two political crises: the drought in the Zaraysk province and the "плачевно[е] состояни[е]" (lamentable situation) (*PSS* 18:302) of the *inorodtsy* in Central Asia.[48] His political plans are couched between glancing at Anna's portrait that hangs in his study, the action progressing from writing her a letter to glancing at her portrait to drafting notes for the ministry to glancing at her portrait again. Just as the image of Anna's mangled body haunts the volunteer movement in the epilogue, so her portrait oversees Karenin's statesman duties regarding Russia's colonies. Karenin feels pleased with the letter he writes to Anna, but when he looks at her portrait, she seems to look back at him "насмешливо и нагло" (mockingly and insolently) (*PSS* 18:300), causing him to turn away with a shudder. By contrast, looking at her again after attending to state business he "презрительно улыбнулся" (smiled contemptuously), and when he lies down in bed afterwards, "событие с женой, оно ему представилось уже совсем не в таком мрачном виде" (the incident with his wife, it no longer presented itself to him in the same gloomy light) (*PSS* 18:303). The wife and the nation become interchangable concepts as drafting solutions to one problem eases the pain of the other.

Karenin's initial reaction to Anna's affair, as well as to the child born from it, bears examining in a brief return to the porno-prophetic theme because of the peculiar similarities between this nineteenth-century Russian statesman and the ancient Hebrew prophet Hosea. Although there is no evidence of Tolstoy's purposeful fashioning of such parallels, their *post factum* discovery is still worth exploring within the theoretical paradigm of this study and especially in a novel that is framed by an Old Testament verse. The Old Testament book of Hosea describes the prophet as being commanded by God to marry an adulterous woman and to adopt her illegitimate children in order to perform, in his own home, Israel's adultery in worshipping the gods of other nations: "When the Lord first spoke through Hosea, the Lord said to Hosea: 'Go, take for yourself a wife of whoredom and have children of whoredom, for the land commits great whoredom by forsaking the Lord.'"[49] When Hosea confronts the unfaithful Gomer, he demands the following: "You must remain as mine for many days; you shall not play the whore, you shall not have intercourse with a man, nor I with you."[50] This is where the uncanny similarity to Karenin occurs. In the letter he writes to Anna before drafting solutions to the problems plaguing Russia, Karenin insists that "наша жизнь должна итти, как она шла прежде" (our life must go on as it went before) (*PSS* 18:299), while in the subsequent face-to-face confrontation he requests the following:

> Мне нужно чтоб я не встречал здесь этого человека и чтобы вы вели себя так, чтобы ни *свет*, ни *прислуга* не *могли* обвинить

> вас . . . чтобы вы не видали его. Кажется, это не много. И за это вы будете пользоваться правами честной жены, не исполняя ее обязанностей.
>
> I want not to meet that man here and that you behave in such a way that neither *society* nor *the servants* would be *able* to accuse you . . . that you not see him. It doesn't seem like much. And for that you will enjoy the rights of an honest wife, without fulfilling her duties. (*PSS* 18:338; emphases Tolstoy's)

His demands seem an exact replica of the ancient prophet's: his insistence that their life together continue as before echoes Hosea's injunction to Gomer that she "remain as [his] for many days"; his request that she not see Vronsky is the polite equivalent of "not play[ing] the whore"; and his absolving her of the duties of an honest wife can only pertain to sexual intercourse, of which Hosea also absolves Gomer in the last clause of the above quoted verse.

A further similarity between these two men separated by epochs and literary genres is their treatment of their unfaithful wives' progeny. In addition to taking "a wife of whoredom," Hosea is instructed to "have children of whoredom," which becomes the situation in the Karenin household once Anna delivers Vronsky's baby there. Karenin not only temporarily adopts that baby, but he is also credited with saving her life as the new creature is all but ignored during Anna's nearly fatal postpartum illness. Finally, because of the circumstances just described, Vronsky's baby carries Karenin's last name, which becomes especially uncomfortable for the former once he, Anna, and the baby move into his estate Vozdvizhenskoe and commence life together as a family.

Anna's New Friends

Only a few chapters after Karenin deals with wife and empire, Anna's new circle of affair-promoting friends is described, with names and features that carry connotations of both sexual and national otherness. In chapter 17 Princess Betsy Tverskaya invites Anna to a croquet match, which "должно было состоять из двух дам с их поклонниками" (was to consist of two ladies and their admirers) (*PSS* 18:310). The setup provides a way for Betsy to ease Anna's conscience by introducing her to other adulterous women, ones not "склонны[е] смотреть на вещи слишком трагически" (inclined to view things too tragically) (*PSS* 18:315), as Betsy accuses Anna of doing at the end of the chapter. The two ladies are Sappho Stolz—whose first name alludes to one of the first known sexually rebellious women in history, and whose last name only intensifies the effect with its German meaning "proud"—and Liza Merkalova—whose description as "худая брюнетка с восточным ленивым типом лица и прелестными, неизъяснимыми, как все говорили, глазами" (a thin brunette with a lazy Eastern type of face and charming, unfathomable, as everyone said, eyes) (*PSS* 18:316) is matched by her last name, the linguistic derivative of "мрак" (darkness). Sappho Stolz is, obviously, the one with the stranger first name, utterly non-Russian and atypical in general, with only one possible connotation, which means that Tolstoy's choice for it was no coincidence but a purposeful designation that seemed fitting to him for Betsy's immoral circle. One might wonder why he chose Liza Merkalova and not Sappho as the person who "бредит" (raves) about Anna, as Betsy informs her in their pre-party chat: "Она говорит . . . что, если б она была мужчиною, она бы наделала за вас тысячу глупостей" (She says . . . that if she were a man, she would have committed a thousand follies for you) (*PSS* 18:314). The author does, however, avail himself of one stereotype in the next chapter, where he describes Sappho's handshake as "по-мужски" (mannish) (*PSS* 18:315).

The conflation of sexual and national otherness in the Greek-German Sappho Stolz and the dark, Eastern Liza Merkalova seems fitting for the novel of adultery that condemns Russia's foreign policy, especially because the national allusions contained in the names and features of these two adulterous women point to the international complications associated with the Slavonic Question. Once again, there is no evidence that this was part of Tolstoy's plan for the book, but the parallels match up so well that they are worth mentioning. In the March 1877 issue of his *Writer's Diary* Dostoevsky explores a possible consequence of Ottoman surrender: Greek ascendancy in the region, bolstered by Western European support. He cites the 1870 conflict between the Greek and Bulgarian patriarchs—one identified by him as well as by contemporary historians as a national dispute in ecclesiastical disguise—in support of the need for Russian protection and supervision in the area. In order to illustrate that Greek ties with Western Europe are stronger than those with its Bulgarian or Russian Orthodox brothers, Dostoevsky declares, "В международном городе, мимо покровителей англичан, все-таки будут хозяевами греки—исконные хозяева города. Надо думать, что греки смотрят на славян еще с большим презрением, чем немцы" (In the international city [i.e., Constantinople], aside from the protection of the English, the Greeks will still be the masters, who were originally the masters. One must realize that the Greeks regard the Slavs with even more contempt than the Germans do) (*PSS* 25:72). The combination of anxieties expressed in that statement—that Greece would only cooperate with Western Europe in diminishing Russia's influence in the Balkans and that Greek contempt for Slavs outmatches even German contempt for them—is encapsulated perfectly in Sappho Stolz's Greek-German name. The effect is greater given the meaning of the German word, conjuring a proud, Western woman who looks down on Slavs and men. On the other hand, the designation of Liza

Merkalova's face as "Eastern" is, in the general Russian context, most likely an allusion to Turkey, whose rule in the Balkans occasioned the Eastern Crisis. From this perspective and within the theoretical framework that reads Anna as an anthropomorphized Russia, these two women form the appropriate new social circle for the adulterous heroine.

Women Slavophiles

The Slavonic Question had not yet gathered mass interest in Russia when Tolstoy wrote the first sketches for "the novel concern[ing] an unfaithful wife and the whole drama resulting from this" on March 18, 1873,[51] or when the *Russian Herald* published the first installments in its January–April 1875 issues. The Herzegovinian uprising that started the wave and got the attention of Europe took place that summer, when Tolstoy was on a long break from writing.[52] Yet the Slavonic Question was on his mind, since already in the first part of the novel—chapter 32, published as part of the second installment in February 1875—Countess Lydia Ivanovna receives a letter from a "известный панславист" (famous Pan-Slavist) and rushes off to a Slavonic Committee meeting (*PSS* 18:115). In part 5, chapter 23—published in December 1876, after the crisis was in full swing—the Countess is not only portrayed as an enthusiastic Pan-Slavist in more detail, but her political infatuations blur the lines with romantic ones:

> Графиня Лидия Ивановна давно уже перестала быть влюбленною в мужа, но никогда с тех пор не переставала быть влюбленною в кого-нибудь. Она бывала влюблена в нескольких вдруг, и в мужчин и в женщин; она бывала влюблена во всех почти людей, чем-нибудь особенно выдающихся. Она была влюблена во всех новых принцесс и принцев, вступавших в родство с Царскою фамилией, была влюблена в одного митрополита, одного викарного и одного священника. Была влюблена в одного журналиста, в трех славян, в Комисарова; в одного министра, одного доктора, одного английского миссионера и в Каренина.
>
> Countess Lydia Ivanovna had long ago ceased to be in love with her husband, but had never since ceased to be in love with somebody. She was in love with several [persons] at once, both men and women; she had been in love with almost every one who was particularly prominent. She was in love with all the new princesses and princes who became connected with the Tsar's family, she was in love with a metropolitan, a bishop, and a priest. She was in love with a journalist, three Slavs, Komisarov, a minister, a doctor, an English missionary, and Karenin. (*PSS* 19:82–83)

Lydia's infatuations are never to be physically consummated, like Anna's is, but are sublimated, as evidenced in the quoted passage, through her involvement in benevolent causes. She proves to be aware of this when, several sentences later, "она ясно видела, что не была бы влюблена в Комисарова, если б он не спас жизни Государя, не была бы влюблена в Ристич-Куджицкого, если бы не было Славянского вопроса" (she saw clearly that she would not have been in love with Komisarov if he hadn't saved the Tsar's life and that she would not have been in love with Ristich-Kudzhitsky if it were not for the Slavonic Question) (*PSS* 19:83).

Despite these lofty reasons, the description of Lydia's infatuations and the description of the conduct of Tolstoy's last heroine, the prostitute Katiusha Maslova prove to have a lot in common. Chapter 2 of *Resurrection* describes Katiusha's

> прелюбодеяния с молодыми, средними, полудетьми и разрушающимися стариками, холостыми, женатыми, купцами, приказчиками, армянами, евреями, тартарами, богатыми, бедными, здоровыми, больными, пьяными, трезвыми, грубыми, нежными, военными, штатскими, студентами, гимназистами—всех возможных сословий, возрастов и характеров.
>
> adulteries with the old, middle-aged, half-children and feeble old men, bachelors, married men, merchants, clerks, Armenians, Jews, Tartars, rich, poor, sick, healthy, drunk, sober, rough, gentle, military men, civilians, students, high schoolers—of all possible classes, ages, and characters. (*PSS* 32:11)

In both cases a long list of various types of persons is presented and the main difference between the two women is that of class: Lydia Ivanovna's title allows her contact with the highest echelons of society, with "everyone who was particularly prominent"—princes, doctors, and ministers—while Katiusha is obliged to entertain anybody who pays for her services. Further, while Katiusha's list, proportionate to her profession, connotes heavier degrees of national adulteration in that it incorporates the disenfranchised ethnic groups of the Russian empire, Lydia's love fantasies center on trendy current events, such as the Slavonic Question. The latter is alluded to in the figures of the three Slavs on Lydia's list—and perhaps also the journalist that precedes them, since the Slavonic Question occupied the headlines at the time—as well as Ristich-Kudzhitsky, based on Jovan Ristich, the well-known Serbian political activist involved in the independence movement. Karenin, Lydia's latest infatuation, is the appropriate person to end the long list as a man who expects his ideas to "принести величайшую пользу государству" (be of greatest use to the state) (*PSS* 18:301) and whose doctor, invited by Lydia to check up on him after Anna's betrayal, cares for his health "для России" (for the sake of Russia) (*PSS* 18:214).

Tolstoy's tainting of the Slavonic cause with connotations of romantic profligacy through the character of Lydia Ivanovna becomes even more interesting when considered in comparison to the earlier drafts and in light of a probable real-life model for the countess. Manuscript 46 (*PSS* 20:369 ff.) shows that Lydia Ivanovna was originally intended to be Karenin's sister, Katerina Aleksandrovna, which allowed her to move in with him after Anna moved out but prohibited the possibility of her infatuation. Her mock-worthy hyperspirituality and love of Slavdom are present from the start, however, for she is described as one of the "дамы того высшаго Петербурскаго Православно-Хомяковского-добродетельно-придворно-Жуковско-Християнскаго направления" (ladies of that higher Petersburg Orthodox-Khomikovian-virtouous-courtly-Zhukovskian-Christian trend) (*PSS* 20:370–71). The lengthy designation is a form of the shorter, yet equally ridiculous, "филантропическое, религиозно-патриотическое учреждение" (philanthropic religio-patriotic society) (*PSS* 18:115) to which Lydia Ivanovna belongs in the published novel, and it is located in the same chapter—32 of part 1—where she rushes off to a Slavonic Committee meeting. Although the reference to the prominent Slavophile Khomiakov from the draft is removed from later versions describing Lydia Ivanovna, his name appears in the final version of the epilogue in the form of yet another disappointment in Levin's quest for spiritual enlightenment.

Subsequent versions of the section describing Lydia Ivanovna's relationship to Karenin give her the name she bears in the final version, do not designate her as family, and have her falling in love with him,[53] but it is only in the final version, written in the week preceding November 20, 1876, that Tolstoy penned the section describing Lydia's multiple infatuations.[54] The timing is significant, because the section under discussion appeared in the first installment published in the *Russian Herald*—in December 1876—after Serbia and Montenegro declared war on Turkey the previous summer with expectation of Russian support. Immediately preceding the writing of that section Tolstoy traveled to Moscow with the express purpose of finding out more about the war, as he informs both Fet and Strakhov in letters dated November 12 (*PSS* 62:288, 291). Tolstoy had been corresponding with Fet regarding the war for a year by this time, since November 1875, when Fet informed him that his brother had joined the fight in Herzegovina. In the letters of November 12, 1876, Tolstoy confesses to both Fet and Strakhov that "всё это волнует меня очень" (all this disturbs me a lot), but to Fet he also brings up, as an example of a Slavophile, "какая-нибудь Аксакова с своим мизерным тщеславием и фальшивым сочувствием к чему-то неопределенному" (some kind of Aksakova with her meagre vanity and false sympathy toward something indefinite) (*PSS* 62:288). Anna Fedorovna Aksakova was married to Ivan Sergeevich Aksakov, president of the Slavic Committee during the Eastern Crisis, and she was the daughter of the poet and outspoken Slavophile Fedor Ivanovich Tiutchev, which placed her in a visible position within the movement. A reference to her in a letter composed only days before completing chapter 23 of part 5 about Lydia Ivanovna is a strong indicator that Aksakova might have been the inspiration for that particular character description.

Levin's "Tiny Circle"

The Eastern Crisis, as we have seen, affects the book's plot as well as the very process of writing it. The war creeps into the novel slowly, through characters such as Ivanovna, and as the crisis progresses, the references to it not only increase, but come to punctuate extremely important family events, such as the arrival of Levin's long-expected firstborn son. The last full section of the novel printed in the *Russian Herald,* part 7, abounds with hints regarding developments in the Balkans. In chapter 3 Montenegro enters into small talk when Katavasov asks his visitor Levin, "Ну что каковы черногорцы? По породе воины" (How about those Montenegrins? Warriors by nature) (*PSS* 19:254), and a "неумолкаемый разговор о Герцеговине" (never-ending discussion of Herzegovina) (*PSS* 19:261) takes place in the following chapter. Finally, Levin loses his composure in chapter 14, when the doctor who is to deliver Kitty, rather slow for the panicked father-to-be in getting his things together, casually remarks, "Однако Турок-то бьют решительно. Вы читали вчерашнюю телеграмму?" (However, the Turks are certainly being beaten. Have you read yesterday's telegram?) (*PSS* 19:289).

The epilogue opens with the din of patriotic activities, as already discussed in relation to Vronsky, and that din is then carried over from the train station into Levin's estate through visitors Koznyshev and Katavosov, who unsuccessfully attempt to convert its residents to Pan-Slav ideology. The very name of Levin's estate—Pokrovskoe—illuminates the national position allegorized in his family home, as *pokrov* means "shelter," "cover," and "protection." In her excellent book *Unattainable Bride Russia*, Ellen Rutten notes "the cult of the so-called *pokrov*—the intercession or protection of the Mother of God" in medieval Russia.[55] Tolstoy's shrinking of this ecclesiastical and national concept to the borders of Levin's estate confirms the earlier observation that his home "был целый мир для Левина" (was the entire world for Levin) (*PSS* 18:101). The author's mouthpiece realizes by the end of the novel that nothing outside of this home-world matters much and that not much can be done to effect meaningful change beyond its borders.

Shortly after the heated political debate between Levin and his guests, an intimate family moment occurs when the former is called into the nursery, where Kitty demonstrates to him how their infant son, Mitya, "очевидно, несомненно уже узнавал всех своих" (obviously, undoubtedly already recognized all of his own [people]) (*PSS* 19:396). This private scene of family bliss and the discussion of the Eastern Crisis that takes place outside it both engage the topic of boundaries: the question of who one's own people are and how to recognize them. Mitya begins to recognize his own parents at the end of the day during which his uncle had argued on behalf of the Southern Orthodox Slavs, while his grandfather proclaimed that he felt no love for his brother Slavs and was, together with Mitya's father, interested only in Russia (*PSS* 19:388).

An earlier draft of the epilogue creates a direct link between the family moment in the nursery and the question of Slavonic brotherhood. In the published version Mitya's recognition is followed by Levin's own realization that he loves his son, an emotion that, contrary to his expectations, he did not experience immediately upon his son's birth. In a draft version Mitya's recognition prompts Levin to think about the Slavonic Question he had just discussed with his visitors, and his thoughts bring the entire novel to its end:

> "Сербы! говорят они. Нетолько Сербы, но в своем крошечном кругу жить не хорошо, а только не дурно. Это такое [счастье], на которое не могу надеяться один, а только с помощью Бога, Которого я начинаю знать," подумал он. Конец.

> "Serbs! they say. Not only the Serbs, but to live in one's own tiny circle, if not well, then at least not badly. That is such [happiness], for which I cannot hope on my own, but only with the help of God, Whom I am beginning to know," he thought. The End. (*PSS* 20:571–72)

In this somewhat incoherent conclusion to the novel Levin affirms the desire of all people, "not only the Serbs," to enjoy the moments of intimacy that he had just experienced and that can only be realized in a "tiny circle." This universalization of experience negates any kind of uniqueness in the case of the Serbs, while the isolationist politics expressed in the metaphor of the "tiny circle" prohibit any grand-scale action.

The question of who is *svoi* (one's own) and who is *chuzhoi* (a stranger)[56] can be traced all the way back to the famous opening line, which sets up a definition of sameness and difference: [57] "Все счастливые семьи похожи друг на друга, каждая несчастливая семья несчастлива по-своему" (All happy families resemble one another, each unhappy family is unhappy in its own way) (*PSS* 18:3).[58] A closer look at the subsequent portrayal of the novel's families justifies reading the first half of that line not only as "this happy family resembles another happy family" but also as "members *within* a happy family resemble one another." Nowhere is this more obvious than in the relationship between Levin and Kitty, the model happy family that comprises the real ending of the novel. Levin and Kitty's union is seamless, as described in another oft-quoted passage, where he cannot tell where she ends and he begins (*PSS* 19:50). It even borders on the incestuous, since the Shcherbatskys are the only family Levin has ever known (*PSS* 18:24–25) and Kitty associates him with memories of her dead brother (*PSS* 18:51). Following the same logic, the members of an unhappy family are strangers to each other, as exhibited by the Oblonskys when Dolly repeatedly uses—and shudders at—the word *chuzhoi* to describe her unfaithful husband (*PSS* 18:14, 16). The same happens to the Karenins. After Anna confesses her affair, she and her husband become "совершенно чужды друг другу" (completely estranged from each other) (*PSS* 18:372), the repetitve ending of that phrase recalling and comprising a meaningful contrast to the opening definition of happy families, who "похожи друг на друга" (resemble one another). Parenthetically, the opening line also offers a hint as to the number of the novel's happy and unhappy families, as it employs the word *happy* once and its opposite twice.

The "family idea" and the story of the consequences of breaking family boundaries turn out to be especially appropriate for the novel that ends up debating Russia's own familial obligations to her South Slavic "братьев, единокровных и единоверцев" (brothers of the same blood and faith) (*PSS* 19:387). Levin certainly feels no familial connection with the Serbs, and in a section of the epilogue that echoes the ending of the novel's draft cited above, he does indeed define his circle of *svoikh* along tiny perimeters:

> когда он старался сделать что-нибудь такое, что сделало бы добро для всех, для человечества, для России, для всей деревни, он замечал, что мысли об этом были приятны, но сама деятельность всегда бывала нескладная . . . теперь же, когда он после женитьбы стал более и более ограничиваться жизнью для себя, он . . . видел, что оно спорится гораздо лучше.
>
> When he had tried to do something that would be good for everyone, for mankind, for Russia, for the whole village, he had noticed that thinking about it was pleasant, but the doing itself was always awkward . . . while now, after his marriage, when he began to limit himself more and more to living for himself, he . . . saw that it turned out much better. (*PSS* 19:372)

Nestled inside the country, in the very core of Russianness, Levin remains unimpressed with the writings of the Slavophile philosopher Khomiakov and exhibits indifference, as Dostoevsky bemoans, to the all-uniting Slavophilic cause that is to redeem Russia.

The distinction between Levin's "tiny circle" inside Mitya's nursery and the political posturing taking place outside can further be illuminated by employing Gary Saul Morson's insightful insistence on the distinction between intimacy and romance that is presented through Levin and Kitty's relationships on the one hand and Anna and Vronsky's on the other. "Romance depends on mystery,"[59] Morson claims, on separation, distance, obstacles, on not knowing. Romance imbues the language of the Slavophiles, including Dostoevsky's enthusiastic support for them in his *Writer's Diary*, where the emphasis on purity, selflessness, and the willingness to suffer for another is evocative of the language of romance. As soon as all of the distance and obstacles are traversed, however, the romance ends, as it did for Russia at the Congress of Berlin and as it eventually does for Anna, who thinks to herself during the fateful ride to the train station, in English, "The zest is gone" (*PSS* 19:343). It is the culmination of fears that began as soon as she moved with Vronsky to Vozdvizhenskoe—an estate whose name aptly, in keeping with the idea of romance, suggests upward movement[60]—where she continually tried to keep everything "оживленное и веселое" (lively and happy), as she explained to Dolly, "чтоб Алексей не желал ничего нового" (so that Aleksei would not wish for anything new) (*PSS* 19:195). By contrast, "prosaic love," to use Morson's favorite phrasing, which he interchanges with intimacy, "thrives on closeness."[61] It is encapsulated in the very prosaic notion of the "tiny circle," in which one is "to live . . . if not well, then at least not badly," and demonstrated in the marital and parenting experiences of Levin and Kitty, as well as in the functioning of Pokrovskoe as a whole. If Tolstoy defamiliarizes war in *War and Peace* by describing it as a series of crimes and defamiliarizes romance in *Anna Karenina* by first foreshadowing and finally depicting its grim ending, then the Serbian war in the latter novel, backlit as it is by the extramarital affair, shows that what Tolstoy would later repeatedly call "суевери[е] патриотизма" (the superstition of patriotism) (*PSS* 37:241, 90:44) is as dangerous as the superstition of forbidden love.

Tolstoy disappointed his compatriots and his brother Slavs by protesting Russia's involvement in the Serbo-Turkish War and then disappointed them once again three decades later, when Austria annexed Bosnia and Herzegovina in 1908 and the Bosnian Serbs, as in the past, looked to Russia for help. A letter he originally sent as a private reply to a "сербская женщина" (Serbian woman) (*PSS* 37:222), who appealed to him directly, grew into an essay that critiqued the superstition of patriotism. Fully a pacifist at that point, as well as a Christian anarchist, Tolstoy not only refused to entertain the idea of Russian intervention, but implored the Serbs also to "освобождаться всеми силами от губительного суеверия патриотизма, государства и сознать каждому человеку свое человеческое достоинство, не допускающее отступления от закона любви" (free themselves with all might from the destructive superstition of patriotism, the state, and acknowledge in every man his human dignity, not allowing a departure from the law of love) (*PSS* 37:241). Russia's other tsar[62] did not live long enough to see that "the superstition of patriotism" would soon bring about the Great War, which was triggered precisely inside annexed Bosnia by a young Serbian patriot's assassination of the Austrian archduke. His essay endured a slightly better fate than the unpatriotic epilogue to *Anna Karenina* in that it saw the light of day in *Golos Moskvy* (the Voice of Moscow) but in a heavily redacted edition.

Returning to the Soviet critic Babaev's observation, discussed in the beginning of the chapter, we can conclude that this novel that opens with a distinction between happy and unhappy families weaves a parallel lesson, by the end, on the difference between happy and unhappy nations. The recipe for happy nations, like the one for happy families, requires a tight circle of mutually resembling members. By contrast, Anna's "избыток чего-то" (surplus of something) (*PSS* 18:66), that quality that first attracts Vronsky to her, and Russia's surplus of feeling for the South Slavs both lead to ruin.

Part II

Nations

Chapter 4

The Goldsmith's Gold

The Origins of Yugoslavism and the Birth of the Croatian Novel

August Šenoa, father of the Croatian novel and, concomitantly, Croatian realism, is virtually unknown in international literary circles. Nineteenth-century literature of the South Slavs in general pales in renown compared to that of the Western Slavs, as the disparity in name recognition between August Šenoa and Henryk Sienkiewicz, the author addressed in the next and last chapter, testifies. Twentieth-century Yugoslav authors, such as the Nobel laureate Ivo Andrić and, to a somewhat lesser extent, Miroslav Krleža and Danilo Kiš, enjoy a certain degree of recognition within the European literary canon, but the educated reader would be loath to recall an author that predates them. Yet Šenoa's importance in Croatian literature and the politics of the nineteenth-century proto-Yugoslav movement cannot be overstated. The impact he made in the brief span of sixteen years (1865–81) during which he was intellectually active was so powerful that the period is referred to in Croatian literary history as *Šenoino doba* (Šenoa's time). He completed four novels;[1] wrote short stories, poetry, and literary manifestos; and worked as a city senator, as well as the artistic director of the national theater. Perhaps most important for the development of Croatian literature and national sentiment, he edited the leading literary journal, the weekly *Vienac* (Garland), which was at the height of its success under Šenoa's charge (1874–81). *Vienac* serialized both domestic novels, including Šenoa's, and foreign ones, many of them translated by Šenoa; it also featured lesser known parts of Croatia for its mostly urban audience and generally provided a political platform for questions pertaining to the South Slavs. Since most of Šenoa's literary fiction tends to center on Zagreb, he fulfilled the role of the capital city's faithful chronicler, as Fontane did for Berlin. In the context of the present study, he is significant for his vision for the South Slavs in the age of nationalism and his depiction of Croatia's problems through the trope of adultery in his first novel. Turning away from the anti-Ottoman national epic that dominated the literary sensibilities of the South Slavs and inspired their liberation movements in the first half of the nineteenth century, Šenoa gave birth to the modern Croatian novel in the second half and, at the same time, redirected the politics of suspicion toward the Habsburg Empire.

When William Gladstone described Montenegro to his English readers as a buffer zone between the Islamic East and the Christian West, he captured the sentiment that was foundational to the self-perception of all South Slavs. Even as far back as the twelfth century, before the Ottoman Empire came into existence, the founder of the Serbian Orthodox Church, St. Sava Nemanjić, wrote about being "doomed by fate to be the East in the West, and the West in the East."[2] While the nineteenth-century Orthodox Slavs could count on Russia for protection, the case of the South Slavic Catholics was most poetically rendered by the early twentieth-century British historian Robert Seton-Watson: "During the long Turkish night these provinces pinned all their hopes upon the House of Habsburg."[3] Rebecca West was less forgiving in her tone when in her Yugoslav travelogue she wrote that "there developed among the Croats one of the most peculiar passions known in history: a burning, indestructible devotion to the Habsburgs."[4] Neverthelss, both statements perfectly capture the political sentiment that Šenoa was determined to combat in his fiction: instead of casting the enemy in the mold of marauding, raping, kidnapping Jannisaries, he presented *her* as an enticing Western woman, a move that would be copied in the further development of Croatian realism even by his ideological adversaries.

Though I have demonstrated briefly in the introduction how Ferida Duraković's poem in the epigraph relates to the book in its entirety, and I return to it in the conclusion, her poem about Yugoslavia's dissolution makes a most obvious fit, if a bit of a nostalgic one, with the current chapter, which addresses the inception of the idea of South Slavic unity. The heroines of the previous three novels of empires are decidedly not cast in the mold of "the deceiving beauty" by their authors, all of whom exhibit sympathy and portray them as victims of societal bigotry or hypocrisy rather than illicit desires. Those beauties who cause "boys" to "die for them," whether in duels or in war, certainly do so without forethought.[5] The adulterous woman of Šenoa's novel, however, fits the mold very well. She attempts to use her beauty in order to seduce the hero; when that fails, she employs her political power in attempts to destroy the peasant heroine. She is also "the deceiving beauty" on a national level. As a representative of one of the oppressive empires that rule the South Slavs, she is the foreign "homeland" that has been imposed on them and that entices Croatian "boys" to die for "her" in battles against the Turks. As a semicolony inhabiting what was perceived by the West as the border between civilization and barbarism, between Christianity and Islam, and eager to prove that it belonged to the former, nineteenth-century Croatia, as Šenoa shows, was particularly vulnerable to the charms of "the deceiving beauty" that was Austria.

The Illyrian Movement and the National Epics

South Slavic nationalism was born against the Ottoman Empire as a common enemy in the first half of the nineteenth century and redirected, largely through Šenoa's efforts, toward the Germanic West in the second half. What is known as Croatian National Rebirth or Revival (*Hrvatski narodni preporod*) was led by the so-called Illyrian movement, which predated Šenoa by one generation, beginning in the late 1820s, after Napoleon's fall and the return of the coastal parts of Croatia to Austrian jurisdiction. The Illyrians took their name from the ancient tribes that occupied, roughly, the northeastern quadrant of the Adriatic shore and were eventually assimilated into the Slavic peoples that settled on the territory. Under the linguistic leadership of Ljudevit Gaj and poetical inspiration of Ivan Mažuranić, the Illyrians promoted South Slavic brotherhood with the rest of the peoples who would in the twentieth century unite, as well as break up, in the form of Yugoslavia. The word *sloga*, which means "agreement" and "unity," was, as one Croatian literary historian points out, one of the most frequently encountered words during the national revival.[6] The movement issued a call for the collection of national treasures and customs and founded the Zagreb University as well as the national theater in the capital. Most important, it worked toward establishing a common literary language, bolstered by the publication of grammar and orthography books, Croatian journals and newspapers, and other means by which print media unites a people into a common identity, well known to us since the publication of Benedict Anderson's *Imagined Communities*.

The political opposition to the initial Illyrians came in the form of the so-called Magyarones, and the split became formal in 1841 when the two movements organized themselves into Croatia's first two political parties, Hrvatsko-ugarska—or, as it was pejoratively known among the people, Mađaronska—and Ilirska. In contrast to the Illyrian leaders, such as Ivan Mažuranić and, later, August Šenoa, who came from the common people and promoted their education and enlightenment and the awakening of a sense of a unique national identity among them, the Magyarones consisted mostly of pro-Hungarian nobility. They called themselves "stari Horvati" (old Croats), and they found their political and economic interests threatened by a surge in Slavic nationalism and insistence on autonomy.[7] Due to the Ottoman presence in the Balkans, those in power were keen on aligning themselves with the western empires for protection; moreover, as will be shown in the example of Mažuranić's unlikely post as governor, one could play the ruling Austrians and insurgent Hungarians against each other to achieve certain political goals.

Ljudevit Gaj was an Illyrian cultural pioneer who realized—both in the sense of comprehending and in the sense of accomplishing—the value of a unified language for establishing a unified national identity. Croatia, in comparison to the other South Slavic states, was particularly fragmented in its language, which consists of three dialects named after the word each uses for "what." Gaj chose the *štokavski* dialect (among, in addition, *kajkavski* and *čakavski*) for the official Croatian language, which was significant because it encompassed the dialects used in Bosnia, Herzegovina, Serbia, and Montenegro, thereby demonstrating Croatian unity with the other South Slavs. In making this choice, he followed the lead of Vuk Karadžić, who chose the *štokavski* Herzegovinian dialect for his 1818 Serbian dictionary. Vuk, it ought also to be noted, is considered the father of the now-defunct Serbo-Croatian language since his translation of the New Testament propelled Serbo-Croatian into common usage and gave it the same impetus that Martin Luther's Bible gave to modern German.

If Gaj's choice of dialect embraced the broadest possible spectrum of South Slavs, then his important orthographic decision demonstrated a sense of camaraderie with other smaller Slavic groups going through their own national revivals. By instituting diacritical marks (e.g., *č*, *ž*) as replacements for the previously used combinations of letters (e.g., *cs, zs*), Gaj spurned the Hungarian influence in Croatian orthography in favor of the Czechs, who were Croatia's comrades in their common belonging to the House of Habsburg as well as a major inspiration for Croatia's national rebirth.[8] The year 1830, when Gaj's *Pravopis* (Orthography)[9] was published, is considered the official beginning of the Illyrian movement. Gaj was also personally significant in Šenoa's development, since the young Šenoa used to visit Gaj and borrow collections of Croatian poetry from him. Like Gaj, Šenoa drew inspiration from the Czechs and made overtures of camaraderie. As a student in Prague he was fluent in Czech and his first publication was in Czech—an article in January 1861 for the journal *Národní listy* (National Papers), in which he lauded the election of Ivan Mažuranić as Croatian court chancellor.

Along with Gaj, Mažuranić is the figure who is most commonly associated with the Illyrian movement, as both poet and politician. Mažuranić entered the Croatian political scene in 1848, when the Hungarian revolution frightened the Austrian Empire into seeking Croatian help by allowing common Croatians to participate in politics. After serving as Croatian court chancellor, Mažuranić in 1873 became the first *ban* (governor) to come from the common people. His literary style was influenced by the likes of George Gordon Byron and Aleksandr Pushkin, and he published poetry in Gaj's literary journal *Danica* beginning with its establishment in 1835. Prior to the political appointments, he was best known for his 1846 epic poem, *Smrt Smail-age Čengića* (The Death of Smail-aga Čengić), which is a prime example of the rise of South Slavic nationalism against the rule of the Ottoman Empire in the region.

The Death of Smail-aga Čengić describes an actual event that took place in October 1840—the ambush and murder of the eponymous Turkish general and ruler in Herzegovina by a group of Montenegrins. The poem opens with the aga bestowing the "Turkish gift" (i.e., impaling) on the "Mountain people" (*Brđani* in the original, *brdo* meaning "mountain") but failing to experience any satisfaction in the spectacle because of their stoic response. The line "Niti pisnu, niti zubi škrinu" (Made no sound, nor gnashed their teeth) repeats throughout the third stanza, while the fifth describes the aga's frustration at the scene—or, more accurately, at the lack of a scene—"Posmica ih, srca ne iskali / Što bez straha svi su pred njim pali" (He killed them, but he did not appease his anger / Because all fell fearlessly before him).[10] Mažuranić expresses his South Slavic camaraderie with the suffering brave Montenegrins by romanticizing them in the same way that Gladstone and Tennyson do on the English side and that Tolstoy's characters in *Anna Karenina* do on the Russian side. A much more recent Croatian historical novel, Nedjeljko Fabrio's *Vježbanje života* (Practicing Life), published in 1985, describes a group of Croatian children at a ball in 1859 "playing" Turks and Montenegrins. Those playing the Turks pretend to fall "šireći ruke, na uglačanom parketu, pod sabljama dječaka što su bili preodjeveni u nesmiljene Crnogorce" (spreading their arms, onto the polished parquet, under the swords of the boys who were dressed as merciless Montenegrins). The paragraph-long description ends with the following sentence: "U modi su bili Tursko-Crnogorski ratovi!" (Turko-Montenegrin wars were in vogue!).[11]

The notorious Smail-aga had, in fact, murdered the nephew of Petar Petrović Njegoš, the man who played an almost identical role in nineteenth-century Montenegro politics and literature as the one Mažuranić played in Croatia. He was a statesman as well as a poet, with his own epic piece about Montenegro's fight for freedom. He was not yet eighteen years old when he assumed the role of Montenegro's *vladika* (ruler), after his uncle, Petar I, named him his successor on his deathbed in 1830. Three years later his appointment was celebrated and confirmed in St. Petersburg, thus cementing the relationship between the Russian Empire and her little brother. The benefits of this relationship for Montenegro would most strongly be felt a little less than half a century later, in the late 1870s, when Russia declared war on and defeated the Ottoman Empire. Official Yugoslav as well as contemporary Montenegrin histories and literary anthologies laud Njegoš for the role he played in assuring Russia's protection of Montenegro's interests against Austria-Hungary and Turkey, and even Serbia.

Njegoš's anthologized poetic masterpiece is *Gorski vijenac* (The Mountain Wreath), published in 1847, only a year after Mažuranić's poem about the Smail-aga's death. The content of the epic poem is so vehemently anti-Muslim that the work has been connected, as an artistically valorized historical precedent, to Serbia's aggression against the Muslim populations of Bosnia and Kosovo in the 1990s.[12] How Mažuranić has managed to escape this weighty historical assessment when Croatia had its own vested interests in Bosnia in the 1990s is beyond the scope of the current project, but suffice it to say that his (typical) pitting of the strong Turks against the small Montenegrins creates a clear distinction between the oppressor and the underdog, which makes the latter the easy moral choice in terms of taking sides. Njegoš's *Mountain Wreath* tells a slightly different story, as it is devoted to the issue called "istraga poturica"—literally, the investigation, but more accurately the eradication, of Slavic converts to Islam. The poem offers a justification of the actual historical event, which occurred on Christmas Eve and early Christmas morning in 1707, with the idea that converts to a religion are worse than its original inheritors. The epic heroes, who go in search of the converts, debate among themselves whether to allow their "brothers of the same blood"—to borrow the phrasing from *Anna Karenina*—who have become *inovertsi* (those of different faith) to convert back before being sentenced to death. According to popular Yugoslav readings, this kind of vacillation endows the hero-murderers of the poem, which refrains from describing the actual slaughter, with lofty Hamlet-like attributes,[13] but it makes a post-Yugoslav appreciation for it all the more difficult.

Be that as it may, Mažuranić's and Njegoš's epic poems are the canonical proto-Yugoslav works and the two most notable examples of the so-called Haiduk-Turkish theme that dominated the literature of the South Slavs prior to realism and the novel. Their style and theme was hardly suitable for the circumstances of Austria's Slavs, however, and ceased to resonate more generally as the decline of the Ottoman Empire began increasingly to seem inevitable. The famed Balkan historian Barbara Jelavich observes that "unlike the Ottoman Christian, the Habsburg peasant was not well situated to express his desire either legally or by revolt. . . . [T]here were no peasant armed forces like those formed by the armatoles and haiduks."[14] Two out of Šenoa's four completed novels do depict Croatian acts of revolt, however, one by sixteenth-century peasants in the Zagreb region and the other by the Uskoks—the Croatian version of the Haiduks, to put it most generally—on the Adriatic coast in the seventeenth century. *Čuvaj se Senjske ruke* (Beware of the Senj Hand), published in 1876, might be described as the typical Haiduk-Turkish epic in novelistic form, except that the enemy in it is the Venetians rather than the Ottomans. The Croatian novelist and literary scholar Julijana Matanović notes that Šenoa changed the title of this novel from the originally intended *General Rabata i Uskoci* (General Rabata and the Uskoks) because "Beware of the Senj hand" was a well-known catchphrase in the region that survived into the nineteenth century. Matanović points out the novel's similarity with the entire corpus of "our national epic" in which "the national storyteller . . . celebrates Uskok heroism, war expeditions, and glorifies their leaders," while the title itself already reveals "whose side the author is on."[15] *Seljačka buna* (The Peasant Revolt), published in 1878, describes a historical event that stands out as a rare exception to Jelavich's conclusion about the Habsburg peasant: a massive, though ultimately quashed, uprising of 1573 under the leadership of Matija Gubec, who is occasionally referred to in the national history as a Croatian Spartacus.

Šenoa's intention with these two novels was certainly not to encourage revolt, at least not an armed one, though the argument could be made that he spent his career advocating a sort of intellectual revolt. His dedication of a novel about a sixteenth-century peasant rebellion in the Zagreb region to Mihovil Pavlinović, his contemporary who was the leader of the national revival movement in Dalmatia, speaks to this effect. Šenoa, in fact, uses the language of heroism that is present in his novel for the dedication. Addressing Pavlinović directly, he praises him with rhetorical questions: "Nijesi li se Ti digao na junačke noge da oda sna preneš drijemnu dušu primorskoga puka, da ga gromom glasa svojega budiš u svijest, da korov iščupaš iz vinograda rodnoga, pravi zatočnik našega prava, pravi apostol nehinjene slobode?" (Did you not rise up to your heroic feet to startle the slumbering soul of our coastal people from its sleep, to wake it into consciousness with the thunder of your voice, to pull out the weed from the native vineyard, [you,] the real champion of our right, the real apostle of unfeigned freedom?) (*SD* 4:10).[16] In *The Peasant Revolt*, the rebelling peasants and their supporters thunder with their voices, while their leader, Matija Gubec, issues the following statement after being captured and before he is about to be tortured and executed: "Za pravo i slobodu sam se digo, za nju mrem" (For right and freedom did I rise up, for it I die) (*SD* 4:285). If the sixteenth-century peasants raised up the "kuka i motika" (hook and hoe) (*SD* 4:90, 196, 232) for their right and freedom, then Šenoa employed his pen for the same purpose. The dedication of his novel to the Dalmatian cultural pioneer reinforces his call for Croatian political and linguistic unity and emphasizes the education of the people about their own history as integral to national rebirth. He proved to be successful in this last regard, since his novels—more accessible to the average reader than the long and, frankly, boring epic poem[17]—were the first artistic works in Croatia that managed to reach a mass audience.

Šenoa's Time

Although Šenoa had previously published journalistic pieces, the official beginning of his writing career is marked by his 1865 manifesto titled "Naša književnost" (Our Literature), in which he points out the "glavni grijeh u naših pisaca" (cardinal sin of our writers) as the following: "Ne umiju ili neće birati zgodna gradiva, te mjesto novelističkog obično uzmu epički čin. Ta svako znade da dvije trećine naših izvornih pripovijesti pričaju o turskom ratu" (They do not know or do not want to choose appropriate subjects, and instead of the novelistic take the epic act. Everybody knows that two-thirds of our original tales tell about the Turkish war) (*SD* 9:522). In his manifesto, Šenoa lays out the task of literature in shaping society "dok se duh narodni ne uvriježi ne samo u svakom gradu, u svakom uredu i u svakoj školi, već upravo i u obitelji koja je pravi temelj i narodnog i državnog života" (until the national spirit inhabits not only every city, every office, and every school, but especially the family, which is the true foundation of both national and state life) (*SD* 9:517). The national spirit was to be manifested in public places through the speaking of a codified South Slavic literary language instead of the official German, but its foundation was to be in the home, a practice Šenoa himself embraced. Two years after publishing "Our Literature" he wrote several love letters to his fiancée in which he urged her to be "svojoj Hrvatskoj domovini iskrena kćerca" (a true daughter of her Croatian homeland), to read Croatian, and to write to him in the native tongue because it is the only means of truly expressing what is in one's heart.[18]

His patriotic appeals to his fiancée constitute an inverse relationship from a romantic liaison of his student days, when he was "zabludjel[a] ovc[a]" (a lost sheep) (*SD* 5:8, 12) and a young Slovenian girl "ga povratila Slavenstvu" (returned him to Slavdom) (*SD* 5:44). Titled "Karanfil s pjesnikova groba" (The Carnation from the Poet's Grave), this later autobiographical story, published in 1878, is worth examining here briefly for its insights into the first political stirrings of young Šenoa, the political climate in which his education took place, and the tale's embodiment of the national spirit as female—in this particular case, the case of an oppressed nation, an innocent and fragile female from the peasant class. As he recalls his student days, Šenoa describes the director of his Zagreb lyceum as "feljbaba germanizacije" (a sergeant of Germanization), who "nije ljubio Hrvate" (did not like Croatians), uttered "fraze of veleaustrijskom patriotizmu" (phrases about great Austrian patriotism) (*SD* 5:9), and who once scolded him for possessing literature typed in the Cyrillic alphabet. The author's use of a Turkicized (Bosnian, specifically) word—*feljbaba*—for the German word *Feldwebel* (sergeant) to describe a western administration's aggressive effort at Germanization is a wonderful bit of syncretism that would have been offensive to Austrian and upper-class Croatian sensibilities. The author continues in this vein when he writes, nearer the end of the story, about how he and his schoolmates offended "ponijemčen[e] Sloven[ce]" (germanized Slovenes) in a pub not only by speaking Croatian, but by throwing "cijelu litaniju turskih fraza" (an entire litany of Turkish phrases) (*SD* 5:42) into their conversation.

Šenoa writes that Zagreb children were "i kod kuće tuđim duhom odgojena" (even at home brought up in a foreign spirit) and describes himself at the time as "zagrebački Švapčić" (a little Zagreb German boy)[19] who spoke Croatian "kao kakva piljarica" (like some kind of greengrocer) (*SD* 5:12). The family of his Slovenian schoolmate Albert "govorili su . . . samo sa služavkom materinjim jezikom, inače uredovnim, da ne bude sumnje o panslavizmu" (spoke only with the servant girl in their mother tongue, otherwise using the official [German] language, so there would be no suspicion of Pan-Slavism) (*SD* 5:10). The events described in this story take place in the summer of 1857, and it was in the fall of that same year that the young Šenoa was denied entry into Vienna's Oriental Academy precisely because he was suspected of being a Pan-Slavist.[20] Over the summer holidays he traveled with his friend Alfonso Moše—Albert in the story—to visit the latter's relatives in the Slovenian region of Kranj. In the story both the narrator and his friend fall in love with the servant girl of the Kranj household, Neža, who mocks their German poetry and introduces them to the works of the Slovenian national poet, France Prešeren. Neža takes the two young men to Prešeren's grave, where they swear "da ćemo dizati s drugim poštenjacima domovinu iz ropskog praha" (that we will raise with other honest men the homeland out of the ashes of slavery) and "služit ćemo velikoj ideji Slavenstva do svoga groba" (we will serve the great idea of Slavdom until our graves) (*SD* 5:29). Šenoa, as this chapter shows, kept his oath and worked on behalf of Yugoslavism. One of the many ways in which he served the idea of (South) Slavdom was in his role as Croatia's first anthologist: he issued two collections that included both Croatian and Serbian poetry; the first one—*Vienac izabranih pjesama hrvatskih i srbskih* (A Garland of Selected Croatian and Serbian Poems)—for the 1873 World Fair in Vienna, and the second—*Antologija pjesničtva hrvatskoga i srbskoga, narodnoga i umjetnoga* (An Anthology of Croatian and Serbian Poetry, National and Artistic)—in 1876.

The story of young Croatian and Slovenian subjects—both student and peasant—of the Habsburg Empire awakening to their common Slavic spirit and shunning German poetry was serialized in *Vienac* only a few months before the summer 1878 Congress of Berlin. When the congress curtailed the gains Russia had made for her Orthodox Balkan brothers in the war with Turkey, it did so largely in response to Austria's qualms about the size of the new independent Slavic states in its neighborhood. Šenoa took the opportunity to reference the events in Berlin in his support of another argument for a South Slavic union. In an article titled "Ime *Slovinac*" (The Name *Slovinac*) he endorses the idea, proposed previously by a Dubrovnik-based literary journal, that *Slovinac* ought to be the correct ethnic and linguistic designation for "svi Slovenci, Hrvati, Srbi i Bugari" (all Slovenes, Croats, Serbs, and Bulgarians) (*SD* 11:442–43). He points out that Ljudevit Gaj had already proposed the same in 1835, but under the name "Illyrian," and he expresses a pragmatic reservation about a state as large as Bulgaria accepting the common designation and the Herzegovinian dialect. Despite the great loss that Bulgaria suffered at the Congress of Berlin, by being divided into three parts, Šenoa expresses optimism that "oni [će] imati svoju državu, jer Bugara ima do 6 milijuna" (they will have their own state, because there are up to six million Bulgarians) (*SD* 11:443). For the sake of comparison, Croatia's population numbered around two million at the time.

Referencing the Congress of Berlin, Šenoa bemoans the fact that "u taj par, gdje se u Berlinu riešava ponajvažnije za sva jugoslavenska plemena pitanje, biesni boj medju Hrvati i Srbi s jedne, a medju Bugari i Srbi s druge strane" (at the same time that the most important questions for all Yugoslav tribes are being resolved in Berlin, a battle rages between Croats and Serbs on the one side and between Bulgarians and Serbs on the other side) (*SD* 11:443). He describes the Serbs, for his Croatian *Vienac* readers, as a "narod, koj govori, pjeva ko i mi, koj se nosi ko i mi, koj u Šumadiji ima one običaje, što ih ima turopoljski Kajkavac, koj ima iste krvne protivnike, što nam rade o glavi" (people, who speak, sing as we do, who dress as we do, who in Šumadija have those same customs as the *kajkavian* speaker from Turopolje has, who have the same blood enemies that are putting our lives in danger) (*SD* 11:443). To use Tolstoy's imagery from his famous opening line, as I have rendered it in the previous chapter, Serbs and Croats, according to this essay, *resemble one another*. They should, therefore, belong in the same family/nation. Šenoa uses the image of one hand with separate fingers as a symbol of Yugoslav—as distinct from South Slavic, since it excludes Bulgaria[21]—oneness and condemns the intertwining of religious affiliations with politics and literature.

While resisting German linguistic and cultural imperialism, he still looks at the recently unified Germany as a model of a people crossing religious boundaries and even suggests that some other Slavic groups might have survived and prospered had they followed the same model:

> Stara je to rana, šaka i prst nas razdvaja, mi pletemo vjeru u politiku i literaturu. To je zlo. Zato propade Češka na Bieloj gori, zato izbrisa poviest baltičke Slavene s površja zemlje. A Niemac? Katolik Bavarac jurišao je zajedno sa protestantom Prusom na parižke obkope. To je mudro.
>
> It is an old wound, the hand and the thumb separate us, we interweave faith with politics and literature. This is evil. That is why the Czechs were destroyed on the White Mountain, why history erased the Baltic Slavs from the face of the earth. And the German? The Catholic Bavarian stormed the Parisian embankments together with the Protestant Prussian. That is wise. (*SD* 11:443–44)

The German example highlights the idea that the best uniting force for an ethnically related group of people prone to emphasizing their differences from each other is a common enemy, as were the Catholic French for both the Catholic Bavarians and the Protestant Prussians. In the preceding quote, Šenoa unites Serbs and Croats through—in addition to language and custom—common "blood enemies," who, based on his reference to the happenings in Berlin at the time, are the Western powers.

The political climate of Šenoa's time, as has been expounded up to this point, was marked by a call for South Slavic unity, but the disagreements between Serbs and Croats or the threats from the surrounding superpowers were not the only obstacles in the achievement of this goal. On the home turf Croatians themselves divided into various factions, not only between those who were willing to lean on Austria-Hungary and those who, like Šenoa, saw all the danger of that kind of political alliance, but also between those who, like Šenoa, promoted what was to become the future Yugoslavia and those who sought Croatian sovereignty that excluded other South Slavs, especially the Orthodox Serbs.

In 1843, thirteen years after the publication of Gaj's *Orthography* and the inception of the Illyrian movement, the name "Illyrian" was prohibited by the Hungarian authorities. The movement did not cease to exist, however, but continued under the new name Narodnjaci and functioned politically as Narodna stranka (People's Party). Its political opponents were the Pravaši, who formed the Stranka prava (Party of Right).[22] The Party of Right, which advocated Croatia's sovereignty, was founded by Ante Starčević, who is today considered Croatia's "otac domovine" (father of the homeland). The split between the Narodnjaci and the Pravaši over national belonging became official at the meeting of the Croatian parliament in 1861. The third Croatian political party, which was the enemy of both the Narodnjaci and the Pravaši was the former Hrvatsko-ugarska stranka, now named Unionistička, which had no Slavic sensibilities and supported so-called Magyarization. Since the Croatian *ban* was, as Seton-Watson explains, "appointed by the Crown on the nomination of the Hungarian premier," he often came from the ranks of this political party.[23]

The Croatian People's Party, to which Šenoa belonged, held the majority and reached its peak when its member Ivan Mažuranić became the first *ban-pučanin* (governor from the common people) from 1873 to 1880. These were also, roughly, the years of Šenoa's literary peak. Another one of the party's prominent members that ought to be mentioned was the bishop of Đakovo, Josip Juraj Strossmayer. He is credited with the founding of the Jugoslavenska akademija znanosti i umjetnosti (Yugoslav Academy of Sciences and Arts), which operated from 1867 until the breakup of the last Yugoslavia in 1991 and is now known as the Hrvatska akademija znanosti i imjetnosti (Croatian Academy of Sciences and Arts). Although disagreeing vehemently on the role of other South Slavic nationalities in Croatian political development, the People's Party and the Party of Right could agree on one goal: freedom from Austro-Hungarian management.

The Historical Novel

As a realist author, Šenoa differs in some significant ways from the mainstream European realists, and these differences can be directly connected to his politically inferior historical circumstance. He and the Polish Henryk Sienkiewicz both share, as will become more evident in the following chapter, a predilection for the remote historical novel. I use the adjective *remote* for the sake of comparison with *War and Peace*, perhaps the historical novel par excellence, which is only half a century removed from its author's milieu. George Eliot also rarely ventured beyond the half-century mark, and the Napoleonic wars were as far back into history as Theodor Fontane was willing to delve. A subject's proximity to the present, one might expect, would only be in the service of the successful execution of a realist project. Šenoa's two best-known novels, *The Goldsmith's Gold* and *The Peasant Revolt*, are both set in the sixteenth century; the other two he completed cover events from the seventeenth and the eighteenth century. The most obvious reason for this remoteness is that addressing current political events too critically could be dangerous; if even the great Count Tolstoy could be censored, then an author writing from the semicolonized peripheries had double the reason to fear the authorities. Another reason is that the subjugated nation's reading public needed to be reminded of and emboldened by a real or fictional "glorious past." Since Poland had once, in fact, been a medieval European force, that past was easier to conjure for Sienkiewicz, while Šenoa somewhat sanctimoniously defended the historical novel of those nations that had never been "great" and emphasized that the point was to learn from history rather than to revel in it. In an 1874 issue of *Vienac*, three years after his own first historical novel had been serialized in the journal, he writes:

> U historijskom romanu moraš analogijom između prošlosti i sadašnjosti narod dovesti do spoznaje samoga sebe. Za to ima sto prilika. Pusto je hvalisanje praotaca, krvava slava prošlih vremena nije zadaća našeg historičkog romana. Prikazati valja sve grijehe, sve vrline naše mi[nu] losti, da se narod uzmogne čuvati grijeha, slijediti vrline. Ciceronova riječ: Historia vitae magistra—malo će gjde boljeg mjesta naći no u povijesti Hrvata i Srbalja.
>
> In the historical novel you must use the analogy between the past and the present to bring the people to an awareness of itself. There are a hundred opportunities for this. In vain is the boasting of the forefathers, the bloody glory of the times gone by is not the task of our historical novel. One must depict all the sins, all the virtues of our past, in order to enable the people to guard from sin, follow virtue. Cicero's saying: Historia vitae magistra—will not find a better place than in the history of the Croats and the Serbs.[24]

As the subsequent reading of *The Goldsmith's Gold* shows, Šenoa depicts "all the sins" of his nation through sixteenth-century events that resonate exactly with those occurring in his own, nineteenth, and he extols his readers to "follow virtue" by putting speeches in the mouths of his characters that are just as relevant for his contemporary audience.

Regardless of one's historical status, however, describing events of the distant past also gives a nation whose culture, language, and very existence are under threat a historical continuity and, therefore, the important quality of perseverance. Just as Langhans's inclusion of Poland in the *Deutscher Kolonial-Atlas* increased Germany's status as an empire, so Šenoa's and Sienkiewicz's novelistic output increased the mere validity of their stateless nations. Further, what glories Šenoa could not find in Croatia's political past he made up for in its artistic riches. The sixteenth century was the time of the Croatian Renaissance, when the first great Croatian literary works were written in the two main cities of the Dalmatian coast, Split and Dubrovnik. The majority of the Croatian coast was under Venetian rule at the time—with the exception of Dubrovnik, which enjoyed an independent city-state status—and benefited from the Italian artistic spillover. Although the action in Šenoa's novels tends to take place around Zagreb, the informed Croatian reader would recall the Dalmatian Renaissance in connection with the period described in the novels.

The Dalmatian Renaissance is also linguistically significant: its authors used the *štokavian* dialect, which means that its choice by Ljudevit Gaj for the official Croatian language, in addition to linguistically uniting it with Serbs and other South Slavs, solidified Croatia's historical link with its earliest poets. Šenoa extends this link into the new genre of the novel, which brings us to another significant distinction between him and the mainstream European realists. When it comes to language, George Eliot, for example, takes pains to emulate the English of the working-class characters in her fiction through particular spelling and the abundant use of apostrophes, which often slows down the speed of the modern-day reader, while Theodor Fontane is known and admired for his faithful emulation of various Prussian provincial dialects. By contrast, every character in Šenoa's novels, from the highest aristocrat to the lowest peasant, speaks in the official *štokavian* Croatian that the author and other inheritors of the Illyrian ideology sought to promote. The plots of Šenoa's novels tend to center on the Croatian capital city of Zagreb, where even today the average person speaks *kajkavian*, whereas the aristocracy of Šenoa's time would have spoken German or Hungarian, just as in Tolstoy's Russia they spoke French, which the author includes in his novels. Šenoa himself, born in Zagreb into a petit bourgeois family, had German and Hungarian roots from his parents, who were new to Zagreb and signed their last name in the German orthography, "Schönoa." In a trajectory opposite to Fontane's—whose French family, we recall, dropped the identifying *i* from their name, while their celebrated son went by his middle name rather than Henri—Šenoa embraced his Croatian side to the point of keeping his knowledge of Hungarian a secret[25] and made sure to distinguish both his name and his fiction from the dominant culture. Since he saw the education of the widest possible spectrum of his people as the main goal of his fiction, he consciously sacrificed the aesthetic precepts of the realist movement for didactic political purposes and employed the desired official literary language in every one of his lines. When in *The Peasant Revolt* a peasant woman scolds a noblewoman's clerk for openly verbalizing his attraction to a young peasant girl, it is not the high register of his language but its inappropriate content that she ascribes to his closeness to the nobility: "Vidi vam se po govoru, da se uvijek međ gospodom miješate i nekrštene riječi slušate" (One can see by your speech that you're always mingling with the aristocracy and listening to unsanctified words) (*SD* 4:42).

Two works from the Dalmatian Renaissance are of note for how they reverberate in Croatian realism. While much less explicit than Sienkiewicz in his reliance on biblical allegories to illustrate national struggles, Šenoa's historical novel belongs to a literary tradition whose inception is steeped in those allegories. The poet from Split who is considered the father of Croatian literature, Marko Marulić, wrote his epic poem *Judita* in 1501. First published in Venice twenty years later, it was the first Croatian literary piece to appear in print. Named after the fourth book of the Old Testament Apocrypha, in which the beautiful Israelite heroine bewitches and then slays King Nebuchadnezzar's army general Holofernes in order to rescue her people from Babylonian occupation,[26] *Judita* tells the story of Croatians whose city is under Turkish attack. Marulić's second best known work is *Molitva suprotiva Turkom* (A Prayer against the Turk), which, together with *Judita*, demonstrates that even prior to the time of the nineteenth-century South Slavic national epic, Croatian literature was born against Turkophobia. This makes the sixteenth-century setting of Šenoa's novels all the more significant, as if the author is rewriting Croatia's history of political struggles. As I discuss in relation to *The Goldsmith's Gold*, Šenoa took enormous pains to portray Croatian historical events as truthfully as possible, but the menacing foreign power he chose to focus on in depicting a period when the Ottoman Empire was at the height of its power was Austria. It was how he managed, and impressively so, to fulfill his mission of "us[ing] the analogy between the past and the present to bring the people to an awareness of itself."[27]

Farther south along the Adriatic coast and about a half a century later, Marin Držić—the Dubrovnik cleric, poet, playwright, and briefly rector of Sienna University—was the first to portray the West as the national foe in female form. Držić's best-known comedy, *Dundo Maroje*, written between 1550 and 1556, may be read as a version of the Prodigal Son story with national overtones. Dundo Maroje is the betrayed father, who gives his son, Maro, five thousand gold coins for an education in Florence. Maro travels to Rome instead, where he spends his money on a bewitching woman named Laura. Choosing the name Laura is an audacious move by Držić, since it turns the fourteenth-century perfect love object of *the* poetical representative of the Italian Renaissance, Francesco Petrarca, into a femme fatale. Držić, who was known for some of his own petrarchist poetry, makes Laura's role in the Maroje family particularly damaging as Maro's infatuation with her, in addition to divesting him of his fortune, involves unfaithfulness to his fiancée back home in Dubrovnik.

As the section below elaborates in detail, Šenoa returns to this theme in *The Goldsmith's Gold*, although he depicts a morally upright Croatian hero, who resists the charms of the wicked woman. Subsequent Croatian realists copied this reestablished pattern, most significant among them Šenoa's greatest political nemesis and literary competitor, Ante Kovačić. If Šenoa was the literary figure of the People's Party, then his equivalent in the Party of Right was Kovačić. As an opponent of the idea of Yugoslavism, Kovačić wrote spoofs of Šenoa's and other, earlier Illyrian works, but in allegorizing Croatia's political foe, he followed in Šenoa's footsteps and depicted the fall of a Croatian hero under the simultaneously enchanting and repellent spell of a Western(ized) femme fatale. His most famous novel, *U Registraturi* (In the Registry), published seventeen years after *The Goldsmith's Gold*, presents what was by that point a typical love triangle imbued with national overtones. The evil foreign woman is named Laura, thus recalling Držić's Italian femme fatale, and she engages in acts more gruesome than what the more moderate Šenoa was willing to portray: whereas Šenoa settles for poisoning as the tragic end of his Croatian peasant heroine at the hands of her Germanic adversary, Kovačić's Laura orchestrates the slaughter of the Croatian couple's entire wedding party, during which she herself cuts off the bride's breasts.

The Goldsmith's Gold

Šenoa's most successful work remains his first novel, *Zlatarovo zlato* (The Goldsmith's Gold), which was serialized in *Vienac* between August 5 and December 30, 1871 (nos. 31–52), and came out as a book in 1872. Šenoa marginalizes the Turks in the novel's sixteenth-century setting and focuses on another historical upheaval, the overtaking of the office of Croatian *ban* (governor) by an Austrian in 1578. The parallels with Šenoa's own time are glaringly obvious, since in the years immediately preceding the novel's publication (1868–71), the office of the Croatian *ban* was held by Levin Rauch, whose last name testifies to his Germanic heritage. The entire Rauch family, who settled in Croatia in the seventeenth century, was known for the numerous *bans* it had produced both before and after Levin Rauch, including his great-grandfather Adam and his son Pavao. Levin Rauch was the founder of the Union Party that vehemently persecuted the Narodnjaci. He assumed the post of *ban* shortly after the Austro-Hungarian *Ausgleich*, so it fell on him to integrate Croatia into the new order, which he did by forcing the Croatian-Hungarian Agreement in 1868, which lasted until 1918.[28] The political climate became more optimistic for Croatia a year after the publication of *The Goldsmith's Gold*, however, when Ivan Mažuranić became the *ban* in 1873. Such an auspicious turn of events seems to endow Šenoa's literary masterpiece with political powers it did not actually possess, although the temporal coincidence of the first piece of literature to reach a mass audience and the election of the *ban* from the ranks of common Croatians is worth pointing out.

It is of note that Šenoa's other novel set in the sixteenth-century also marginalizes the Turks as its main action is the peasant revolt against Croatia's aristocracy, which was of Hungarian descent. The uprising was provoked by Franjo Tahi's mistreatment of the peasants, which included forced conscription into his army that was engaged in battles against the Turks. One of the heroes, Ilija Gregorić, who is Matija Gubec's closest ally as the military commander of the revolt, tells a lengthy tale toward the beginning of the novel, its fourth chapter (out of forty-five), of all his successes against the Turks, as if the author is trying to get it out of the way before getting to the real story. The historical Ilija Gregorić escaped Turkish captivity twice, but in *The Peasant Revolt* he tells of three escapes and wonders if a fourth one is possible: "Do tri puta Bog pomaže, a četvrti put bi mogao odmoći Đavo" (Up to three times God helps, but the fourth time the Devil could hinder) (*SD* 4:59). Like Matije Gubec, Ilija Gregorić is captured and executed in the end, which invites several interpretations in light of his foreshadowing statement—that he has spent his good fortune fighting the wrong fight, a question pondered also, as we shall see below, by the characters of *The Goldsmith's Gold* regarding their own allegiances; that God himself could not help when the enemy is the magyarized nobility; and that this nobility has the Devil on its side.

The title of Šenoa's first novel refers to the goldsmith Krupić's daughter, Dora, who is her father's true gold and the embodiment of national as well as sexual purity, the two being metaphorically related. Dora's evil foil is the beautiful, wealthy, bewitching, and immoral young widow, Klara Grubar, later—after she marries the new Austrian *ban*—Ungnad, while the man caught in the love triangle between them is the virtuous young Croatian nobleman named Pavle Gregorijanec. Pavle's father, Stjepko, was an actual historical figure whose legal struggle with the city of Zagreb and its inhabitants over property rights was the historical event that initially inspired the novel, though it proves less significant in the completed work. What Šenoa's realism lacks in the uniform language that all of his characters speak, it makes up for in the historicity of the plot. He prefaces his novel with a paragraph-long note "Štiocu" (To the Reader), in which he states: "Gledao sam da bude to vjerna prilika onoga vremena . . . da se je sve što evo pripovijedam s veće strane uistinu zbilo" (I sought to make it a faithful picture of that time . . . that all that I tell of here had, for the most part, verily happened) (*SD* 2:106). He backs up his claim by describing what he discovered while rummaging through the dusty archives of the city of Zagreb, "u koje od sto godina nije bila ruka dirnula" (which had not been touched by a [human] hand in a hundred years) (*SD* 2:105), and by providing a glossary that exceeds twenty pages in length at the end of his novel for the sake of identifying all of the historical characters, places, and events and describing them down to the minutest detail. Šenoa's historical novel, then, comes with its own footnotes, as if the faithful author did not trust this task to a later editor, and these footnotes constitute more than 10 percent of the entire novel. The author was so concerned about including historical details in his fiction that he attempted, though failed, to become the city archivist[29] and issued multiple appeals in *Vienac* for better management that would aid those authors who wanted to avail themselves of precious historical documents.[30]

The promotion of Yugoslavism, to which Šenoa was devoted, included a preliminary step within Croatian politics of reconciling the disparate classes, which constitutes a significant part of the didactic agenda of *The Goldsmith's Gold*. Pavle Gregorijanec is a nobleman who falls in love with a simple artisan's daughter, much to the dismay of his father, who pushes for Pavle's union with the wealthy Klara. Pavle's brazen answer to his father on this matter is telling of the novel's national anxieties: "što je njemačkim plaćenikom ručkom, ne može hrvatskomu velikašu večerom biti" (what was lunch for the German employee cannot be supper for a Croatian nobleman) (*SD* 2:227). The "German employee" refers to Klara's first husband, and Pavle proudly, if crudely, refuses what he identifies as German leftovers.

Although Pavle's father, Stjepko, plays a negative role when it comes to his son's love choice and even goes so far as to orchestrate a (failed) kidnapping attempt of the helpless Dora, he is no fan of the Austrians when it comes to Croatian political life. Early on in the novel he chides other Croatians in positions of power for relying too heavily on Austrian help while being blind to the fact that their country and its soldiers are merely being used as a buffer zone: "Turčin ne vidi nego leđa tih mušketira i arkebuzira, a vi Hrvati gubite glave, dok se oklopnici napale vaših sela i napitaju vašeg blaga, dok kus po kus naše banovine ne strpaju pod svoju komandu" (The Turk sees nothing but the backs of those musketeers and arkebuzeers, but you Croatians get decapitated while armored soldiers burn out your villages and steal all your cattle until, piece by piece, they shove our region under their command) (*SD* 2:124). The "musketeers" and "arkebuzeers" are the Austrian soldiers carrying the guns known as muskets and arkebuzes, portrayed as cowardly and fleeing the Turks, since the latter only see the backs of the former. Their cowardice is intensified by their portrayal as armored, whereas the Croatians, who lose their heads, obviously lack proper equipment for battle. Moreover, the choice of "villages" and "cattle" to depict Croatian lands expands the contrast between poor and rich, victim and oppressor, all the more poignantly for the fact that the old Croatian word for "cattle"—*blago*—doubles as "treasure." The oppressor, in the end, is not Turkey but Austria.

Stjepko points out a political reality that has subsequently been confirmed by historians of the Balkans. Barbara Jelavich, for example, shatters centuries of prejudice when she describes everyday life under the Ottomans, who installed locals as rulers and allowed local culture to thrive, as better than everyday life under the micromanaging Austrians. Stjepko asserts, "neću da igram u tom kolu" (I will not take part in that dance) (*SD* 2:124), his use of the word *kolo* for dance, in its national specificity, emphasizing Croatia's responsibility for partaking in the role intended for it by the greater powers. It is a corrupt priest, one who hopes to gain personal advantages by supporting Austrian designs, who attempts to convince Stjepko that "ne da nam turska bujica da odahnemo. Dogorjelo do nokata" (the Turkish flood won't let us catch our breaths. It is the eleventh hour [literally, "our fingernails are burning"]) (*SD* 2:125). Stjepko has heard enough, however, and he withdraws from Zagreb into his castle on the outskirts of the city. Later in the novel, the Croatian governor tells an Austrian minister directly and without any use of metaphorical language, "U zemlji najviše nereda pravite vi . . . jer vaši ljudi ne imaju uzde; plijene, pale kao Turci i gore nego Turci" (In [our] country you make the greatest mess . . . because your people have no limits; they plunder, burn like the Turks and worse than the Turks) (*SD* 2:235).

The discrepancy between Stjepko Gregorijanec's goals for Croatia and his wishes for his son's matrimonial choice is a more complicated aspect of Šenoa's novel and should be lauded for its realism. The class tensions portrayed in the father-son disagreement over Klara and Dora are the tensions between the *gospoda* and the *građani*, the former meaning "aristocracy," the landed gentry that owned small towns located around their fortresses on the outskirts of Zagreb, and the latter meaning "city inhabitants," the artisans and merchants of and living in the capital city. Stjepko Gregorijanec, a respected member of the nobility, rightfully chides his own class for its greatest political weakness, but his patriotism ends at the prospect of accepting a lower-class Croatian for a daughter-in-law. The politics of the home and the state are supposed to converge in the next generation, through Pavle's marriage to Dora, but those plans are thwarted by the jealous Klara. The wealthy beauty is offended by the idea that her competition comes from a lower class, and the tragic end of the love story prophesies doom for the nation as a whole.

Dora Krupić is first introduced to the reader as "po duši dobra" (good in her soul) (*SD* 2:110) and one who has not seen evil. Her simplicity is moral in nature only, since, even though a commoner, she learned to read and write from a country teacher—"a nije to za ono doba šala" (no small feat for those times), as the narrator, loath to miss any opportunity for encouraging Croatian literacy for all classes, remarks—and people in town call her "zlatarovom mudrijašicom" (the goldsmith's smart one) (*SD* 2:111). Klara Grubar, on the other hand, has a habit of easing her widowed loneliness by entertaining Austrian officers in her castle, though this practice predates her widowhood. The narrator relates that "za to znala su razna gospoda, samo tupoglavi pokojnik joj nije" (all kinds of gentlemen knew about this, except for her dimwitted late husband) (*SD* 2:186). She dresses in low-cut silk gowns, while Dora wears a white apron, another signifier of both simplicity and purity.

The most interesting and nationally significant contrast between the two women, however, is the style and color of their hair. Dora has thick black hair, which she wears in two braids, thus conveying modesty and restraint. Klara has blond hair, which is depicted by the phrase "zlatni uvojci" (golden curls) (*SD* 2:185) and brought up five times in chapter 8, which describes her appearance, character, and abode. Klara's golden—as opposed to blond—curls can be interpreted as indicators of her wealth and, more broadly, when extended to the political milieu, as Habsburg wealth and decadence. They also connote her moral looseness as they "padahu joj niz šiju" (fell down her neck) (*SD* 2:185) and "razletiše se oko bijelih ramena kao zlatne zmije" (flew all around her white shoulders like golden snakes) (*SD* 2:193). The sexual and political signifiers converge in this hair as it is also her means of seduction when she throws herself at Pavle Gregorijanec, whose principled heart grows icy on feeling her golden curls on his face. As the novel's title indicates, it is Pavle's love object, the modest dark-haired Dora, who is the true gold. The image of Klara's snakelike tresses is an obvious reference to Medusa, the terrifying snake-haired woman of Greek mythology who turns men who look directly at her into stone. Klara's seductive powers do not extend into such magic, but Pavle's heart turning icy on feeling their touch is another obvious parallel with the ancient myth. The actual meaning of the Greek *Médousa* is also significant for the political tensions of Šenoa's time. The Greek word means "protectress," which is what Croatians were erroneously hoping to obtain from Austria against the Ottoman Empire.

The difference in hair color between the two female protagonists is significant for its ethnic stereotyping and its accompanying reversal of conventional moral signifiers in European literature. The South Slavic Dora is a brunette, while the Germanic Klara is blond. In combination with delineating ethnic differences between the southeast of Europe and its northwest, this contrast reverses the traditional association of light with good and dark with evil. Morally superior blonds and their corrupt brunette foils are female character types deeply ingrained in European literature. This is not limited to Anglo-Saxon or Western European fiction; it is also the case in the novel discussed in the previous chapter. Tolstoy's Anna Karenina has "черны[е]" (black) tresses—although, like Klara's, they are curly and escape all over the nape of her neck, apparently being a general connotation for moral looseness—while the innocent Kitty Shcherbatskaya is blond. One must pause here to pay credit to the ever-perspicacious George Eliot in this regard. Her Dorothea Brooke of *Middlemarch* is a brunette, and Lydgate pays dearly, as I pointed out in chapter 1, for falling for the "perfect blond loveliness" (252) of the wicked Rosamond. Also, in *The Mill on the Floss*, the brunette

Maggie Tulliver makes the explicit wish that, in contrast to convention, the dark-haired girl would once prove superior to the light-haired one. To her childhood friend and book supplier, Philip Wakem, she proclaims, "I'm determined to read no more books where the blond-haired women carry away all the happiness. I should begin to have a prejudice against them. If you could give me some story, now, where the dark woman triumphs, it would restore the balance."[31] The young Maggie might have enjoyed the morally superior brunettes of South Slavic fiction, provided that she understood their "triumphs" in exclusively spiritual terms. Their blond-haired foils do not necessarily "carry away all the happiness" for themselves—their lives are hardly enviable but for their material comfort—but "carry away all the happiness" of others, as both Šenoa's Klara and Kovačić's Laura do.

Šenoa's inversion of the traditional paradigm, together with his ethnic stereotyping, speaks volumes within the theoretical framework of gendered nations: as embodiments of Croatia and Austria-Hungary, the brunette Dora and the blond Klara not only engender a reversal of the broad association of light with good and dark with evil, but, more important in the context of Šenoa's novel, between an empire as superior and its colony as inferior, between the economic center and its destitute periphery. Šenoa holds fast to this ethnic stereotyping for both his female and his male protagonists. In addition to Dora, the Slovenian Neža from "The Carnation from the Poet's Grave" also "bijaše crnka" (was a brunette) (*SD* 5:15). Albert from the same story, although raised in a German-speaking household, demonstrates, among other features, "crnima žarkima očima, po bujnoj vrankosi . . . da ne polazi ni od Hermana ni od Thuznelde" (by the black bright eyes, by the thick black hair . . . that he comes neither from Herman nor from Thunzelda) (*SD* 5:9–10).

Pavle and Dora meet and fall in love, in the third chapter of the novel, in the most clichéd manner: he rescues her from underneath the horses' hoofs during a stampede caused by a large crowd's commotion over a public execution in the city square. Pavle, himself on a horse, gallops away with Dora and brings her to her home, where her godmother falsely attributes her fever to the near-death experience she just had. The chapter ends with the godmother's erroneous assessment and the narrator's correction of it: "'Umiri se, dijete, vrućica je.' Da, vrućica, koju svaki nas tek jednom za svoga vijeka oćuti—*ljubav*." ('Calm down, child, it's fever.' Yes, the fever that every one of us feels but once during our lifetime—*love*) (emphasis Šenoa's) (*SD* 2:135).

The more interesting aspect of this chapter is the execution around which the stampede takes place: it recalls Njegoš's *Mountain Wreath* and its "istraga poturica," as the man sentenced to death is a convert to Islam. Yet, unlike Njegoš's controversial poem, this scene in Šenoa's novel carries no obvious political agenda, nor does it constitute the moral lesson of the story. It merely serves to create the emotional intensity necessary for the two protagonists to fall in love. There is a subtle political agenda that can be read into this scene, however. It occasions the falling in love of a Croatian man with a Croatian woman, whereas, in the political sphere, Turkophobia typically instigated Croatia's "running off" with Austria. In this case, it unites the disparate Croatian classes in the figures of a nobleman and a goldsmith's daughter, which is, on a broader scale, the necessary step toward standing up to the western empire that was only too happy to exploit its colony's inner differences.

As already hinted, however, the story does not end well. While the scene described above places Turkophobia in the background, it reemerges, much like in Tolstoy's novel, as a remedy for a broken heart. Klara, already married to the new Austrian *ban* yet still making her designs on Pavle, manages to end Dora's life by poisoning her. She thus destroys the budding young love and the symbol of Croatian class unity. Pavle's reaction is to go fight the Turks; only, unlike Vronsky, his reasons are a bit loftier than a simple desire to die. When Klara challenges him to avenge Dora's death by killing her, Pavle boldly declares, "Ovaj mač proslavih u slavu svoje vjerenice, ovaj mač podigoh za spas kršćanskoga svijeta i prije bih si odsjekao desnu ruku i prije bih ga razlomio na dvoje nego da ga okaljam gadnom tvojom krvi" (I made this sword famous for the glory of my fiancée, I raised this sword for the deliverance of Christendom and I would rather cut off my right hand and break my sword in two than sully it with your repugnant blood) (*SD* 2:328). The first part of Pavle's proclamation makes the all-important link between the woman and the nation, both fought for by means of the symbolically phallic sword. The symbolism can be extended to the second half of his speech, where Pavle refuses to "penetrate" Klara with his sword, claiming that he would rather divest himself of this symbol of his manhood than to "sully it" with another woman's blood, which would symbolically verge on adultery, both sexual—being unfaithful to Dora—and national—being unfaithful to Croatia. Yet he proves unfaithful within Šenoa larger political program, since, even though he virtuously refuses the Medusa of Croatian modern politics, her destroying his Croatian love object causes him to fight the wrong fight. The fact that his own father warned his Croatian compatriots against this makes his mistake all the more poignant. Further, he goes off to fight the Turks just around the time that an Austrian—labeled in the novel "Štajerac," after the Austrian region of Styria—takes over the function of *ban* of Croatia, thus sealing the irony.

Krsto Ungnad was appointed *ban* of the Kingdom of Dalmatia, Croatia, and Slavonia in 1578 and is best remembered for overseeing construction of the picturesque town of Karlovac, located on four rivers and a little less than forty miles southwest of Zagreb. Ungnad is described in the novel as a "čovjek tuđe krvi" (man of foreign blood), with the added explanation, "nije se dakle bilo bojati da će njegovo srce planuti za staro hrvatsko pravo" (there was no fear, therefore, that his heart would burn for old Croatian rights) (*SD* 2:263). Klara marries him immediately after his political ascent in order to gain more power for herself; as she still continues to pursue Pavle and design schemes for removing Dora, she symbolizes the nineteenth-century Austro-Hungarian power schemes and exploitation of its Slavic provinces.

In conclusion, Šenoa's novel fulfills its task of educating its audience by placing the turbulent events of his time within a broader chronological framework and thus giving the South Slavic cause historical continuity. His literary and political importance for Croatia and the larger proto-Yugoslav movement cannot be overestimated. The drama of the love triangle in *The Goldsmith's Gold*, which probably kept the average reader turning the page more quickly than the political turbulence described in the historical parts of the novel did, nevertheless reflects that turbulence in the hero's choice between two national signifiers embodied in Dora and Klara. The death of the former at the hands of the latter paints a bleak picture of the future, but as such, it serves as a warning to those readers who, in the tradition imparted to them by Šenoa's literary predecessors, still demonized the ailing Ottoman Empire while being seduced by the West.

A Serbian Perspective

Nineteenth-century South Slavic literature, as mentioned in the beginning of the chapter, has not had the impact on the world scene as that of the Western Slavs. This is especially unfortunate when it comes to the Serbian author Laza Lazarević, whose small but powerful oeuvre of nine completed short stories deserves wider recognition. His life story is comparable to Anton Chekhov's, since he was a physician—in which capacity he was involved in the Serbo-Turkish War—in addition to an author. And like Chekhov, he died young, of the same ailment, tuberculosis at age thirty-nine in early 1891. He is known for introducing psychological depth into Serbian fiction, and his psychological insights, as well as his promotion of traditional patriarchal values, are comparable to Tolstoy's. Within the Yugoslav canon he is actually known as the Serbian Turgenev, but his endorsement of traditional values and his anti-Westernism especially render such a comparison to a Russian Westernizer false.

If the Russian Slavophile Aleksei Khomiakov wrote a "Letter to the Serbs" warning them against Westernization in 1860, their own master psychological realist did so in an autobiographically based short story titled "Švabica" (The German Girl), which was published posthumously in his collected works in 1898. Lazarević was a realist in the truest sense of the word, meaning that he did not use any mythological devices to portray the evil of the ruling empires. Markers of wealth in his fiction are Turkish, as demonstrated in his first published story, "Prvi put s ocem na jutrenje" (First Morning Service with Father, 1879), in which the middle-class merchant and gambler father, at the expense of basic supplies for his family, "nosio se, razume se, turski" (dressed, naturally, in the Turkish fashion).[32] Just like the Croatian intelligentsia, however, the gifted young Serbs studied abroad in the West, in Germanic lands mostly, as did the author himself, obtaining his medical degree in Berlin. The hero of "The German Girl" meets and falls in love with the eponymous heroine during his medical studies in an unspecified German city that is merely marked by the letter *H*.

The story is written in epistolary form, as a collection of letters that the narrator, in a very brief introductory paragraph, claims to have found on his return from Italy. The letters are written by a young medical student, Mišo Maričić, to his closest friend (*pobratim*) in Serbia. They include some comical parts, such as the letter writer's recollection of educated Germans who ask him whether Serbia is in Asia Minor and are surprised to hear "da i mi pijemo kravlje mleko, da mesimo hleb isto kao i oni, da imamo čak pozorište i da smo hrišćani" (that we also drink cow's milk, that we knead bread just as they do, that we even have a theatre and that we are Christians).[33] As the letters progress, the student's love for the German girl, named Ana, becomes more and more serious, but so do his doubts, which consist of two main entities, regularly listed in tandem: Serbia and his mother.

After the first lengthy flirtation with the German girl, the medical student, as he recalls her image while lying in bed that evening, exclaims, "Dalje od mene! Imam ja svojih poslova. Ja sam Srbin, ja imam staru mater " (Away from me! I have my own work. I am a Serb, I have an old mother).[34] The first time he comes close to confessing his feelings and kissing her, he flees the scene: "Ja se nagnuh njojzi. U isti mah sinu mi kao munja kroz glavu: Švabica, sirota moja mati, Srbija. Skočim, i, ne uzdajući se u svoj glas, bez zbogom ostaj odem u svoju sobu." (I leaned towards her. At the same moment, like lightning it flashed through my head: a German girl, my poor mother, Serbia. I jump up and, not trusting my voice, without taking leave I go to my room).[35] In the last clause it is only the comma that makes the distinction between his human mother and his mother Serbia. A couple of pages later he imagines Ana in his Serbian hometown and "moja mati, crvenih očiju, koja svoje sopstvene snahe ne razume" (my mother, red-eyed, who cannot understand her own daughter-in-law),[36] implying by the mother's red eyes that her son's choice of a bride would bring her to tears.

When he convinces himself, as well as the recipient of his letter, that he has come to his senses, Maričić resorts to Christian imagery: "Mene je mimoišla čaša, koja je, istina, slađa od one koju služe u Getsimanskom Vrtu. Đavo me je terao, dva-triput sam lupnuo da srknem iz nje, no moj dobri genije držao me je za njušku!" (The cup that is, truth be told, sweeter than the one they serve in the Garden of Gethsemane, has passed me by. The Devil pursued me, two or three times I almost slurped from it, but my good genius held me by the snout!).[37] This is the only instance where Lazarević resorts to using mythological features to describe the transnational romance. The conflation of ethnicities with religious faiths in the Eastern European imagination makes the above metaphor appropriate, if seemingly exaggerated. We can assume that the Serbian Maričić is Orthodox and the German Ana either Catholic or Protestant; this is never clarified, but the idea that Ana would have to give up her faith, among other things, for a relationship with Maričić does enter his musings about her. The analogy he draws between pursuing the romance with the German girl and drinking of the Devil's brew adds further weight to the metaphorical reading of that particular romance as national betrayal.

Despite his best intentions to avoid this nationally illegitimate romance, Maričić ends up pursuing it briefly, which includes teaching Ana some Serbian, but another letter from his friend and one from his sister convince him to put an end to it. Not intentionally, like Šenoa's Klara, Lazarević's Anna still manages, unintentionally, to ruin the hero, to make him no good to the homeland he was to return to and serve. The last letter of the story, appropriately the thirteenth, informs us that "danas je upravo dve godine kako je Ana umrla" (today is exactly two years since Ana died) and goes on to describe the letter writer's loss of "ideali i ideje . . . patriotstvo, rad" (ideals and ideas . . . patriotism, work).[38] Sadly, the medical books he brought back from Germany still lie in the suitcase in which he brought them home, his neighbor is using one of his chemical solutions to die Easter eggs, his scalpels have become instruments for peeling potatoes and gutting fish, and his nieces and nephews examine bugs under his microscope. The riches he should have brought back from Germany in the form of medical knowledge have gone to waste because of a forbidden infatuation. In the last line of this last letter, Maričić describes taking back Ana's picture from his sister, who had confiscated it in the hope of curing his lovesickness, and thus demonstrates that he has no hope of recovery. Although the Šenoa-type evil schemes of kidnapping and poisoning do not enter Lazarević's story, the message—beware of the bewitching Western woman—is the same.

Chapter 5

Quo Vadis

Polish Messianism and the Proselytizing Heroine

Like August Šenoa, Henryk Sienkiewicz broke with the romantic tradition of his predecessors from the first half of the nineteenth century and charted a new course for the Polish novel. He was not the first Polish novelist, as his path was already paved by the likes of Józef Korzeniowski (not be confused with Józef Teodor Konrad Korzeniowski, a later writer, much better known as Joseph Conrad) and Józef Kraszewski, but these and other predecessors are usually discussed merely as preludes to Sienkiewicz. Sienkiewicz is often lauded as the Polish Sir Walter Scott, and it is under his pen that the Polish novel reached its apotheosis as well as international recognition. Unlike the Croatian and Serbian novelists, Sienkiewicz had a glorious Polish national—even imperial—past to look back on and revive in his popular historical novels. The trilogy that first secured him fame consists of his first, enormously popular epic novel, *Ogniem i mieczem* (With Fire and Sword, 1884), followed by *Potop* (The Deluge, 1886) and *Pan Wołodyjowski* (translated into English as *Fire in the Steppe* and *Pan Michael*, 1888). All three works describe Poland, that is, the Polish-Lithuanian Commonwealth, during the course of the seventeenth century. This was a period shortly after the Commonwealth had reached its zenith and could withstand the invasions—though it was significantly weakened by them—described in the *Trilogy*: in chronological order of the invasions as well as the novels' publications, first by the Cossacks (who were, to be more accurate, revolting rather than invading), then the Swedes, and finally the Ottomans. As Agnieszka B. Nance reminds us, "Before the first partition of 1772, Poland had been the third largest independent kingdom in Europe."[1] Sienkiewicz's *Trilogy*, published in the decades after the second failed Polish uprising against Russia, was intended to have—and achieved—the effect of uplifting the quashed Polish patriotic spirit.

In 1772, shortly after the first partition, the philosopher Jean-Jacques Rousseau published an essay titled "Considerations on the Government of Poland." In yet another point of contention with Voltaire, his lifelong nemesis from the Enlightenment movement and a great admirer of Catherine the Great, Rousseau found his romantic aesthetic in sympathy with Poland.

Intended as a letter of encouragement, the essay addresses the Polish people directly and includes the following memorable statement:

> You will never have offensive force; for a long time you will not have a defensive one; but you will soon have, or to say it better, you already have the preservative force which, even if subjugated, will safeguard your government and your freedom in its sole and true sanctuary, which is the heart of the Poles.[2]

Such consolation is just what one would expect from the author who is considered the father of romanticism. Larry Wolff, in his discussion of this essay, rightly notes that "when Rousseau relocated Poland in the hearts of the Poles, he also liberated it from the constraints of cartography,"[3] as this was to be Poland's fate with the following two partitions. A century later, after two brutally quashed rebellions, all that a national author like Sienkiewicz could do was to fan the flames of patriotism in "the heart of the Poles" by reminding them of their glorious past. In her discussion of Sienkiewicz's success in this endeavor, Beth Holmgren quotes Poland's other great novelist of the nineteenth century and veteran of the second Polish uprising, Bolesław Prus, who, perhaps enviously, proclaimed that "the sun never sets on the books of Sienkiewicz."[4] Prus saw it fit to amend the famous statement about the enormity of the British Empire to characterize the enormity of Sienkiewicz's influence, but his statement also, as Holmgren notes, "suggest[ed] that the act of buying Sienkiewicz was tantamount to building a Polish empire."[5] Sienkiewicz's novels thus rebuilt the Polish empire in the hearts of the reading Polish public, and they continued to do so under future occupiers as well. As Stanislaw Eile notes, "Even during the Second World War the names of many characters from that cycle were among the most popular codenames in the underground movement."[6]

With Fire and Sword remains the most successful novel from the *Trilogy* and a staple on the Polish school curriculum. It has variously been called the Polish *War and Peace* and the Polish *Gone With the Wind*, and its importance for the nation, beginning with the time of its publication and extending through today, cannot be overstated. The reviewer of the first English translation directly from Polish—Sienkiewicz's first English translator, Jeremiah Curtin, translated it from the Russian version—called it, in a statement that has been repeated elsewhere, "the greatest prose epic of Polish literature" and asserted that "no other book in the history of Polish letters has become such an integral part of Polish culture."[7] By far the most dramatic assessment of the importance of this work came from a contributor to *The Trilogy Companion*, which was published in 1992, that is, shortly after Poland became independent from the Eastern Bloc: "There is no doubt that this great work, written to uplift the hearts in 1883, inspired that nation in its modern struggle to reestablish political pluralism, rebuild their democratic institutions and return to a free economy."[8] It ought to be noted, however, that this novel's immense popularity has not made it immune to criticism, some of it already uttered in its own time, of its treatment of the Ukrainian Cossacks.[9]

For the purposes of the central argument of this study, the most interesting aspect of *With Fire and Sword* is the fictional love story woven throughout the historical events described. It involves the liberation of the beautiful orphaned princess Helena Kurcewiczówna from the Cossack leader Bohdan Khmelnytsky, to whom she was promised in marriage by her mercenary aunt. Bohdan Khmelnytsky is a real historical character, leader of the Cossack uprising that is also named after him and known in Polish history as the Khmelnytsky Uprising, while Helena and her rescuer, the Polish knight Jan Skrzetuski, are fictional. The two fall in love at first sight and, after Helena avoids a series of dangers that span the length of the novel, she and Jan end up happily together. This is another intra-European love triangle that relies on the popular colonialist trope of the white woman under threat of "adulteration" by the subjugated native and, thus, in need of rescue by the white male colonizer. Sienkiewicz heightens the emotional effect of this trope by putting an actual infamous historical figure in the role of the threatening villain.

While *With Fire and Sword* and the following two novels in the *Trilogy* were enormously successful in Poland, it is *Quo Vadis* (serialized in 1895 and published in book form in 1896) that brought the author international fame. As Holmgren observes, compared to the Russian masterpieces of Tolstoy, Dostoevsky, and Turgenev, "Polish literature did not enjoy the same rapid translation into other languages until the novelist Henryk Sienkiewicz took Europe by storm in the late 1890s."[10] *Quo Vadis* is also considered instrumental in securing Sienkiewicz the Nobel Prize in literature in 1905 and he is frequently, though erroneously, described as receiving the prize for this particular work. The Nobel Prize in literature, in fact, is never awarded for a singular work and Sienkiewicz earned his "because of his outstanding merits as an epic writer."[11] The international duration of the effect of *Quo Vadis* was exemplified best by the 1951 Hollywood motion picture of the same name, starring Robert Taylor, Deborah Kerr, and the wonderful Peter Ustinov as Nero. The film was an enormous commercial success, though it did not win one of the eight Academy Awards for which it was nominated.

Quo Vadis, as its subtitle reveals, is *A Tale of the Time of Nero*, and its focus is the persecution of the early Christians in Rome, including Nero's blaming of them for the great fire that nearly destroyed the city in its entirety in 64. *Quo Vadis* has been read as both an apologia for the Christian faith and, more important for my argument, an allegory for the persecuted Poles under Russia's rule. Sienkiewicz engaged in extensive historical research for the novel and relied most heavily on the writings of the Roman historian Tacitus, including the latter's claim, disputed by modern historians, that it was Nero who commanded that Rome be burned. Sienkiewicz also admitted the following regarding his fiction: "It is indisputable that the persecution suffered by the Poles under the yoke of Prussia and especially under the yoke of Russia had a significant influence on my projects."[12] Russia, as previously mentioned, obtained the largest parts of partitioned Poland, and Sienkiewicz, who grew up in Warsaw, was one of her subjects. While the persecution of ancient Christians works well as an allegory for the nineteenth-century nation that saw itself in the role of the suffering Messiah, the Roman Empire as an allegorized Russia is also fitting in light of the age-old Russian pretentions, dating to the destruction of Constantinople in 1453, to Moscow—more accurately, Muscovy, which refers to medieval Russia in its entirety—as the Third Rome. Regarding the reception of the novel by the religious, Pope Pius X, who became pope two years before Sienkiewicz won the Nobel Prize, saw in it a fine apologia for Christianity and commended *Quo Vadis* as such, and the first Polish pope, John Paul II, made the following statement about it in 1996: "I enjoy it as a Pole, but also as a Christian."[13] Pope John Paul II made the order of his allegiances in the case of Sienkiewicz's novel doubly clear when he placed "Pole" before "Christian" and then weakened the latter category by prefacing it with "but also," as if the "Christian" part was a mere appendage required of the head of the Catholic Church.

In its unique history, the Polish nation had the experience of both enjoying the status of empire, in the Middle Ages, and suffering the fate of subjugation, in the eighteenth and nineteenth centuries. Sienkiewicz covered both extremes in his novelistic output, which could in and of itself comprise a book divided into two sections titled "Empire" and "Nation," the *Trilogy* belonging to the first and *Quo Vadis* to the second. The "Empire" section could also include the novel *Krzyżacy* (The Teutonic Knights or The Knights of the Cross, 1900), which, much like *With Fire and Sword*, features a national heroine in the hands of the enemy. *Krzyżacy* has been read in the context of Bismarck's *Kulturkampf*, against which it uplifted the national spirit by depicting the opposite of its present-day political situation: the Polish victory over the Prussian knightly order in the 1410 Battle of Grunwald, a battle that signaled the rise of the Polish-Lithuanian Commonwealth and the decline of the Teutonic Knights. Since the present study draws parallels between the love triangles of nineteenth-century European novels and the nineteenth-century political exigencies in which these stories are steeped, it is *Quo Vadis*, as an allegory of Polish oppression and as a complement to the trials of South Slavic nations discussed in the previous chapter, that is the focus of this chapter on the Polish novel.

Polish Messianism and *Quo Vadis*

The two dominant literary schools of the nineteenth century, romanticism occupying roughly the first half and realism the second, were linked with the two uprisings in the case of Poland. Polish romanticism, which is almost synonymous with Polish messianism, developed in the wake of the November Uprising of 1830, while Polish realism—which was influenced heavily by positivism, though that is beyond the scope of this project[14]—developed in the wake of the January Uprising of 1863. It might be useful to define Polish messianism in contrast to Russian messianism, which was alluded to in chapter 3 through the figure of Dostoevsky and his take on the Slavonic Question. The difference between the two messianisms could not be greater, as it constitutes the difference between a powerful empire and a stateless nation. The one factor they have in common is that each sees its own country as suffering for the redemption of others, as Jesus did, but what precisely that sacrifice involves is where the similarities end. In the Russian case, we recall, Dostoevsky saw the war with the Ottoman Empire on behalf of the South Slavs as Russia's "self-sacrifice," one that was "almost unprecedented among other nations . . . in its pious religious thirst to *suffer for the right deed*" (*PSS* 23:50). Tolstoy, on the other hand, reminded his readers through the mouthpiece of Levin that this salvation of the South Slavs "expresse[d] itself in revenge and murder" as it involved "killing Turks" (*PSS* 19:392, 391). He saw through the grand apocalyptic narrative for what it really was—imperial competition and conquest.

The Polish romantics had absolutely nothing to gain, at least not materially or in this life, from thinking of Poland as "the Christ of nations." The phrase was popularized by the Polish romantic par excellence, the poet Adam Mickiewicz, and is worth contrasting to the figure of the Russian savior, who typically took the form of the Virgin Mary rather than her son. It was, as mentioned in chapter 3, the icons of the Virgin that the Russian armies carried into battle. As the Russian philosopher Nikolai Berdiaev observed, "The people have felt the nearness of the interceding Mother of God more vividly than that of Christ."[15] It was the same Berdiaev, though in a different work, who discussed the difference between the two messianisms. In an essay called "The Russian and the Polish Soul" he claims that "it is with the Polish namely that the idea of a nationalism messianism has reached its highest upsurge and intensity." "The Polish," he continues, "have conveyed into the world the idea of sacrificial messianism," while "the Russian messianism always has to seem to the Polish as something non-sacrificial, greedy, with pretensions to seizing territory." His distinction between the role of Christ in Polish messianism and the role of Mary in the Russian is worth citing at length:

> In the Polish soul there is an experiencing of the path of Christ, the sufferings of Christ, and the sacrifice on Golgotha. At the summits

> of the Polish spiritual life the fate of the Polish people is experienced, as the fate of the Lamb, offered in sacrifice for the sins of the world. Suchlike is Polish messianism, first of all sacrificial, not connected with state power, nor with success and dominance in the world . . . Hence there is born in the Polish soul the pathos of suffering and sacrifice. Everything is different in the Russian soul. The Russian soul is connected moreso with the intercession of the Mother of God, than with the path of Christ's sufferings, with the experience of the Golgotha sacrifice. In the Russian soul there is a genuine humility, but little of the sacrificial victim.[16]

It bears consideration that the image of the all-embracing mother is more apropos for the all-encompassing empire—the "protectoress . . . leading lady . . . mother," to use Dostoevky's phrasing (*PSS* 23:49)—rather than that of the crucified Christ. The Poles, given their national fate, could relate better to the latter and developed the allegory to such a degree that even the placement of the innocent Jesus's cross between those of two criminals has been likened to Poland's "crucifixion" between Germany and Russia.[17] The omission of Austria, the third participant in the partitions, is not amiss, since Austrian Poland, or Galicia, did not experience the kind of repressive measures that were implemented by Germany and Russia. On the contrary, the Polish language was not banned and local administrators were Polish and even had their own Diet, so that the Galician province was the only part of partitioned Poland where native culture could flourish. Righteous indignation was, therefore, reserved for Germany and Russia. In contrast to Russian messianism, the messianic gains the Poles reaped were exclusively spiritual: an otherworldly reason for their suffering—that it would ultimately redeem the entire world, thus giving the quashed nation a leading role—and a hope for a future resurrection.

Like the denizens of most nations and empires, the Poles experienced their homeland as a mother; if the Russians had their *mat' Rossiia*, then the Poles had their *matka Polka*. The idea of Mother Poland did not die out with Poland's downfall; as mentioned in the introduction, Mickiewicz himself invoked it, though the political circumstances compelled him to write of her as being laid in the grave. The death of Poland and the tremendous suffering of its people, the hope for its resurrection and the need to believe that it was not all senseless, made Christ the most relatable figure for the Polish nation during this time. Poland's Catholicism, the religion whose symbol is the crucifix—as opposed to the Orthodox Church, in which the figure of the risen Christ is more prevalent—contributed to the relevance of the image. *Quo Vadis* employs the more typical female image of the nation and casts her—appropriately, a slave girl and Christian convert with occasional visions of martyrdom—in the role of the suffering Christ.

The biblical figure that for Poland best embodied Russia, and a figure that is tacitly present in the novel about the early Christians, is the Whore of Babylon. Written in the decades that followed the 70 c.e. destruction of Jerusalem by Rome, the last book of the New Testament names the aggressor Babylon, referring thereby to the earlier, destruction of Jerusalem in 586 b.c.e. The epithet "whore" recalls the Hebrew prophets' characterization of Israel as an adulteress who was punished for her sins by the Babylonian destruction. The author of Revelation employs the link in admonishing the early Christians, as the new Israel, against pledging their allegiance to the secular Roman authorities and thus committing a metaphorical sexual breach with the Whore of Babylon. Revelation 17:6 explicitly identifies the Roman persecution of Christians through the image of the Whore that embodies the empire: "And I saw that the woman was drunk with the blood of the saints and the blood of the witnesses to Jesus."[18] The secular powers of the earth, by contrast, are her willing accomplices, as stated in Revelation 18:3: "For all the nations have drunk of the wine of the wrath of her fornication, and the kings of the earth have committed fornication with her, and the merchants of the earth have grown rich from the power of her luxury."[19] Since biblical times, the image of the Whore of Babylon has been used to depict one's enemies, especially if they were more powerful. If this was Rome for the early Christians, then it was the Roman Catholic Church for the Protestant reformer Martin Luther, and it was more recently England for the contemporary Irish singer Sinead O'Connor.[20] Rome is referred to as Babylon twice by the Christians in *Quo Vadis*: while taking shelter in a cave from the great fire, two people, one of them the apostle Peter, declare that the fire is God's punishment on "Babylon."[21] Since the typically male-ruled nation is regularly perceived as female, the embodiment of the Whore tends to be assigned to the enemy emperor's wife. The reference is employed in *Effi Briest*, though in the context of a victorious unified Germany at that point: a party host refers to Napoleon III's wife Eugénie as "das Weib von Babel" (the Whore of Babylon) (*SW* 7:224) and contrasts her to German women, with an accompanying bow to Effi. In *Quo Vadis*, as discussed further below, it is Nero's wife, Poppaea, who is to the novel's Christian heroine what Klara is to Dora in *The Goldsmith's Gold*.

The famous Polonist Andrzej Walicki called Poland "a classic country of romantic nationalism" and messianism "the phenomenon of irrational hope."[22] The "irrational hope" and the potential spiritual gains of Polish messianism reached their limits, however, with the second insurrection, whose failure and calamitous aftermath knocked the wind out of "the Christ of nations" doctrine and demanded a new approach. Sienkiewicz belonged to that second, more pragmatic generation, which sought an "organic"—a term frequently associated with the new response following the second insurrection—approach to the Polish problem. For Sienkiewicz this meant turning to the national events based in history for the purpose of bolstering, but also educating, his compatriots. He was so successful that, as Holmgren notes, his popularity in his own lifetime eclipsed that of Mickiewicz's.[23] The two are often mentioned in tandem, the two bards of nineteenth-century Polish literature, with Sienkiewicz as Mickiewicz's inheritor in the realist tradition. The late Sienkiewicz scholar Julian Krzyżanowski deemed him as such and the Polish literary historian and contemporary of Sienkiewicz's, Ignacy Chrzanowski, credited the author with being the first to inspire Polish patriotism since the time of the romantics.[24]

Despite the turn toward positivism and pragmatism following the second Polish insurrection, Sienkiewicz was not completely immune to messianism. His inheritance of the Mickiewicz doctrine is most obvious in *Quo Vadis*. To begin with, first-century Rome as the historical setting of the plot and the role of the persecuted Christians in it as allegorized Poles cannot escape such a reading. Like the Polish romantics, the Roman Christians of *Quo Vadis* put their hopes in the afterlife, which is why they have no fear of the mad Caesar. Two of the main Roman characters discussing the Christians observe that "że są ludzie, którzy się cezara nie boją i żyją tak spokojnie, jakby go na świecie nie było" (there are people who have no fear of Caesar, and who live as calmly as if he were non-existent) (*QV* 1856) while "nasze zaś życie czymże jest, jeśli nie ciągłym strachem?" (our life, what is it if not constant fear?) (1858). When one of them ponders Nero's possible revenge on him, we are informed that he, as a true Roman, "był człowiekiem odważnym i śmierci się nie bał" (was a courageous man and did not fear death), but "nie spodziewając się od niej niczego" (expecting nothing from it) (*QV* 1971)—in distinction to the Christians, for whom "życie . . . zaczyna się wraz ze śmiercią" (life . . . begins together with death) (1839)—he "nie chciał jej wywoływać" (did not want to invite it) (1971) by angering Caesar. The two privileged Romans look upon Christianity, with all of its hope placed in the hereafter, as "nieprzyjaciółką życia, bo nakłada na nie więzy" (an enemy of life, because it places chains on it), yet wonder, "a czyż mogą być twardsze niż te, które nosimy" (but can theirs be stronger than the ones we wear?) (1983).

The two interlocutors discussed above are the Roman patrician Marcus Vinicius, recently returned in the opening of the novel from war in Asia Minor, and his uncle, Gaius Petronius. As in the *Trilogy*, in *Quo Vadis* also Sienkiewicz uses a mix of real and fictional characters, and Gaius Petronius belongs to the former. The historical Petronius was a member of Nero's court and the presumed author of *Satyricon*, which the character Petronius hands to Marcus to read in the second chapter of the novel. Petronius is featured heavily in *Quo Vadis* as he listens to, mocks, and worries about his nephew's incurable infatuation with the young Christian woman and his resulting interest in Christianity. The Christian heroine is Ligia. An orphan of a conquered people, she has been taken in by a loving Roman family, where, together with her adoptive mother, she has become a follower of Christ's teachings. The fictional Ligia's adoptive parents were, like Gaius Petronius, actual historical figures. Her father, Aulus Platius, was the famous general who led the Roman conquest of Britain and served as the new province's first governor in the 40s. In *Quo Vadis*, situated in the 60s, he is retired and lives with his family at home. His wife, Pomponia Graecina, is also known to history and long suspected of having been a Christian. The nineteenth-century archaeologist of the Roman catacombs, Giovanni Battista de Rossi, identified her as the Catholic saint Lucina, Lucina being Pomponia's baptismal name in his theory and not to be confused with the more famous third-century saint Lucia or Lucy.[25]

In addition to portraying the plight of Christians in first-century Rome, a further messianic theme emerges in the novel's plot development: the Christian heroine, instead of functioning as an inspiration for the national hero—in the manner of Croatian peasant girls vis-à-vis the intelligentsia or noblemen—converts one of the imperial oppressors. To use more popular, contemporary terminology, we might say that she engages in the practice of missionary dating. This arrangement leads to a happy ending, at least for the couple who play the lead roles, which is another major difference between *Quo Vadis* and the South Slavic novels. The happy ending also involves the toppling from power and eventual suicide of the cruel Nero, in contrast to *The Goldsmith's Gold*, whose political plot ends with the election of a foreigner as the new governor of Croatia. The difference between the two novels' endings speaks to the overall difference between the two authors and their missions. Sienkiewicz's novels in general, like the ones in the *Trilogy* and *The Teutonic Knights*, tend to end happily, since his purpose is, after all, to uplift the Polish spirit. Šenoa, on the other hand, in the absence of a compelling otherworldly doctrine and intent on warning the Croatian reading public that their reliance on the Habsburgs is misguided, uses the scare tactic of an unhappy ending.

The very title of Sienkiewicz's novel is important to discuss for its messianic implications, especially because it has nothing to do with the major story—the couple's romance and their tribulations—but refers to a minor episode that takes place toward the very end. Chapter 69 (out of 74, including the epilogue) recounts an old Christian legend stemming from one of the writings that did not make it into the New Testament canon, the apocryphal Acts of Peter. On his way out of Rome, fleeing persecution, Peter encounters the risen Christ as a brightly lit figure on the road and, falling on his knees, asks him, "Quo Vadis, Domine?" (*QV* 4088), or "Where are you going, Lord?" He receives the following answer: "Gdy ty opuszczasz lud mój, do Rzymu idę, by mnie ukrzyżowano raz wtóry" (If you desert my people, I am going to Rome to be crucified a second time) (*QV* 4090), upon which he turns around and goes back into the city, where the praetorian guards have been searching for him. In chapter 70, as Peter is led to his place of crucifixion, he is described as "nie ofiara idzie ku straceniu, ale zwycięzca odbywa pochód tryumfalny" (not a victim going to execution, but a victor making a triumphal procession) (*QV* 4102). This triumph is accomplished some centuries later, when Rome becomes the seat of the Catholic Church, which considers Peter to have been the original pope. The text of the novel anticipates this historical development by describing Peter among the crowds on the way to his place of crucifixion as one who "spoglądał na nie tak, jakby spoglądał władca i król na swe dziedzictwo" (looked at them as a ruler and king looks at his inheritance) (*QV* 4109). While the following three chapters and the epilogue depict Vinicius and Ligia's happiness in Sicily, Petronius's suicide in Rome, and the fall of Nero, the novel concludes with two sentences describing Peter's victory:

> I tak minął Nero, jak mija wicher, burza, pożar, wojna lub mór, a bazylika Piotra panuje dotąd z wyżyn watykańskich miastu i światu. Wedle zaś dawnej bramy Kapeńskiej wznosi się dzisiaj maleńka kapliczka z zatartym nieco napisem: Quo vadis, Domine?
>
> And so Nero passed, as a whirlwind passes, a storm, a fire, war or plague, but the basilica of Peter rules till now, from the Vatican heights, [over] the city and the world. Near the ancient gate of Capena rises today a little chapel with the somewhat worn inscription: Quo Vadis, Domine? (*QV* 4231–32)

The "somewhat worn" condition of the inscription testifies to the enduring victory of the church over the Roman Empire and, by allegorical extension, we can assume, Poland's eventual eternal victory over its oppressors. Since the religion of Poland's oppressors is Orthodox in the case of Russians and Protestant in the case of Prussians, the eventual Catholic victory in Rome gains an additional Polish significance in the novel.

Sienkiewicz's own attitude toward Poland's oppression and the kind of Polish response to it that he advocated also contains messianic overtones. Of note is his reaction to a renewed wave of Germanization of Prussian Poles in the early 1900s. On September 28, 1902, the *New York Times* published an appeal Sienkiewicz had made to his compatriots in Prussia on the previous day regarding the "anti-Polish agitation" to which they were being subjected by the German government. In its entirety, it reads as follows:

> At present, glowing hatred of the Poles, their traditions, language, and ideals, is spreading in Germany. The movement has one good effect, namely, it renders our Germanization impossible. The Germanism which is thrust upon us through force and hatred will nevermore pass into Polish blood. It is at best but varnish, which can be immediately removed.
>
> The real danger for the Polish people is hatred against Germanism. Hatred begets hatred, and here begins the task of every decent, intelligent newspaper. Protect the Polish popular mind from hatred,

> in order not to be poisoned like the Prussians. Protect them morally and politically. Remember that only God knows what evolutions are impending for the Prussian kingdom, which with all its power may only be a transient, political phenomenon. Whatever great changes may come, you must always live with the Germans in the eastern provinces. Remember that hatred is a fever. Whoever does not want to die of fever must overcome it.
>
> One must be bereft of all political or historical perception not to see that the treatment you are receiving from your enemies not only lacks dignity, but the equipoise and intelligence which characterize actions as reasonable. Intelligent Germans see this. You, too, must feel that logic is lacking in the measures applied against you, and that the authorities themselves are not clear regarding the success of those measures, and are tormenting you even against your own advantage. Hold fast to your Polonism. Let no power on earth tear it from you. But avoid hatred of the present Government's policy. It is merely a congestion of the Prussian head, causing temporary dizziness.[26]

The parallels between the sentiments expressed in this appeal and those of the Christians and the narrator himself in *Quo Vadis* could warrant an entire separate article, as echoes of *Quo Vadis* can be found in almost every sentence above. To start at the very beginning, the "spreading" of the "glowing hatred" of everything Polish in Germany parallels the spreading hatred of Christians by the Romans in *Quo Vadis*, with the adjective *glowing* being especially appropriate in the context of blaming the Christians for the burning of the city. The assertion in the following sentence, that the "one good effect" of Prussian oppression is that "it renders our Germanization impossible," was equally true for the Russianization of Russia's Poles, since the partitions of the eighteenth century and the further subjugations of the nineteenth only increased and strengthened Polish patriotism. The parallel therein with *Quo Vadis* is that Christianity, also, flourished under Roman persecution, as acknowledged in the novel when Petronius, resistant to the apostle Paul's efforts to convert him, nevertheless admits to Vinicius, "Zadziwiająca jednak rzecz, jak ci ludzie umieją zdobywać wyznawców i jak ta sekta się szerzy" (But it is astonishing how these people are able to gain followers and how that sect is spreading) (*QV* 2213).

The injunctions against returning hatred for hatred in the second paragraph are obviously in accordance with Christ's teaching, and they come out most poignantly in *Quo Vadis* during the post-fire mass executions of Christians. As Kryspus, the most severe of the Christian elders, is about to be nailed to the cross, he encourages the others among the condemned not only by calling on them to be proud of dying the same death as Christ did but also by foretelling a day of God's wrath for the wicked Romans. He is interrupted by the arrival of Paul, however, who reminds him that "Chrystus więcej jeszcze nakazał miłować ludzi niż nienawidzić złego, albowiem nauka Jego miłością jest, nie nienawiścią" (Christ commanded [us] to love people even more than to hate evil, for His teaching is love, not hatred) (*QV* 3573). When Sienkiewicz requests of the Polish newspapers that they "protect the Polish popular mind from hatred," he is asking them to do what his *Quo Vadis* apostles sought to do among the early Christians in Rome. The statement following the two sentences beginning with "protect," that "only God knows what evolutions are impending for the Prussian kingdom," echoes Vinicius's words as he rescues Ligia from the burning city: "Bóg jeden wie, jakie jeszcze klęski mogą spaść na Rzym" (God only knows what disasters may yet fall on Rome) (*QV* 2685). Sienkiewicz's completion of the sentence about the Prussian kingdom—that "with all its power" it "may only be a transient, political phenomenon"—has proven true for Prussia as it had for Nero's Rome, which, as discussed previously in regard to the novel's ending, became the center of Western Christianity.

The phrasing "Hold fast to your Polonism" toward the end of the third paragraph has a spiritual ring to it, especially since it is followed by "Let no power on earth tear it from you," thereby generating a contrast between earthly powers, such as the German government, and Polonism as something heavenly, which has no end. This sentiment is most closely expressed in *Quo Vadis* through a troubling insight Vinicius gains prior to his conversion: "Porwać Ligię wydawało mu się rzeczą możliwą i tego był prawie pewien, ale również pewien był, że wobec nauki on sam, jego męstwo, jego potęga są niczym i że z nią sobie nie poradzi" (To kidnap Ligia seemed to him a possible thing and he was almost certain of it, but he was equally certain that, in view of her religion, he himself, his bravery, his power was nothing and that with it he could not succeed) (*QV* 1345). Such a line of reasoning is equally applicable to Poland's situation, if we replace "him" and "he" referring to Vinicius in the sentence with either "Prussia" or "Russia," "Ligia" with "Poland," and "religion" with "Polonism." Just as Vinicius realizes that his great Roman power "could not succeed" when pitted against Ligia's Christianity, so Prussia and Russia, although they easily managed to "kidnap" Poland, proved powerless in any attempts at quashing Polonism. Finally, the "congestion of the Prussian head" in the last sentence in Sienkiewicz's appeal is reminiscent of the mentally imbalanced Nero, implying that nobody in the right state of mind—nobody with "the equipoise and intelligence which characterizes actions as reasonable," to quote an earlier line from the same paragraph—would treat an already oppressed people as the ancient Roman or the modern Prussian rulers did.

Who Is the Barbarian?

While Eastern Europe was for the Germans a place of "so many little wild peoples" (according to Herder) and "barbaric remnants" (Hegel), Sienkiewicz's appeal discussed above contributes to the reversal of this view. His call to the Polish people to guard themselves against hatred and his recognition that "you must always live with the Germans in the eastern provinces" clearly constitutes what would be considered the more "civilized" mind-set, especially as it contrasts so sharply with the Prussian conduct of seizing land that belonged to others, which we might deem "barbaric." When it came to the Poles and the Russians, they considered each other barbaric, with the Poles, given their closer proximity to Western Europe, relying on the stereotypes learned from their western neighbors. Sienkiewicz makes use of these mutual accusations in *Quo Vadis* through his portrayal of a Roman patrician, as well as Rome more generally, and a Christian barbarian.

In the second chapter of the novel, as Petronius and Vinicius pass through the city on their way to Aulus's house, they discuss the death sentence that was issued to all four hundred slaves belonging to a Roman prefect, another historical figure named Pedanius Secundus, who was murdered by one of them. Petronius, the *arbiter elegantiarum*, has protested the imposed punishment to be meted out on the entire *familia* as "barbarzyńska rzeź, godna jakichś Scytów, nie Rzymian" (a barbarous slaughter, befitting some Scythians, not Romans) (*QV* 139). The Romans of *Quo Vadis* were, as many readers and critics understood, allegorized Russians, but the reference to ancient Scythians is also significant because it was a widespread belief that Russians were their descendants. As revealed by Petronius's statement, the reputation of the Scythians in the ancient world was that of barbarians—Herodotus and Ovid both described them as such—and the belief that the Russians were their descendants bolstered eighteenth- and nineteenth-century Western European anti-Russian prejudices. Needless to say, this caused considerable resentment on the Russian side, already vexed by the fact that Western Europeans considered them "Asiatic," and was most notably expressed in Aleksandr Blok's 1918 satirical poem, "The Scythians."[27] The "Asiatic" reference is also used in *Quo Vadis*, just a few chapters after the "Scythian" reference, when Petronius and Vinicius discuss Nero's murders of his brother, mother, and first wife. Vinicius describes it as "rzeczą godną jakiegoś azjatyckiego królika, nie rzymskiego cezara" (a thing worthy of some petty Asiatic king, not a Roman Caesar) (*QV* 343), thus further invoking that widespread perception that was painful for the Russians.

The two references cited above could not have been lost on Sienkiewicz's Polish readers, not only because such a judgment supported the view of Russians as barbarians, but also because the Polish nation had endured an ordeal comparable to that of Pedanius's slaves under the Russian tsar three decades earlier and was still suffering the consequences. Pedanius is described as an "okrutnik" (monster) and his murder by his slave as committed "w chwili rozpaczy" (in a moment of despair) (*QV* 139). It is, therefore, not too great a stretch to suggest that this brief episode of *Quo Vadis* might be read as an oblique allusion to the brutal quashing of the second Polish uprising. Another allusion to Polish uprisings in general might be seen in the apostle Paul's efforts, mentioned above, to convert Marcus when he uses the following argument: "Przed wami drży świat cały, a wy drżycie przed własnymi niewolnikami, wiecie bowiem, że każdej godziny mogą podnieść przeciw waszemu ciemięstwu wojnę straszliwą, jaką już nieraz podnosili" (The whole world trembles before you, but you tremble before your own slaves, because you know that every hour could raise a terrible war against your oppression, such as has been raised many a time) (*QV* 2283). The contrast posited between the Romans and the barbarians in the two discussions had by the uncle and the nephew—the contrast between the Scythians and the Romans in the first and between a petty Asiatic king and a Roman Caesar in the second—is all the more effective for the Russian pretentions to Muscovy as the Third Rome. Russia, as the conversations between Marcus and Petronius seem to suggest, is no more worthy of the title than Nero is of the title of Caesar.

Nineteenth-century Russians, in turn, saw the rebellious Poles as barbarians, minus the erroneous ethnic underpinning. Sienkiewicz exploits and subverts this view by casting Ligia, the allegorized Poland and "Christ of nations," as a barbarian princess; she is the daughter of the murdered king of Ligians, whence she gets her Roman nickname (her original name is Kallina but is rarely used in the novel). When Petronius realizes, near the beginning of the novel, just how deep his nephew's infatuation is, he feels compelled to remind him of his rank in the empire and how different it is from Ligia's: "Uspokój się, szalony potomku konsulów. Nie po to sprowadzamy barbarzyńców na sznurach za naszymi wozami, byśmy mieli zaślubiać ich córki" (Calm thyself, mad descendant of consuls. We do not lead in barbarians bound behind our cars to make wives of their daughters) (*QV* 225). Yet, in the preceding chapter—chapter 2, the same one where the discussion of the fate of Pedanius's slaves takes place—when the two visit Ligia together in Aulus's home and Petronius meets her for the first time, he is already forced to check his assumptions. In a show of attempting to impress her, he recites to her the greeting Odysseus offers the Phaeacian princess Nausicaa in book 6 of *The Odyssey*. When Ligia answers him with the very words Nausicaa recites in reply to Odysseus, Petronius is astonished, "nie spodziewał się bowiem usłyszeć Homerowego wiersza w ustach dziewczyny, o której barbarzyńskim pochodzeniu był przez Winicjusza uprzedzony" (for he had not expected to hear verses of Homer from the mouth of the girl whose barbarian origins he had previously been warned of by Vinicius) (*QV* 187).

Not only is it impressive for Petronius to hear the verses of Homer uttered by a barbarian, but this knowledge of hers also presents another point of distinction between her and Marcus. Petronius—a more refined man, though still one given to sensual enjoyments—makes several allusions throughout the novel to his nephew's lack of appreciation for literature and art. One of the occasions on which he comments on these deficiencies is toward the middle of the novel, when he observes that art might also be a possible cure for Marcus's lovesickness, but realizing that his urging is probably hopeless, offers the following piece of advice: "Jeśli nie potrafisz być Grecją, bądź Rzymem: władaj i używaj!" (If you cannot be Greek, then be Roman: rule and enjoy!) (*QV* 1921). Back in chapter 3, Marcus decides on the following remedy for quenching his passion: "Rozkażę ćwiczyć którego z niewolników i będę słuchał jego jęków" (I will give command to flog one of the slaves and listen to his groans) (*QV* 222). The horrific remedy is referenced again in chapter 11, after Ligia has escaped and he finds that, much like the Turkish Smail-aga in his torturing of the Montenegrins, "jęki smaganych niewolników nie mogły ukoić ani jego bólu, ani wściekłość" (the groans of the whipped slaves could allay neither his pain nor his rage) (*QV* 732). It is, thus, made obvious to the reader over and over again that it is the temperamental Roman tribune, Marcus Vinicius, who is the greater barbarian, though not one beyond redemption; Ligia's love softens and "civilizes" him over the course of the novel. By chapter 28, when he returns home before his slaves expect him to and, consequently, finds the house in disorder and the slaves drunk and feasting on his goods, Marcus discovers, to his own surprise, that he is unable to punish them. In a letter to his uncle, after announcing forgiveness to his slaves, he attributes his unusual response to Ligia's influence: "Wydało mi się, że w tej chwili widzę słodką twarz Ligii i jej oczy zalane łzami, dziękujące mi za ten postępek" (It seemed to me that at that moment I saw the sweet face of Ligia and her eyes filled with tears, thanking me for this act) (*QV* 1786).

Parenthetically, the Greek element present in Roman culture can be likened to the French element present in eighteenth- and nineteenth-century Russia. Ligia has picked up Greek from listening to the instruction of "mały" (little) Aulus, Aulus Platius's biological son, who has a Greek tutor. The presence of a Greek teacher in a wealthy Roman home is akin to the ubiquitous presence of French tutors in wealthy Russian homes, as is the accompanying patriotic discomfort with this arrangement. Ligia's Homeric reply to Petronius is followed by a description of Aulus's pride at her display, together with the information that "mimo swych starorzymskich uprzedzeń, które kazały mu przeciw greczyźnie i jej rozpowszechnieniu piorunować, uważał ją za szczyt towarzyskiej ogłady" (in spite of his old Roman prejudices, which ordered him to thunder against Greek and its prevalence, he considered it the pinnacle of social polish) (*QV* 188). Following the reforms of Peter the Great, French came to be considered "the pinnacle of social polish" in imperial Russia, and the cultural ambivalence felt by the old Roman general is comparable to the kind experienced by more traditional Russians, especially those portrayed by Tolstoy, who was himself known for his propensity to "thunder against [French] and its prevalence."

Christ as a Romantic Rival

When Marcus tells Petronius, in the beginning of the novel, about first meeting Ligia, while healing his disjointed arm at Aulus's house, he recalls that "ona słuchała słów moich . . . ze schyloną głową, kreśląc coś trzciną na szafrannym piasku" (she listened to my words . . . with bent head, drawing something with the reed on the saffron-colored sand) (*QV* 123). The drawing turns out to be a fish, the early secret symbol for Christianity. Though Marcus remarks that "i w Grecji, i w Rzymie nieraz dziewczęta kreślą na piasku wyznania, których nie chcą wymówić ich usta" (in Greece as in Rome girls frequently draw on the sand a confession which their lips will not pronounce) (*QV* 131), there is only one connotation for the common reader of a person drawing in the sand, and that is Jesus. In the eighth chapter of the Gospel of John—in the story of the woman taken in adultery, which was already discussed in relation to Fontane's novel of the same name in chapter 2—"Jesus bent down and wrote with his finger on the ground."[28] The use of this line in *Quo Vadis* is significant on several levels. First and most obviously, it identifies Ligia with Jesus and, by allegorical extension, with Poland, "the Christ of nations" who is supposed to be the redemption of the whole world. The identification of Ligia with Christ as the original Christian martyr is confirmed later on when she, taken against her will to Nero's palace, imagines herself "męczennicą, z ranami w rękach i stopach, białą jak śniegi" (a martyr, with wounds on hands and feet, white as the snows) (*QV* 355).

On the other hand, considering that Roman girls might draw on the sand the name of their beloved, Ligia's symbol also reveals what is to become, as yet unbeknownst to Marcus, the greatest obstacle in his winning of her affection—a love triangle, in which Marcus's competition is none other than Jesus. The suggestion of a love triangle is confirmed by Petronius's erroneous assumptions about what Ligia must have written in the sand: "Czy nie imię Amora, czy nie serce przeszyte jego grotem lub nie coś takiego" (Was it not the name of Amor or a heart pierced with his dart, or something like that) (*QV* 130). Related to this complication, the evocation of the New Testament story of the woman taken in adultery reminds us of the moral danger that Marcus presents for Ligia. The scene ends, in fact, because she "nagle uciekła jak hamadriada przed głupowatym faunem" (suddenly fled like a hamadryad before a dull faun) (*QV* 123), an act she repeats several times when Marcus attempts to get close and she fights her own budding desire for him. Finally, the evocation of this particular tale from the life of Jesus stands out in a novel that frequently refers to the many and multiple-times-divorced women of Rome, thus highlighting, by contrast, Ligia's virtue. Like Jesus, she is the one without sin and the one capable of forgiveness. The entire household of Aulus, in fact, is described in idyllic terms, starting with Marcus's observation, when he and Petronius visit there together a little later, that "odźwierny tu bez łańcuchów" (the door keeper here is without chains) (*QV* 151). Petronius responds with, "To dziwny dom" (It is a wonderful house) (*QV* 152), and goes on to describe Pomponia's loyalty to her husband in the following terms: "Univira! . . . Łatwiej dziś w Rzymie o półmisek rydzów z Noricum" (A one-husband woman! It is easier today in Rome to get half a bowl of mushrooms from Noricum) (152).

A class complication in *Quo Vadis* that resembles the one in *The Goldsmith's Gold*—whose aristocratic father, we recall, is disgusted by his son's love for a merchant's daughter—is that the Christian heroine of barbaric origins is viewed as an unsuitable match for a Roman patrician, at least in the role of wife. From the other side, her Christian mentors fear for her purity in Vinicius's hands, and not merely her sexual purity, but even more the religious. In that sense, although the adulteress of *Quo Vadis* is Caesar's wife, Poppaea, Ligia is also, prior to Vinicius's conversion, in danger of being unfaithful to Christ. When she confesses her love for Vinicius to Kryspus—the severe Christian elder and a father figure to Ligia as one who had confirmed her in the faith—he scolds her mercilessly. In his scolding he employs the kind of rhetoric that reinforces the image of Ligia in a love triangle between Vinicius and Christ by portraying the two as rivals: "Bóg umarł dla cię na krzyżu, by krwią własną odkupić twą duszę, lecz ty wolałaś umiłować tego, który chciał cię uczynić swoją nałożnicą. Bóg cudem ocalił cię z rąk jego, lecz ty otworzyłaś serce żądzy nieczystej i pokochałaś syna ciemności" (God died for you on the cross, so that he would redeem your soul with his own blood, but you chose to love the one who wanted to make you his concubine. God miraculously saved you from his hands, but you opened your heart to impure desire and began to love the son of darkness) (*QV* 1751). Interestingly, the 1951 film accentuates the rivalry by having Marcus issue the following ultimatum to Ligia: "Yes, choose, because I'd no more share you with your Christ than I would with any other man."[29]

Yet it is the messianic message of the story, steeped in the proselytizing nature of the Christian religion, that not only allows for such a mismatch but also turns it into a positive outcome for all. Kryspus's ill treatment of Ligia is interrupted by Peter, who reminds him that Christ forgave Mary Magdalene, that he forgave Peter himself for denying him thrice, and that, regarding Vinicius, "Chrystus kruszył twardsze jeszcze serca" (Christ has shattered even harder hearts) (*QV* 1775). In the end, the endangered Christians gain an additional follower and from none less than the ranks of those who threaten them the most. When Vinicius invites the Christian elders to teach him, they "poczęli się naradzać, myśląc z radością o zwycięstwie swej nauki i o znaczeniu, jakie dla pogańskiego świata mieć będzie nawrócenie się augustianina i potomka jednego z najstarszych rodów rzymskich" (began to confer, thinking with joy of the victory of their religion and of the significance for the pagan world that the conversion of an Augustian and a descendant of one of the oldest Roman families will have) (*QV* 2083). His own Christian slaves benefit directly, as he, to Petronius's astonishment, decides on the following: "Każę im jeszcze zejść się w ogrodzie i kreślić przed sobą znaki, jakie chcą. Tych, którzy nakreślą rybę, wyzwoli Ligia" (I will tell them to meet again in the garden, and to make such signs on the ground as they want. Ligia will free those who draw a fish) (*QV* 2192). In return, as a new convert, Vinicius gains eternal salvation, that is, entry into the heavenly kingdom, which is to outlast the Roman Empire.

Sienkiewicz and Tolstoy

Marcus Vinicius's gradual conversion, including the nature of his attraction to Ligia, can best be described using Tolstoy's language from his last novel, *Resurrection*, which was briefly discussed in chapter 3 and published a few years after *Quo Vadis*, in 1899. The protagonist, Nekhliudov—whose name, minus the *kh* sound, means "not human"—is described as a person in whom, "как и во всех людях" (as in all people), according to Tolstoy, "было два человека" (there were two men):

> Один—духовный, ищущий блага себе только такого, которое было бы благо и других людей, и другой—животный человек, ищущий блага только себе и для этого блага готовый пожертвовать благом всего мира.
>
> One—the spiritual, seeking only that kind of happiness for himself, which would also be the happiness of all people, and the other—the animal man, seeking only happiness for himself, and ready to sacrifice for that happiness the happiness of the entire world. (*PSS* 32:53)

When, ten years after he had seduced a peasant girl on his aunts' estate, Nekhliudov unexpectedly faces the same woman—now a prostitute and one framed for murder—from the juror's seat in a courtroom, his spiritual man begins to awaken, and he decides to do everything in his power to help her, including following her and the other convicts to Siberia.

Marcus initially thinks that he can have Ligia, a Roman hostage, much like Nekhliudov has the peasant Katyusha. He displays his selfish animal man and his willingness to sacrifice others for his happiness when he rants of his desire to his uncle: "Muszę ją mieć. . . . Chciałbym zabić Aula i Pomponię, a ją porwać i zanieść na ręku do mego domu" (I must have her. . . . I would like to kill Aulus and Pomponia, and kidnap her and carry her on [my] arm to my house) (*QV* 222). Petronius prevents him from doing anything so rash by convincing Nero to present Ligia to Vinicius as a gift—thus also thwarting Nero's own potential designs on her—and she is taken to the palace, accompanied by her gigantic servant and bodyguard, Ursus, who is also a Christian. The latter comes to Ligia's rescue and carries her out of the palace when Vinicius gets drunk at Nero's celebration and begins to force himself on her. The two fugitives go into hiding among destitute Christians and Vinicius begins a mad search for them, displaying again his animal man, as he "rozumiał tylko, że musi ją znaleźć" (understood only that he must find her) (*QV* 1114) and attempts a kidnapping. Ursus saves Ligia a second time and is prepared to kill Vinicius, but she prevents him by reminding the mighty giant of Christ's teaching.

As the Christians forgive Vinicius and nurse him back to health from his injuries, his gradual conversion begins; his spiritual man awakens and the effect of this awakening on his feelings for Ligia is described thus:

> Pierwej pożądał jej, teraz poczynał ją kochać pełną piersią. Dawniej, jak w ogóle w życiu, tak i w uczuciu, był, jak wszyscy ówcześni ludzie, ślepym, bezwzględnym egoistą, któremu chodziło tylko o siebie, obecnie poczęło mu chodzić i o nią.
>
> At first he desired her, now he was beginning to love her with a full breast. Previously, as generally in life as in feeling, he was, like all people of that time, a blind, ruthless egotist, who thought only of himself, at present he began to think also of her. (*QV* 1702)

While Nekhliudov slowly begins to feel "всю жестокость, подлость, низость не только этого своего поступка, но всей своей праздной, развратной, жестокой и самодовольной жизни" (all the cruelty, turpitude, baseness not only of that act of his [bringing Katiusha to ruin], but of his whole idle, dissolute, cruel and self-satisfied life) (*PSS* 32:78), Vinicius informs the Christians, "Wiedzcie, że sam siebie nie poznaję, ale zbrzydły mi uczty, zbrzydło wino, śpiewanie, cytry i wieńce, zbrzydł dwór cezara i nagie ciała, i wszystkie zbrodnie" (Know that I do not recognize myself, but I am disgusted by feasts, disgusted by wine, singing, citharae and garlands, disgusted by the court of Caesar and naked bodies, and all crimes) (*QV* 2069). The all-important difference between the two novels, however, is that *Resurrection* is written by a Christian universalist who has long abandoned belief in any national allegiances, whereas *Quo Vadis*, where the Romans represent the Russians and the Christians represent the Poles, cannot but be read apart from its national signifiers. Moreover, Sienkiewicz makes a point of attributing his hero's original "animal man" to his national origins when he draws a contrast between Vinicius's "dawne surowe i samolubne, prawdziwie rzymskie i zarazem wilcze serce" (former harsh and selfish, truly Roman and at the same time wolfish heart) and the "uczuci[e] słodki[e] nauki chrześcijańskiej" (sweet sentiment of Christian teaching) (*QV* 1734).

Nekhliudov's conversion experience includes giving away all of his property, the possession of which he begins to deem sinful. This change reflects Tolstoy's own spiritual crisis, which compelled him to want to get rid of his property as well as his copyright, while his distressed wife argued that he had a financial responsibility to their eight surviving children. Vinicius's conversion does not go this far; in fact, his villa in Sicily provides a safe haven for him and Ligia away from the bloodbath that Nero's Rome turns into by the end of the novel. The older Tolstoy's views on property, however, concern a different part of Sienkiewicz's writing, the one piece of correspondence that transpired between the two authors. In early December 1907 Sienkiewicz sent a letter to a number of popular European figures, including Tolstoy, asking them to voice their opposition to the Prussian government's seizure of Polish farmers' lands in the province of Posen (Poznań in Polish). Tolstoy's reply, which was later published in several international, including Polish, newspapers, was a great disappointment and generated some harsh criticism, though none from Sienkiewicz, who went on to praise the Russian author in November of the same year, on the occasion of his eightieth birthday.[30] In a response that is as unsatisfactory as Rousseau's idea of rebuilding partitioned Poland in the hearts of her people, Tolstoy stated that he felt greater pity for "тех людей, которые устраивают это ограбление" (those people who arrange that robbing) than for those "кого ограбят" (whom they rob) (*PSS* 77:273), since the robbers are obviously morally inferior. Any moral man, Tolstoy insisted, would undoubtedly choose to be a Pole rather than a Prussian under the current circumstances. As frustrating as such a reply was, it should not have been surprising, coming from an author whose answer to the question, "How much land does a man need?," discussed in his 1886 story of the same title, was, as much as is needed for the grave that awaits him at the end of his life.

A little over a year after Sienkiewicz's appeal, in March 1909, a Polish woman wrote to Tolstoy, protesting his answer, not to her national novelist, but to the Serbian woman who, we recall from chapter 3, appealed to him after Austria annexed Bosnia and Herzegovina. Tolstoy, as is to be expected, defended his position on nonviolent resistance and exhorted her to "признать всех людей, как своих поляков, так и чуждых и враждебных русских, немцев, одинаково ближними, братьями" (acknowledge all people, one's own Poles as well as the foreign and hostile Russians, Germans, as equally neighbors, brothers) (*PSS* 38:151). Since the Tolstoy of *War and Peace* supported the Russian quashing of the second Polish rebellion while the Tolstoy of the *Resurrection* advocated pacifism and property-less-ness, the Polish cause could not have found a satisfactory answer from the great Russian author at any point in his life. Tolstoy claimed, according to N. N. Gusev's diary entry from July 1908, that because his childhood environment developed in him a hatred for the Poles, he felt all the more affection for them in his old age, as if “отплачиваю за прежнюю ненависть” (I am repaying them for the former hatred).[31] The “особенная нежность” (special affection) of his later years, however, prevented any political action.[32]

The Whore of Babylon

Jesus is not the only or the most daunting figure that stands in the way of Marcus and Ligia’s love. Jesus, after all, presents an obstacle that is surmountable via conversion, which is what Marcus accomplishes. The more immediate, earthly, and utterly unforgiving danger comes in the form of Nero’s wife, Poppaea, who, as noted above, plays the same role in *Quo Vadis* that the evil Klara plays in *The Goldsmith’s Gold*. She also, like Klara, fits the mold of Duraković’s “deceiving beauty.” The narrator describes her as “złotowłosa, słodka i jakkolwiek po dwóch mężach rozwódka, z twarzą i wejrzeniem dziewicy” (golden-haired, sweet, and though divorced from two husbands, with the face and eyes of a virgin) (*QV* 480). When Ligia first espies her at Caesar’s court, she is stunned by her beauty and “oczom własnym nie chciało jej się wierzyć, albowiem wiadomo jej było, że Poppaea Sabina jest jedną z najniegodziwszych w świecie kobiet” (could not believe her own eyes, because she knew that Poppaea Sabina was one of the vilest women in the world) (*QV* 481). Earlier, when Vinicius returns to Rome in the first chapter and catches up on the news in the city, Petronius gives him a warning that proves prophetic: “Jesteś pięknym chłopcem, więc ci to chyba może grozić, że Poppaea zakocha się w tobie” (You are a handsome lad, so this is what could threaten you, that Poppaea falls in love with you) (*QV* 48). Poppaea, indeed, becomes an enemy of Ligia’s as a rival for Marcus’s affection, just as the Croatian Klara attempts to compete with Dora and uses all of her powers to gain Pavle. As for Klara, in Poppaea’s mind also, “już to samo, że śmiał przenieść nad nią inną, zdawało jej się występkiem wołającym o pomstę” (this alone, that [Vinicius] had dared to prefer another over her, seemed to her an offense crying for vengeance). “Co do Ligii” (As to Ligia), the text continues, “znienawidziła ją od pierwszej chwili, w której zaniepokoiła ją piękność tej północnej lilii. . . . Znawczyni Poppaea od jednego rzutu oka zrozumiała, że w całym Rzymie jedna Ligia może z nią współzawodniczyć, a nawet ją zwyciężyć. I od tej chwili zaprzysięgła jej zgubę” (she hated her from the first moment, in which she was alarmed by the beauty of that northern lily. . . . The expert Poppaea understood from one glance of the eye that in all Rome only Ligia could compete with her, and even prevail. And from that moment she vowed her destruction) (*QV* 2866). The opportunity for destroying Ligia comes when Poppaea’s little daughter dies, a child whom Nero adores, and Poppaea, with the aid of others courting Nero’s favor, accuses Ligia of having bewitched the infant.

Poppaea also turns out to be an enemy of Christians in general and, again, the one who steers Nero in the same direction. The Christians, in turn, consider her "wcielenie zła i zbrodni" (the incarnation of evil and crime) (*QV* 481). When Ligia's distressed parents part from her on Caesar's orders, their main concern is that "dom cezara jest jaskinią hańby, zła, zbrodni" (the house of Caesar is a den of infamy, evil, crime) (*QV* 269). Since the first phrasing, used to describe Poppaea, echoes the second one, used to describe Caesar's house—*zła, zbrodni* (of evil, crime)—it verifies Poppaea as the embodiment of the Whore of Babylon that is Caesar-ruled Rome. As the wife of a hostile emperor, she again resembles the Croatian novel's Klara, who marries the newly appointed Austrian governor. The opportunity for destroying Christians comes when Nero has Rome set on fire and the angry mob demands a culprit; Poppaea convinces him to place the blame on Christians and thus commence the mass executions that constitute part of the Ludi annual festivities in the amphitheater.

Another similarity between Šenoa's and Sienkiewicz's portrayal of the virtuous heroine versus her cunning rival that bears mentioning is the hair color of the women. Šenoa's inversion of the association of light with good and darkness with evil, of that pervasive depiction in European literature, including Russian, of the blond woman as virtuous and the brunette as wicked, was discussed in the previous chapter. Sienkiewicz does the same—just as he reverses the barbarian/civilized dichotomy—and, in his case, the choice runs against ethnic expectations. The various ethnic groups inhabiting the Mediterranean basin, like the Croats, have historically been dark-haired, while those of Germanic origins have tended to be blond, and this meets the expectations one might have of Dora's and Klara's looks in *The Goldsmith's Gold*. In *Quo Vadis*, however, it is the Roman Poppaea that is described as "złotowłosa" (golden-haired) (*QV* 480, 487, 3235), while Ligia, who stems from the northern-based Ligian people (*QV* 195), has "ciemne włosy" (dark hair) (190, 579, 611, 1462). The MGM studios, incidentally, held fast to the established moral signifiers by casting Deborah Kerr as a strawberry blond Ligia and Patricia Laffan as a brunette Poppaea. The specific term used for Poppaea's hair in the novel also recalls the wording associated with Klara's, as the latter's tresses are identified as "golden" and not "blond." Thus both authors, one going against the grain of ethnic stereotyping, endow the embodiment of virginal purity with dark tresses, while the blond hair of the Whore of Babylon is labeled in a manner that symbolizes the empire's wealth and decadence. It is unfortunate that the two great national authors never had a chance to meet or even hear of each other. Šenoa, only eight years older than Sienkiewicz, died prematurely in 1881, before Sienkiewicz became Poland's favorite novelist. The father of the Croatian novel, who felt a connection with the Western Slavs and reported on the developments in Polish literature when he was the editor of *Vienac*, surely would have sought contact and praised Sienkiewicz's works in his journal. The two also would have found common ground in their opposition to the Germanization of their people.

Poppaea's evil scheming against Ligia and the Christians leads to the climactic moment of the novel. It takes place during the Ludi, in chapter 65, as Ursus, Ligia's gargantuan servant and bodyguard, a member of her own people, stands in the arena awaiting his death. Like other Christians and to the great disappointment of the entertainment-hungry crowd, he "postanowił zginąć, jak przystało na wyznawcę Baranka, spokojnie i cierpliwie" (decided to die as becomes a confessor of the Lamb, peacefully and patiently) (*QV* 3970). His plan is thwarted, however, by a sudden appearance in the arena of an aurochs with a naked Ligia tied to its horns. The scene is intensified by the presence of the distraught Vinicius in the audience. The site of his queen stretched out across the bull's body rouses Ursus to action and, after a prolonged struggle to hold the beast by the horns, he manages to break its neck. The audience goes wild as he picks up the fainted Ligia and lifts her up toward Caesar in a gesture imploring mercy, while Vinicius jumps over the barrier into the arena, covers her naked body with his toga, and exposes his chest scars to the crowd as a Roman war veteran. The narrator relates that "od czasu rozpoczęcia widowisk nie pamiętano takiego uniesienia" (since the beginning of spectacles such excitement was not remembered) (*QV* 3992) as the masses demand with increasing fury that Nero spare the lives of the two condemned and he is begrudgingly forced to comply.

Prior to the fire and the persecutions, when Vinicius and Ligia become engaged and Petronius, noticing a happy change in his nephew, asks, "Co ci się zdarzyło?" (What has happened?) (*QV* 2175), Vinicius answers thus: "Coś takiego, czego bym nie odstąpił za imperium rzymskie" (Something which I would not give for the Roman Empire) (2176). While such an expression is not uncommon, equivalent as it is to claiming that one would not give up one's beloved for the riches of the world, there is an additional significance to Vinicius's particular phrasing in the context of Poppaea's evil designs and her embodiment of Rome as the Whore of Babylon. His earlier rejection of Poppaea's advances anticipates and symbolizes his ultimate rejection of Rome and his place in it. Along the same lines, Ligia's eventual victory over Poppaea in the amphitheater is symbolic of Christianity's ultimate victory over Rome, which, as previously noted, constitutes the ending of the novel.

Happy Endings

The messianic theme of *Quo Vadis* slightly alters the theoretical paradigm of adulterous nations, as the love pair of Sienkiewicz's novel successfully overcome national, class, and religious boundaries in order to be together. Since the novel relies on a messianic theme, its moral message is not so much to guard against the foreigner as it is to bring him or her over to the other side. A nation or a religion that sees itself as the redeemer of the world has no reason to fear adulteration but rather sees itself in the function of a cleansing agent. It can, therefore, convert and absorb potential "pollutants," as Peter notes when he defends Ligia from Kryspus's condemnation. Ligia accepts Marcus on the condition that he convert to her religion, which absolves her of religious/national adultery. On the other hand, Marcus accepts a person of much lower rank, one who would otherwise only be fit for him as a concubine, but he gains immeasurably more than she does—eternal life, no less—in the exchange.

There are several ways in which this last chapter on *Quo Vadis* connects to *Middlemarch* and thus brings the entire book full circle. One is the happy ending, connected to the ability of both heroines, their societies, and ultimately the novels to absorb a person of difference. The prerequisite for this seems to be a penchant for martyrdom, which both heroines exhibit. While we might ultimately view Effi, Anna, and Dora as martyrs, none of them consciously entertain those fantasies or feed their imaginations on religious texts, as Dorothea and Ligia do. Unlike Dorothea, Ligia actually lives in perpetual danger of martyrdom, yet like Dorothea she does not eschew the idea of it. The line from *Quo Vadis* quoted previously, when Ligia is taken to Nero's palace and imagines herself "a martyr, with wounds on her feet and hands, white as the snows," ends with "i podobnymi widzeniami lubowała się jej wyobraźnia" (and her imagination delighted in similar visions) (*QV* 355). Dorothea is described in the beginning of *Middlemarch* as "likely to seek martyrdom, to make retractations, and then to incur martyrdom after all in a quarter where she had not sought it" (8). By the end, as suggested in chapter 1, she gets to live out the martyr fantasy on a smaller scale by giving up Casaubon's fortune and incurring the disapproval of her neighbors when she marries the novel's outsider. The English and the Polish heroines' martyr alter egos are built on two different biblical images, which reflect the difference between a large empire that sees itself in the function of "mother" to others—whether those others accept that notion or interpret it differently is another matter—and the subjugated nation interpreting its own suffering. Dorothea is associated with the Virgin Mary throughout *Middlemarch*, while Ligia is associated with Christ. The difference between these two images is analogous to the one that Berdiaev describes between Russian and Polish messiansim, and it can easily be extended more broadly into the difference between the messianism of any Christian empire, such as the British, and that of a subjugated nation, with the former "connected moreso with the intercession of the Mother of God" and the latter "with the path of Christ's sufferings." Both paths ultimately lead to victory, however, and if Ligia redeems Marcus's soul, then Dorothea redeems Will for England (while Will, in turn, satisfies her soul hunger). While Ladislaw could not be further from the brute that Marcus is in the first part of *Quo Vadis*, he is a lost man with no purpose in life and, like Marcus, is made better by the love of a good woman. By the end of *Middlemarch* Ladislaw is put to good use in the empire's service, just as Marcus is turned from an enemy of to an asset for the early Christians in *Quo Vadis*.

If Sienkiewicz's best-known novels had been written and translated before George Eliot died (in 1880), we could assume that the English author, who grew up on Sir Walter Scott's novels and endorsed the idea of nationality as "that sense of special belonging which is the root of human virtues,"[33] would have admired and promoted the Polish Walter Scott. Her observation that "it is this living force of sentiment in common which makes a national consciousness"[34] aptly describes the important role that Sienkiewicz's novels played for Poland. It is unfortunate that we have no record of Sienkiewicz ever having known of or having read Eliot, since his take on Will Ladislaw and other Poles in Eliot's fiction would have been extremely valuable. Suffice it to say that the heroines of *Middlemarch* and *Quo Vadis* would have understood each other very well.

Conclusion

The novels addressed in this study were written during what Benedict Anderson has so cleverly called the "heyday" of "the hyphen that for two hundred years yoked state and nation."[1] Their political milieu is part of the reason why the constellations of their love triangles lend themselves to national readings, more obviously in the novels of subjugated nations, whose primary purpose was to raise national consciousness, but also fairly easily in the mainstream novels of adultery, which reveal that managing an empire can be analogous to keeping a wife in order. The first chapter discussed the grandson of a Polish refugee who is himself initially an aimless wanderer through Europe and is compared (favorably) to a Gypsy by his good friend and the narrator herself while being conflated (unfavorably) with a Jew by his small-minded neighbors. What all three ethnic groups had in common at the time, as the chapter points out, was the lack of a homeland, but why one comparison is favorable and the other is not is instructive of national prejudices. As Deborah Nord has shown in her work, Gypsies were perceived as romantic in the British imagination, and if we can describe such a perception as benevolent racism, then what the English Jews experienced was hostile racism, exhibited in the novel through the manner in which Ladislaw gets slapped with the "label" once the town discovers that his stepgrandfather is an old thief. In her own "insistance on the idea of Nationalities" Eliot promoted the idea of a separate Jewish state, while for her Gypsy-like quarter Pole who had no reason to hope for one at the time she found not only a home, but a meaningful existence in England.

In utter contradiction to Eliot's idea that belonging to a nationality engenders human virtue, Tolstoy argued that patriotism was the opposite of peace.[2] Although he articulated that position almost twenty years after completing his novel of adultery, the seeds of it, as shown in chapter 3, are evident in the epilogue, where Levin feels no love for his Serbian "brothers of the same blood and faith" (*PSS* 19:387) but simply wishes to live in his "own tiny circle, if not well, then at least not badly" (*PSS* 20:571). In other words, the statelessness of the South Slavs and statelessness in general were of no concern to the great Russian moralist; it was, in fact, as he wrote to Sienkiewicz, the preferred mode of existence. Concomitantly, Tolstoy's heroine comes to a completely different end than Dorothea Brooke, whose author kills off the stifling husband instead. And, while it is commonplace to argue that the female author will inevitably feel compelled to grant an unhappily married woman a more generous ending—Eliot, after all, does the same for Gwendolen Harleth, whose sadistic husband drowns in *Daniel Deronda*—it is valuable to consider, within the framework of the present study, how these differing endings affect the nation. Ladislaw, though initially only inspired by the prospect of proximity to Dorothea, works with her uncle on behalf of reform, which Eliot supported. Vronsky, on the other hand, joins a war that Tolstoy condemned.

If Eliot welcomed the dispossessed in *Middlemarch*, while Tolstoy exhibited an active disregard for statelessness in *Anna Karenina*, then Theodor Fontane entirely ignored the problem in *Effi Briest*, the novel whose analysis in this book is conveniently couched between the masterworks of two large empires that were the source of German envy. Yes, he puts high Prussian society to shame in his portrayal of Roswitha, since the character whose name bears the colors of the Polish flag proves to be the most faithful person in the novel focused on unfaithfulness, but he also depicts Effi's marital aspirations as colonial fantasy, which is not critiqued as such but is meant to elicit the reader's pity for the naive child-bride. Kristin Kopp's distinction between "inner" and "outer" German colonialism proved helpful in discussing the novel whose half-Polish seducer takes over the role of a Chinese ghost. Unlike Catherine the Great, who subjugated Poland, though, the mini-Catherine who demanded a fur coat and expected to see a polar bear on the Baltic Sea coast becomes the victim of an unscrupulous seducer whom she did not even love.

Statelessness was *the* issue of the last two novels covered in this book and possibly their raison d'être, all the more interesting for how the two authors approached it differently. Unlike Sienkiewicz, Šenoa did not have a glorious Croatian past to look back on and revive in the minds of his readers, but he nevertheless used significant historical events from the sixteenth century to discuss nineteenth-century oppression by foreign rule. He saw the solution, as did many of his predecessors and contemporaries, in multiple layers of unity: linguistic—not just within Croatia, but Croatia's with the other speakers of South Slavic languages (save the Bulgarians, whose large number, he argued, would assure them their own state)—literary, since the anthologies he edited included Croatian and Serbian works, and political, in the form of what would become Yugoslavia after World War I brought the age of empires to an end.

Sienkiewicz, in recalling Poland's past glory as well as in allegorizing its current suffering, wrote the empire-size novels, comparable in length to the English and Russian masterpieces of the nineteenth century, as opposed to the German and Croatian ones. True to the theme of Polish messianism that characterized the preceding period of romanticism, he fashioned a heroine who was not so much in need of rescue by a good-hearted nobleman, as the fragile Dora of Šenoa's novel, but one who is capable of redeeming the enemy. Ligia's redemption of a Roman warrior highlights the difference between the messianism of the oppressed and that of the oppressor or, to recall Nikolai Berdiaev's words quoted in chapter 5, the difference between sacrifice and dominance. As Eliot demonstrates in *Middlemarch*, however, the lines do not have to be tightly drawn, since her English heroine has much more in common with the Polish one than with either from the other two empires covered in this book.

While this study has focused on Europe and nations within it that are geographically close to each other if not contiguous, the investigation could be extended into other parts of the world, such as the United States, for example, a fascinating case of a colony turned (a twentieth-century version of) empire. The two best-known American novels of adultery flank the second half of the nineteenth century, with Nathaniel Hawthorne's *The Scarlet Letter* in 1850 and Kate Chopin's *The Awakening* in 1899. They each come with their own national anxieties related to parts of the Old World, against which they must define themselves,[3] and it would be interesting to explore how these anxieties play out in their love triangles. It is the crossing from England to Massachusetts that occasions the adultery of *The Scarlet Letter*, as it first separates the heroine from her husband and then leaves her thinking, alone in the New World, that he had been killed by Native Americans at the end of his voyage over. In *The Awakening* two different sets of transplants from the Old World clash as the Anglo-American Edna Pontellier, "though she had married a Creole, was not thoroughly at home in the society of Creoles."[4] Unlike *The Scarlet Letter*, *The Awakening* includes the additional difference in religion, since the young Edna had to contend with "the violent opposition of her father and her sister Margaret to her marriage with a Catholic."[5] Much like the first marriage of Dorothea Brooke in *Middlemarch*, Edna's is an act of defiance against her concerned family, yet in the end it proves untenable.

Crossing into the twentieth century and the burst of literary activity that characterized the 1920s, in the United States Edith Wharton selects a Europeanized divorcée of a brutish Polish count to threaten scandal in New York society of the 1870s, while in England D. H. Lawrence pens *Lady Chatterley's Lover*, a novel whose heroine turns to a wealthy Irishman and ultimately to an impoverished Englishman for what her paralyzed aristocratic husband cannot give her. It is of note that after ending an affair with an Irishman who "had already made a large fortune by his plays in America" but "obviously wasn't an Englishman, in spite of all the tailors, hatters, barbers, booters of the very best quarters of London," Connie Chatterley decides that her next lover will be "a real foreigner: not an Englishman, still less an Irishman."[6] The "real foreigner," however, the lover to whom the single noun in the novel's title refers, turns out to be a gamekeeper from Derby who can code-switch between his vernacular and the "ordinary," "natural," or "normal English," which Connie prefers over "getting his meaning through the fog of the dialect."[7] In Germany, whose literature reenters the world scene through Thomas Mann, the Russian, "leicht asiatischer" (slightly Asiatic),[8] Clawdia Chauchat mesmerizes the visitor into staying on the Magic Mountain and a charming Polish boy captivates a middle-aged author until he meets his death in Venice. It is interesting, in relation to the nations covered in this book, that Aschenbach's first destination is Slavic—a northern Croatian island "mit farbig zerlumptem, in wilde-fremden Lauten redendem Landvolk" (with a colorfully ragged local population that talked in wild-foreign sounds)[9]—but he quickly discovers that he cannot bear "eine kleinweltliche, geschlossen österreichische Hotelgesellschaft" (a provincial and self-contained Austrian society in the hotel) and moves on to Venice.

Writing in 1996 for an edited collection of over a century's worth of essays theorizing the nation, Anderson briefly pondered "two new guises" of nationalism emerging at the end of the twentieth century: "the creation of a congeries of weak, economically fragile nation-states out of the debris of the Soviet system" and "the impending crisis of the hyphen."[10] During my writing of this book, the debris of former Soviet states could be acutely felt in the crisis between Ukraine and Russia, to which I return at the very end. The crisis happening during Anderson's writing in the mid-1990s, though he curiously omitted mentioning it, was the violent dissolution of Yugoslavia, illustrated also through a sexual metaphor by Ferida Duraković in the poem that comprises the epigraph of this study. The grammatical gender in the Bosnian (as well as in the Croatian and Serbian) language allows for an easy equation of the Homeland with the deceiving beauty, since the word *homeland* is feminine: *domovina*. Grammatical gender is yet another category that contributes to the anthropomorphizing of nations as female, because in most languages that have it "homeland" is feminine, as are, for the most part, names of countries and continents. To review the word for "homeland" in the other three languages from the novels covered in this book—English being exempt for its lack of grammatical gender—the German *Heimat*, the Russian *rodina*, and the Polish *ojczyzna* are also all feminine, despite the fact that the last one doubles as "fatherland," as the Polish word for "father" is *ojciec*.

The deceiving attribute of the beauty in Duraković's poem is self-evident, since Yugoslavia, in the end, proved to be a deceptive concept. If it is the deceptive and disappearing Homeland that galvanizes "boys" to die for her, then we might assume that this Bosnian poet writing about the war in Croatia—the fall of the town of Vukovar, to be precise[11]—has Serbian boys in mind, since they were the ones engaged to fight the states that had declared independence from the Homeland. I find this aspect of the poem particularly touching, since the typical objects of pity tend to be the innocent civilian casualties of war, whereas here—one of the only such instances in writing about the Yugoslav wars of succession[12]—sympathy is expressed for the "boys" who have been seduced by the impassioned rhetoric of patriotism, which is exposed beautifully for its sexual connotations. The "beast" from the poem's title, unlike the "beauty," receives no further mention in the poem itself and, hence, acquires no analogous political entity within it. We can only surmise, based on the context, that the beast might refer to the war machine or, based on the marriage metaphor, to the latter half of the nation-state combination, with the concept of the homeland being more akin to nation. If the fairy tale to which the poem's title refers depicts an innocent beauty whose love tames the beast and turns him into a prince, then Duraković's deceptive beauty does the opposite, feeding the state/beast's aggression by supplying it with willing soldiers.[13]

The rhetoric surrounding Yugoslavia's breakup, both from within the country and from the outside powers, bore an eerie resemblance to the Eastern Crisis of the 1870s, all the more for the fact that Ottoman memory was invoked in the ethnic cleansing that took place in Bosnia and Kosovo. Russia, once again, felt compelled to protect its Serbian Orthodox brothers, whether it be from the secessionism that seemed to have infected the other Yugoslav republics or from Western involvement, including NATO's bombing of Serbia in 1999. Russian support did not result in the mobilization of thousands of military volunteers and an eventual war declaration as it did in Tolstoy's time, but there were Russian veterans, estimated possibly in the hundreds by the BBC, who did go over to join the fight.[14] The most celebrated among them was the recently deceased Lieutenant Colonel Anatoly Lebed', a veteran of the wars in Afghanistan and Chechnya whose heroic feats earned him the nickname "Russkii Rembo" (Russian Rambo). After NATO forces attacked Serbia, Lebed' came out of retirement and traveled to Belgrade on a tourist visa. To the news crew cameras asking him for his reasons, he gave a succinct answer that echoes those of the Slavophiles discussed in chapter 3: "соседей, товарищей наших православных давят" (our Orthodox neighbors and comrades are being crushed).[15] We can easily imagine what the sage from Iasnaia Poliana would have had to say on this occasion, not only to the Russians or the Serbs, but equally to the seceding republics demanding their own independent states. It is safe to assume that no side would have been satisfied with his answer. Nevertheless, his assessment of the "суеверие патриотизма" (superstition of patriotism) (*PSS* 37:241, 90:44) and, in its harsher incarnations, the "гипноз" (hypnosis) (*PSS* 90:443), "вред" (harm) (*PSS* 90:425), and especially "обман" (deception) (*PSS* 90:441, 443) of patriotism, "в котором так усердно стараются удержать их все правительства" (in which so diligently all governments strive to hold [their people]) (*PSS* 90:441), is compatible with the sentiment of Duraković's poem.[16] My book about the novel of adultery as an expression of national anxieties also turns out to be largely about the superstition of patriotism, which causes everything from malicious gossip in *Middlemarch* to duels in several of Fontane's novels to war in *Anna Karenina*.

If Russian involvement was welcomed by Serbia at the very end of the twentieth century, it certainly was not by Ukraine in the second decade of the twenty-first. In March 2014, as Russia annexed Crimea in reaction to Ukraine's Euromaidan Revolution, *The Atlantic* (along with many other news venues) reported in a headline, "Ukrainian Women Have Launched a Sex Strike Against Russian Men."[17] Two Ukrainian women, Irina Rubis and Katerina Venzhik, launched the campaign on Facebook and had T-shirts made with the image that quickly circulated the globe: a pair of hands folded as if in prayer, except that the widening gap between the palms creates an image of a vagina. The slogan underneath the pair of hands reads, *Ne dai Russkomu* (Don't give it to a Russian), with an asterisk at the end, which is explained by a line of poetry along the right edge of the image: *Kokhaitesia, chornobryvi, ta ne z Moskaliamy* (Fall in love, o dark-browed ones, only not with Muscovites). It points out that the phrase "Don't give it to a Russian" was inspired by Ukraine's national poet, the anti-imperial Taras Shevchenko, who penned the verse as part of his long 1838 poem, "Kateryna."

The Atlantic article described the campaign as "a strategy as old the time" and invoked the eponymous ancient Greek heroine from Aristophanes' *Lysistrata*, who brought the Peloponnesian War to an end by leading her fellow women in a sex strike against their husbands. The important point that this comparison misses, however, lies in the very aspect of sex that this book has sought to explore—the national allegories it can represent, as in the case of Ukrainian women refusing Russian men, which is a gesture symbolic of Ukraine's refusal of Putin. Clarence A. Manning got it right in the introduction to his English translation of the poem when, in addition to remarking that "the theme of the country girl seduced by a nobleman and deserted by him was very popular in all European literature," he takes care to point out that "Shevchenko followed the tradition in this poem but he added the other idea of making the lover a foreigner."[18] That "other idea of making the lover a foreigner" has been at the center of my study, though Shevchenko's poem demonstrates that it predates the second half of the nineteenth century, in which the novel of adultery and its "fear of the foreigner"—to use Julian Preece's assessment of *Effi Briest* from chapter 2—proliferated.

When the two founders of the Ukrainian campaign were asked in an interview by the American *Elle* magazine, "Why did you decide to choose sex as the center of the campaign?," they answered in a way that caused me to further ponder the implications of my book project:

> First of all, the slogan on the T-shirts is not about sex. This is a claim to protect our country from aggressor.
>
> But sex is known for being one of the most effective elements of [gaining] substantial attention to promo campaigns. To use a provocative message to claim the world's attention and interest to the Russians' aggression was one of [the most] effective ways to be heard.[19]

Adulterous Nations is not about sex, the surface-present topic of the classic nineteenth-century novel of adultery that explored adulterous

"Ne dai Russkomu" ("Don't give it to a Russian"), Facebook campaign, March 2014

sex as a means of dealing with the broader anxiety surrounding women's emancipation. Rather, the focus of my study has been the "aggressor" against the heroine and, more broadly, the nation that she embodies.

Sex is, indeed, "one of the most effective elements of [gaining] substantial attention to promo campaigns," and I have sought to elucidate how it dovetailed in the novel of adultery with the age of imperialism and national revivals. There is no doubt that in writing *Middlemarch*, as Gillian Beer argues, George Eliot "brooded on the curtailment of women's lives,"[20] but in fashioning a character of "dangerously mixed blood" for the heroine's fulfillment, she captured the nation's sympathy with the suffering Poles while at the same time critiquing its insularity. Tolstoy's "provocative message" included the portrayal of adulterous sex as murder but placing Anna's lover-cum-murderer at the train station in the epilogue, where he remembers Anna's mangled body on the way to war, was "one of [the most] effective ways" that the author's opposition to the war could "be heard" (once it finally made it into print). The ambivalent Theodor Fontane, on the other hand, stoked Prussian prejudices in his utterly unromantic portrayal of Effi's half-Polish lover while inspiring magnanimity and sympathy through her kindly servant, Roswitha. August Šenoa, as Julijana Matanović shows, sought a balance between Croatian historical events and the invented love story "by which he made the novels more interesting and acceptable to the wider populace."[21] Henryk Sienkiewicz, finally, uplifted the quashed Polish national spirit and brought the Polish sufferings to "the world's attention" through a heroine who manages to tame a megalomaniacal "aggressor."

NOTES

Introduction

1. "Прелюбодеяние есть не только любимая, но и единственная тема всех романов." From chapter 9 of *What Is Art?* (*Что такое искусство?*), in Lev Nikolaevich Tolstoy, *Polnoe sobranie sochinenii* (*PSS*), 90 vols. (Moscow: Gosudarstvennoe izdatel'stvo khudzhestvennoi literatury, 1928–58), 30:88. Further references are to this edition (*PSS*) and will be given by volume and page number in the text.

2. Herbert Lottman, *Flaubert: A Biography* (London: Methuen, 1989), 137. In addition to Flaubert, the editors of the journal *Revue de Paris* were also the targets of the lawsuit, but all parties were acquitted on February 7, 1857.

3. In a book chapter titled "The Miserable Marriages in *Middlemarch, Anna Karenina,* and *Effi Briest*," Barbara Hardy attributes England's lack of an adultery novel to "the cultural difference, which inhibited the representation of adultery in English Victorian fiction, as both Thackeray and Henry James complained." She concludes, "An English novel's heroine as sympathetic as Edith Newcome or Dorothea . . . could not be led or driven to adultery, but she could be in Russian and German novels." In *George Eliot and Europe*, ed. John Rignall (Brookfield, Vt.: Scolar Press, 1997), 69.

4. George Eliot, *Middlemarch* (New York: Oxford University Press, 1997), 195–96. Further references to *Middlemarch* are to this edition and appear in the text.

5. I have the anonymous Reader 3 for Northwestern University Press to thank for this wonderful phrase.

6. August Šenoa, *The Goldsmith's Treasure*, trans. Neven Divjakinja (Zagreb: Spiritoso, 2015.)

7. Georg Lukács, *Theory of the Novel: A Historico-Philosophical Essay on the Forms of Great Epic Literature*, trans. Anna Bostock (Cambridge: Cambridge University Press, 1971), 41. Lukács's omission of Sienkiewicz, the internationally recognized master of the novelistic epic, is particularly surprising.

8. One study that is contemporary to Tanner's but was far less favorably received is Judith Armstrong's *The Novel of Adultery* (London: Macmillan, 1976). The two more recent ones I have in mind are Bill Overton's *The Novel of Female Adultery: Love and Gender in Continental European Fiction, 1830–1890* (Basingstoke: Macmillan, 1996) and Maria Rippon's *Judgment and Justification in the Nineteenth-Century Novel of Adultery* (Westport, Conn.: Greenwood Press, 2002). The former contains useful sociological information

regarding the Woman Question (the effect of declining birthrates, for example), but the latter discusses Russia with the language of backwardness that appears out of place in contemporary academic discourse, relies on English translations of its non-English-language novels, and even gets part of Tolstoy's name wrong in the bibliography, listing Ilich instead of Nikolaevich as his patronymic.

9. Tony Tanner, *Adultery in the Novel: Contract and Transgression* (Baltimore, Md.: Johns Hopkins University Press, 1979), 12.

10. See Naomi Ritter's review in *Comparative Literature Studies* 19 (1982): 390–93.

11. Tanner, *Adultery in the Novel*, 13.

12. Tanner, *Adultery in the Novel*, 221.

13. Tanner, *Adultery in the Novel*, 12.

14. Benedict Anderson, *Imagined Communities: Reflections on the Origin and Spread of Nationalism* (London: Verso, 1983), 5.

15. Ernest Gellner, "The Coming of Nationalism and Its Interpretation: The Myths of Nation and Class," in *Mapping the Nation*, ed. Gopal Balakrishnan (London: Verso, 1996), 127; emphasis Gellner's.

16. Eric Hobsbawm, "Mass-Producing Traditions: Europe, 1870–1914," in *The Invention of Tradition*, ed. Eric Hobsbawm and Terence Ranger (Cambridge: Cambridge University Press, 1992), 264–65.

17. Hannah Arendt, *Origins of Totalitarianism* (New York: Harcourt, Brace & World, 1966), 163.

18. Friedrich von Schiller, *Letters on the Aesthetic Education of Man*, in *Critical Theory since Plato*, rev. ed., ed. Hazard Adams (Fort Worth, Tex.: Harcourt Brace Jovanovich College Publishers, 1992), 422 (note 5).

19. Hobsbawm, "Mass-Producing Traditions," 268.

20. Arendt, *Origins of Totalitarianism*, 169.

21. Tanner, *Adultery in the Novel*, 235. Regarding the enormity of Flaubert's influence and his novel's generative potential, of note is Priscilla Meyer's article "*Anna Karenina*: Tolstoy's Polemic with *Madame Bovary*," *Russian Review* 54 (1995): 243–59.

22. Gustave Flaubert, *Madame Bovary* (Paris: Gallimard, 1972), 376.

23. Arendt, *Origins of Totalitarianism*, 162. She notes how Boulainvilliers's division of the French nation into the Germanic Franks and the subjugated Gauls indicates that, "paradoxical as it sounds, the fact is that Frenchmen were to insist earlier than Germans or Englishmen on this *idée fixe* of German superiority" (164–65).

24. Arendt, *Origins of Totalitarianism*, 165.

25. Hobsbawm, "Mass-Producing Traditions," 278.

26. A former student of mine, Mary Lingwall, wrote an excellent paper in which she argued that precisely because of the critique of the middle class and its desire for wealth accumulation in *Madame Bovary*, Tolstoy's novella *The Death of Ivan Ilyich*—whose protagonist dies of an injury sustained from a fall during the hanging of curtains in his brand-new house—makes a better companion to Flaubert's novel than *Anna Karenina*.

27. George Eliot, *Impressions of Theophrastus Such*, ed. Nancy Henry (Iowa City: University of Iowa Press, 1994), 160.

28. Anderson, *Imagined Communities*, 5.

29. Gellner, "The Coming of Nationalism and Its Interpretation," 110.

30. Too many books to enumerate have been written on this topic, particularly on the Indo-British relationship, which has perhaps more than any other been cast in terms of rape. I would just like to mention my favorite study on the topic, Jenny Sharpe's *Allegories of Empire: The Figure of Woman in the Colonial Text* (Minneapolis: University of Minnesota Press, 1993).

31. Maria Todorova, *Imagining the Balkans* (New York: Oxford University Press, 1997), 16.

32. Todorova, *Imagining the Balkans*, 17.

33. Todorova, *Imagining the Balkans*, 16.

34. Larry Wolff, *Inventing Eastern Europe: The Map of Civilization on the Mind of the Enlightenment* (Stanford, Calif.: Stanford University Press, 1994), 7, 22.

35. Tanner, *Adultery in the Novel*, 12: "*Adulteration* implies pollution, contamination, a 'base admixture,' a wrong combination."

36. Todorova, *Imagining the Balkans*, 17.

37. Andrzej Walicki, *Philosophy and Romantic Nationalism: The Case of Poland* (New York: Clarendon, 1982), 5.

38. I use George Rapall Noyes's 1917 translation: *Pan Tadeusz or the Last Foray in Lithuania: A Story of Life among Polish Gentlefolk in the Years 1811 and 1812* (New York: Mondial, 2009), 9. His and Jewell Parish's translation of the title of Mickiewicz's other, shorter poem—"Do Matki Polki"—I think misses the point with "To a Polish Mother."

39. Ojdana Koharević, "Nakon 60 godina otkrivena tajna smrti autora pjesme 'Rajska djevo, kraljice Hrvata,'" *Slobodna Dalmacija*, May 15, 2010, accessed Dec. 10, 2013, http://www.slobodnadalmacija.hr/Split-županija/tabid/76/articleType/ArticleView/articleId/ 102669/Default.aspx. The original version of the song begins with "Zdravo" (Hello), instead of "Rajska," but this greeting carries Yugo-Communist connotations and was therefore changed.

40. Regarding the idea of "Mother England," I want to point out Cannon Schmitt's study *Alien Nation: Nineteenth-Century Gothic Fictions and English Nationality* (Philadelphia: University of Pennsylvania Press, 1997), which performs a theoretical twist similar to mine when reading novels of adultery as symptomatic of national anxieties. Schmitt takes the English gothic, which has frequently been read as confronting repressed female sexuality, and reads it as "a nationalist narrative in miniature" (11).

41. Quoted in Gordon A. Craig, *Theodor Fontane: Literature and History in the Bismarck Reich* (New York: Oxford University Press, 1999), 108.

42. Walicki, *Philosophy and Romantic Nationalism*, 2; emphases mine.

43. This discussion occurred on September 4, 2008, and can be accessed by the listserv subscribers in the SEELANGS Archive: https://listserv.ua.edu/cgi-bin/wa?S2=SEELANGS&m=32387&I=-3&L=SEELANGS&X-=6594E170409737D6A2&a=august+2008&b=october+2008&d=No+-Match%3BMatch%3BMatches&q=russia+she+or+it

44. Hobsbawm, "Mass-Producing Traditions," 272.

45. Hobsbawm, "Mass-Producing Traditions," 276.

46. Tolstoy makes a strong point of this when he describes how a real painter feels about Vronsky's work, even employing the word *смешно* (ridiculous), while simultaneously taking the opportunity to draw an analogy to Anna and Vronsky's

inauthentic relationship: "Он знал, что нельзя запретить Вронскому баловать живописью; он знал, что он и все дилетанты имели полное право писать что им угодно, но ему было неприятно. Нельзя запретить человеку сделать себе большую куклу из воска и целовать ее. Но если б этот человек с куклой пришел и сел пред влюбленным и принялся бы ласкать свою куклу, как влюбленный ласкает ту которую он любит, то влюбленному было бы неприятно. Такое же неприятно чувство испытывал Михайлов при виде живописи Вронского; ему было и смешно, и досадно, и жалко, и оскорбительно" (He knew he could not forbid Vronsky to toy with painting; he knew that he and all the dilettantes had a perfect right to paint what they pleased, but he found it unpleasant. One cannot forbid a man to make himself a big wax doll and kiss it. But if this man with the doll were to come and sit before a man in love and begin caressing his doll the way the man in love caressed the one he loved, the man in love would find it unpleasant. Mikhailov experienced the very same unpleasant feeling at the sight of Vronsky's painting; he found it ridiculous, and annoying, and pathetic, and offensive) (*PSS* 19:47).

47. To demonstrate just how far this idea can be taken in places like contemporary Texas, consider the following report by *New York Times* columnist Gail Collins: "There are a couple of conservative-versus-crazy Republican school board primaries, and the results may influence a pending war over requiring social studies students to learn how Moses impacted the founding fathers." February 21, 2014, http://www.nytimes.com/2014/02/22/opinion/collins-texas-strikes-again.html?hp&rref=opinion&_r=1.

48. William E. Gerard Winstanley, "The True Levellers' Standard" (1649), quoted in Laura Doyle, "'A' for Atlantic: The Colonizing Force of Hawthorne's *The Scarlet Letter*," *American Literature* 79 (2007): 250.

49. Conrad Cherry, ed., *God's New Israel: Religious Interpretations of American Destiny* (Englewood Cliffs, N.J.: Prentice Hall, 1971), 65.

50. Eliot, *Impressions*, 150.

51. Eliot, *Impressions*, 150.

52. Milica Bakić-Hayden, "Nesting Orientalisms: The Case of Former Yugoslavia," *Slavic Review* 54 (1995): 918.

53. Julia Kristeva, *Strangers to Ourselves*, in *The Portable Kristeva*, ed. Kelly Oliver (New York: Columbia University Press, 2002), 282. A similar gradation can be depicted in the United States as well. While the North may collectively look down on the South, in the South residents of Georgia tell incest jokes about their neighbors from Alabama, while these in turn reply that if it were not for Alabama, Georgia would have to suffer the indignity of being neighbors with Mississippi.

54. Wolff, *Inventing Eastern Europe*, 15.

55. Quoted in Catherine Brown's "Why Does Daniel Deronda's Mother Live in Russia?," *George Eliot-George Henry Lewes Studies* 58–59 (2010): 28.

Chapter 1

1. Deborah Nord has a chapter on George Eliot in her book, *Gypsies and the British Imagination, 1807–1930* (New York: Columbia University Press, 2006); quote on 107.

2. My information on the two Reform Bills comes from Clayton Roberts, David Roberts, and Douglas R. Bisson, *A History of England,* vol. 2: *1688 to the Present* (Upper Saddle River, N.J.: Prentice Hall, 2002), 572–615.

3. Some of the publications on colonialism and the role of Germany in Eliot's fiction will be referred to throughout the chapter. The monograph on Italy is Andrew Thompson, *George Eliot and Italy: Literary, Cultural and Political Influences from Dante to the Risorgimento* (New York: St. Martin's Press, 1998).

4. Karen Chase, Introduction to *Middlemarch in the Twenty-First Century,* ed. Karen Chase (Oxford: Oxford University Press, 2006), 3.

5. See, e.g., Gillian Beer, "'Middlemarch' and 'The Woman Question,'" in *Middlemarch, George Eliot,* ed. John Peck (Basingstoke: Macmillan, 1992), 155–81; and Kathleen Blake, "*Middlemarch* and the Woman Question," *Nineteenth-Century Fiction* 31 (1976): 285–312.

6. To name only two of the many articles that engage this angle of the novel, see Lilian R. Furst, "Struggling for Reform in *Middlemarch,*" *Nineteenth-Century Literature* 48 (1993): 341–61; and Mark Wormald, "Microscopy and Semiotic in *Middlemarch,*" *Nineteenth-Century Literature* 50 (1996): 501–24.

7. See George Levine, *Darwin and the Novelists: Patterns of Science in Victorian Fiction* (Cambridge, Mass.: Harvard University Press, 1988); and Gillian Beer, *Darwin's Plots: Evolutionary Narrative in Darwin, George Eliot, and Nineteenth-Century Fiction* (Cambridge: Cambridge University Press, 2000).

8. Edward Said, *Orientalism* (New York: Vintage Books, 1979), 12.

9. Wolff, *Inventing Eastern Europe,* 4.

10. Said, *Orientalism,* 18–19; *Middlemarch,* 207.

11. Wolff, *Inventing Eastern Europe,* 359.

12. Wolff, *Inventing Eastern Europe,* 331.

13. Gordon S. Haight, ed., *The George Eliot Letters,* 9 vols. (New Haven, Conn.: Yale University Press, 1954–78), 5:441.

14. Henry James, review of *Middlemarch,* by George Eliot, *Galaxy* 15 (March 1873): 424–28. James's review can currently be found in *George Eliot: Critical Assessments,* vol. 1: *Biography, Nineteenth-Century Reviews and Responses,* ed. Stuart Hutchinson (East Sussex, U.K.: Helm Information, 1996).

15. Jerome Beaty's article on this topic is "The Forgotten Past of Will Ladislaw," *Nineteenth-Century Fiction* 13 (1958): 159–63.

16. Nord, *Gypsies and the British Imagination,* 105.

17. From one of the rare essays that defend Will Ladislaw, especially against doubts pertaining to his masculinity, Gordon S. Haight's "George Eliot's 'Eminent Failure,' Will Ladislaw," in *This Particular Web,* ed. Ian Adam (Toronto: University of Toronto Press, 1975), 24.

18. David Malcolm, "What Is a Pole Doing in *Middlemarch*?," *George Eliot Fellowship Review* 17 (1986): 66.

19. See Peter Brock, "Polish Democrats and English Radicals, 1832–1862: A Chapter in the History of Anglo-Polish Relations," *Journal of Modern History* 25 (1953): 139–56.

20. For more on Russia's suppression of the uprising, consult Nicholas Riasanovsky and Mark Steinberg's *A History of Russia,* 7th ed. (New York: Oxford University Press, 2005).

21. Andrew Halliday, "Beggars," in Henry Mayhew, *London Labour and the London Poor; A Cyclopaedia of the Condition and Earnings of Those That "Will" Work, Those That "Cannot" Work, and Those That "Will Not" Work: Those That Will Not Work, Comprising Prostitutes, Thieves, Swindlers, Beggars* (London: Griffin, Bohn, and Co., 1862), 419. Mayhew's series of articles, published in the *Morning Chronicle* in the 1840s, was compiled into a three-volume book in 1851; the supplementary fourth volume appeared in 1862. My use of "Polish fever" and "fair sex" is borrowed from Halliday.

22. Mayhew, *London Labour and the Poor*, 420–21.

23. Mayhew, *London Labour and the Poor*, 421.

24. Mayhew, *London Labour and the Poor*, 423.

25. George Eliot, *Scenes of Clerical Life*, ed. Graham Handley (Ware, U.K.: Wordsworth Editions, 2007), 33. Further references are to this edition and appear in the text.

26. Haight, "George Eliot's 'Eminent Failure,'" 37.

27. David L. Smith, "Will Ladislaw's Polish Ancestry," *Polish Anglo-Saxon Studies* 3–4 (1992): 57.

28. Haight, *The George Eliot Letters*, 4:102.

29. Haight, *The George Eliot Letters*, 4:117.

30. Haight, *The George Eliot Letters*, 5:89.

31. Smith, "Will Ladislaw's Polish Ancestry," 61.

32. This information comes from John F. Kutolowski's "Mid-Victorian Public Opinion, Polish Propaganda, and the Uprising of 1863," *Journal of British Studies* 8 (1969): 86–110. Kutolowski does not discuss *Middlemarch* or suggest that Count Ladislas Zamoyski could have served as a model for Will Ladislaw; that inference is my own.

33. Brock, "Polish Democrats and English Radicals," 146.

34. Information on the rulers and their accomplishments is from Anita J. Prażmowska's *A History of Poland* (Houndmills, U.K.: Palgrave Macmillan, 2004).

35. Haight, "George Eliot's 'Eminent Failure,'" 37.

36. Nancy Henry, *George Eliot and the British Empire* (Cambridge: Cambridge University Press, 2002), 73. Rosemarie Bodenheimer's book is *The Real Life of Marian Evans: George Eliot, Her Letters, and Her Fiction* (Ithaca, N.Y.: Cornell University Press, 1994).

37. Henry, *George Eliot and the British Empire*, 4.

38. Haight, *The George Eliot Letters*, 4:117.

39. George Eliot, "A Word for the Germans," in *Selected Critical Writings*, ed. Rosemary Ashton (Oxford: Oxford University Press, 1992), 335.

40. Rosemary Ashton, *The German Idea: Four English Writers and the Reception of German Thought, 1800–1860* (Cambridge: Cambridge University Press, 1980), 153.

41. Ashton, *The German Idea*, 148. Eliot's second major publication was also a translation of a German work, Ludwig Feuerbach's *The Essence of Christianity* (1841), which came out in 1854.

42. Eliot, "A Word for the Germans," 334–35.

43. Eliot, "A Word for the Germans," 333.

44. Malcolm, "What Is a Pole Doing in Middlemarch?," 66–67.

45. Ashton, Introduction to *Selected Critical Writings*, xxv.

46. Beer, *Darwin's Plots*, 239.

47. Beer, *Darwin's Plots*, 140.

48. Eliot, *Middlemarch*, 3; Beer, *Darwin's Plots*, 139.

49. Herbert Spencer, *The Principles of Biology*, vol. 1 (New York: D. Appleton and Co., 1904), 541.

50. Spencer, *The Principles of Biology*, 456. To be fair to Spencer, although this hardly diminishes the impact of racial measurements in the nineteenth century, he relates jaw size to nutritional habits and goes on to write in the same footnote that "the Australian and Negro jaws are thus strongly contrasted, not with all British jaws, but only with the jaws of the civilized British." Also, in a much later work, *Factors of Organic Evolution* (1886), he denounced the jaw/brain correlation.

51. These come from Wolff's *Inventing Eastern Europe*; see p. 307 for Hegel, p. 315 for Herder, and p. 334 for Fichte.

52. Wolff, *Inventing Eastern Europe*, 342–43. Wolff claims that the attribution of the pamphlet's authorship to Frederick the Great is erroneous, but I would add that it points to how well known Prussian hostility to Poland was at the time.

53. Wolff, *Inventing Eastern Europe*, 333.

54. Nancy L. Paxton, *George Eliot and Herbert Spencer: Feminism, Evolutionism, and the Reconstruction of Gender* (Princeton, N.J.: Princeton University Press, 1991), 180.

55. Paxton, *George Eliot and Herbert Spencer*, 176.

56. For a history of the novel's compilation, see Jerome Beaty, *Middlemarch: From Notebook to Novel* (Urbana: University of Illinois Press, 1960). To be precise, Lydgate appears in *Middlemarch* prior to chapter 15, in chapters 11–13, but chapter 15 is one where the narrator "make[s] the new settler Lydgate better known" (132), and Eliot devotes the entirety of the chapter to his life story.

57. Anonymous, review of *Middlemarch*, by George Eliot, *Saturday Review* 34 (December 7, 1872): 733–74.

58. According to Paul Robert Magocsi, *Historical Atlas of East Central Europe* (Toronto: University of Toronto Press, 1993), 219,000 Jews lived in Warsaw by 1900, making up one-third (32.5 percent) of the city's population.

59. See Robert A. Greenberg, "The Heritage of Will Ladislaw," *Nineteenth-Century Fiction* 15 (1961): 355–58; and Thomas Pinney, "Another Note on the Forgotten Past of Will Ladislaw," *Nineteenth-Century Fiction* 17 (1962): 69–73.

60. Pinney, "Another Note," 71.

61. Eliot, *Daniel Deronda*, ed. Terence Cave (London: Penguin Books, 1995), 241. Further references are to this edition and appear in the text.

62. In chapter 22 Klesmer is described as "not yet a Liszt" (238) and compared to Mendelssohn (240). Franz Liszt as the main inspiration for Eliot's fashioning of Herr Klesmer has been well documented, especially in Gerlinde Röder-Bolton's book, *George Eliot in Germany, 1854–55: "Cherished Memories"* (Aldershot: Ashgate, 2006); see chapter 4, "Franz Liszt and His Circle."

63. See Pinney's "Another Note" for a review of these. Bernard Semmel might have been influenced by these arguments as well when he proposed the young

Benjamin Disraeli as a possible model for Ladislaw in his work, *George Eliot and the Politics of National Inheritance* (New York: Oxford University Press, 1994), 98.

64. James, review of *Middlemarch*, 426.

65. Röder-Bolton, *George Eliot in Germany*, 4.

66. It is important to keep in mind here that Liszt, being Hungarian and therefore Eastern European, was not, however, Slavic. The two categories are frequently conflated because the majority of Eastern Europe is Slavic. There are several exceptions, however: Hungary, Romania, Albania, and the Baltic States (Estonia, Latvia, Lithuania) have geographically and politically been considered Eastern European, but they are ethnically not Slavic.

67. The essay, published in June 1855, following Eliot's first trip to Germany, ends with her recollection of "Wagner operas presided over by Liszt." *Fraser's Magazine for Town and Country* 51 (1855): 699–706.

68. Kovalevskaya visited Eliot one more time shortly before the latter's death. The Russian scholar's impressions of the English author were translated and published by Raymond Chapman and Eleanora Gottlieb under the title "A Russian View of George Eliot," in *Nineteenth-Century Fiction* 33 (1978): 348–65. Incidentally, in her account, Kovalevskaya reports being introduced to Spencer by Eliot as "a living refutation of your theory—a woman mathematician" (359).

69. Brown, "Why Does Daniel Deronda's Mother Live in Russia?," 30, 36.

70. Brown, "Deronda's Mother," 40.

71. Brown, "Deronda's Mother," 30; Eliot, *Deronda*, 243.

72. Henry, *George Eliot and the British Empire*, 55.

73. Nord, *Gypsies and the British Imagination*, 6.

74. Nord, *Gypsies and the British Imagination*, 100–101.

75. Eliot, *Impressions of Theophrastus Such*, 163.

76. Eliot, *Impressions of Theophrastus Such*, 161. The "Eastern Question" was the designation for the concern over the fate of South Slavic provinces in the Ottoman Empire, and it was used interchangeably with "the Slav(on)ic Question," which I use in the title of chapter 3.

77. Wolff, *Inventing Eastern Europe*, 244.

78. Brock, "Polish Democrats and English Radicals," 141, 145.

79. For more on religious and national divisions in Eastern Europe, see Magocsi's *Historical Atlas*; for Poland specifically, see p. 51.

80. Edith Simcox, review of *Middlemarch*, by George Eliot, *Academy* 4 (January 1, 1873): 2–4.

81. Gary Saul Morson, *Anna Karenina in Our Time: Seeing More Wisely* (New Haven, Conn.: Yale University Press, 2007), 29.

82. Sarah Gates, "'Dim lights and tangled circumstance': Gender and Genre in George Eliot's Realism," *Genre* 31 (1998): 145.

83. Gates, "'Dim lights and tangled circumstance,'" 144. My previous two references to Dorothea's domestication in the Victorian decorum or mode are also inspired by Gates.

84. Gates, "'Dim lights and tangled circumstance,'" 147.

85. Gates, "'Dim lights and tangled circumstance,'" 152.

86. For an interesting take on Kristeva's own positioning vis-à-vis Eastern and Western Europe, see Dušan Bjelić, "Julia Kristeva: Exile and Geopolitics of the Balkans," *Slavic Review* 67 (2008): 364–83.

87. Nord, *Gypsies and the British Imagination*, 105.

88. Kristeva, *Strangers to Ourselves*, 281.

89. Kristeva, *Strangers to Ourselves*, 288.

90. Kristeva, *Strangers to Ourselves*, 277–78.

91. Eliot herself most likely did not realize the ethnic pun she was making when she described Ladislaw's desire that Dorothea "should know that she had one slave in the world" in him (339).

92. Kristeva, *Strangers to Ourselves*, 272, 273.

93. Kristeva, *Strangers to Ourselves*, 270.

94. In addition to appearing in the introduction to *Orientalism*, *Middlemarch* also belongs to Said's list of English novels that participate in the imperial project, in *Culture and Imperialism* (New York: Knopf, 1993). Alicia Carroll argues that Eliot stands out as subversive among her contemporaries in *Dark Smiles: Race and Desire in George Eliot* (Athens: Ohio University Press, 2003). Nancy Henry's book has been quoted earlier, and my discussion of Thornton Lewes's Civil Service exam is partly informed by its second chapter, "'Colleagues in Failure': Emigration and the Lewes Boys."

Chapter 2

1. Todd Kontje, "Introduction: Reawakening German Realism," in *A Companion to German Realism, 1848–1900*, ed. Todd Kontje (Rochester, N.Y.: Camden House, 2002), 1.

2. Jeffrey L. Sammons, review of *The Truth of Realism: A Reassessment of the German Novel, 1830–1900*, by John Walker, *Monatshefte* 104 (2012): 131. The very title of the book under review, with the words *truth* and *reassessment*, reveals the nature of the problem, as does the title of Kontje's introduction cited above, with *reawakening*.

3. Helen Chambers, *The Changing Image of Theodor Fontane* (Columbia, S.C.: Camden House, 1997), 97.

4. Alan Bance, *Theodor Fontane: The Major Novels* (New York: Cambridge University Press, 1982), 6.

5. Henry Garland, *The Berlin Novels of Theodor Fontane* (Oxford: Clarendon Press, 1980), 5.

6. Garland's book (see n. 5 above) is considered the classic work on this segment of Fontane's literary output, and my list of his Berlin novels mirrors his.

7. Thomas Mann, *Gesammelte Werke*, 12 vols. (Frankfurt am Main: S. Fischer Verlag, 1960), 9:34. Mann's more frequently cited comment on Fontane, one that is present in just about any article on *Effi Briest* or introduction to the novel, is that *Effi Briest* belongs among the six most significant novels ever written. See Thomas Mann, *Das essayistische Werk*, ed. Hans Bürgin (Frankfurt am Main: S. Fischer Verlag, 1968), 106.

8. Bance, *Theodor Fontane*, 6.

9. Quoted in the Introduction to *A Companion to German Realism*, ed. Todd Kontje, 4.

10. Tanner, *Adultery in the Novel*, 210.

11. Barbara Everett, "Night Air: *Effi Briest* and Other Novels by Fontane," in *Theodor Fontane and the European Context: Literature, Culture and Society in Prussia and Europe*, ed. Patricia Howe and Helen Chambers (Amsterdam: Rodopi, 2001), 86.

12. Theodor Fontane, *Sämtliche Werke*, 24 vols. (Munich: Nymphenburger Verlagshandlung, 1959–1975), 7:222. Further references are to this edition (*SW*) and will be given by volume and page number in the text.

Regarding my assessment of Anna's age, I base it on her son being eight in the beginning of the novel. Considering her young marriage, typical of Russian women at the time, and the assumption that she conceived shortly thereafter, also typical, I estimate that she is around twenty-seven.

13. Hardy, "The Miserable Marriages," 67.

14. A few examples: Hardy's previously cited "Miserable Marriages"; Christiane Seiler, "Representations of the Loving, Hateful and Fearful Wife in Flaubert's *Mme Bovary*, Fontane's *Effi Briest*, and Tolstoy's *Anna Karenina*," *Germanic Notes and Reviews* 25 (1994): 3–7; and Gisela Zimmermann, "The Civil Servant as Educator: *Effi Briest* and *Anna Karenina*," *Modern Language Review* 90 (1995): 817–29.

15. Gordon A. Craig, *Theodor Fontane: Literature and History in the Bismarck Reich* (New York: Oxford University Press), 196.

16. Kristin Kopp, *Germany's Wild East: Constructing Poland as Colonial Space* (Ann Arbor: University of Michigan Press, 2012), 16.

17. See Henry T. Finck, *Wagner and His Works*, vol. 1 (New York: Haskell House, 1893), 69–70; and John F. Runciman, *Richard Wagner: Composer of Operas* (Charleston, S.C.: BiblioBazaar, 2007), 47.

18. Kopp, *Germany's Wild East*, 15.

19. Quoted in Richard Blanke, *Prussian Poland in the German Empire (1871–1900)* (Boulder, Colo.: East European Monographs, 1981), 8.

20. Kutolowski, "Mid-Victorian Public Opinion," 90.

21. Agnieszka Barbara Nance, *Literary and Cultural Images of a Nation without a State: The Case of Nineteenth-Century Poland* (New York: Peter Lang, 2008), 3.

22. Garland, *The Berlin Novels*, 5.

23. Craig, *Theodor Fontane*, 145.

24. See, e.g., Sean Franzel's "Cultures of Performance, Gender, and Political Ideology in Fontane's *Vor dem Sturm*," *Colloquia Germanica* 41 (2008): 20, 29.

25. Quoted in (and the German translated by) Garland, *The Berlin Novels*, 5–6; emphasis Fontane's.

26. Although *Fathers and Sons* is the more common English translation of Turgenev's title, I use the literal translation here (from the Russian *Отцы и дети*), not only because it is more accurate, but also because it is more appropriate for the generational issues in Fontane's novel. It should also be noted that Turgenev became known to Western Europeans earlier than Tolstoy or Dostoevsky because, unlike the two famous Slavophiles, Turgenev was a Western sympathizer and spent much of his life living abroad.

27. Garland, *The Berlin Novels*, 25.

28. Nance, *Literary and Cultural Images*, 55. Walter Müller-Seidel, for a contrasting example, reads the conclusion of the novel as rejecting the notion that a Pole can ever become a loyal Prussian subject. See "Fontane und Polen: Eine Betrachtung zur deutschen Literatur im Zeitalter Bismarcks," in *Studien zur Kulturgeschichte des deutschen Polenbildes, 1848–1939*, ed. Hendrik Feindt (Wiesbaden: Harrassowitz, 1995), 41–64.

29. Craig, *Theodor Fontane*, 112.

30. See, e.g., Craig, *Theodor Fontane*, 187, though many scholarly works on *Effi Briest* also point out this conversation as such.

31. Garland, *The Berlin Novels*, 70.

32. Craig, *Theodor Fontane*, 113.

33. When his more liberal friend Oblonsky asks, "А слияние сословий?" (And what about the merging of the classes?), Levin answers, "Кому приятно сливаться—на здоровье, а мне противно" (Whoever likes merging—he is welcome to it, but to me it is disgusting) (*PSS* 18:179).

34. I use the years these works came out in book form for their publication dates. Each was serialized prior to that, *L'Adultera* in *Nord und Süd* in 1880 and *Cécile* in *Universum* in 1886.

35. In order to avoid confusion over the designations "Berlin novels" and "Berlin society novels" regarding Fontane's literary output, Fontane's first novel, *Vor dem Sturm*, is also his first Berlin novel and, as such, is the topic of the first chapter of Henry Garland's *The Berlin Novels of Theodor Fontane*. This novel, however, as well as his second one, *Schach von Wuthenow*, belongs to the genre of historical novels. The Berlin society novels, on the other hand, are set in the contemporary Berlin of Fontane's time. *L'Adultera* is, therefore, Fontane's third Berlin novel (and, concomitantly, it occupies the third chapter of Garland's book) but his first Berlin society novel. Garland's chapter on it opens with the following statement: "With *L'Adultera* Fontane abandons the historical setting of the Napoleonic wars, transferring his attention to his own day and so beginning a series of social novels which has for its background the Berlin of Bismarck's heyday and the first years of the young Emperor William II" (45).

36. Garland, *The Berlin Novels*, 62.

37. See, e.g., Fritz Hubertus Vaziri, Levana Oesting, Hans-Georg Wendland, and Imke Barfknecht, *Fontane's "femme fragiles": Effi Briest, Cécile und Frau Jenny Treibel* (Munich: Science Factory, 2013).

38. Michael D. Coogan, ed., *The New Oxford Annotated Bible*, 3rd ed. (Oxford: Oxford University Press, 2001), 162 [New Testament]. All biblical quotations used in this book come from this edition, henceforth abbreviated *NOAB*.

39. John 8:11b; *NOAB*, 162 [New Testament].

40. St. Augustine, *De Conjug. Adult.*, II:6.

41. Craig, *Theodor Fontane*, 190.

42. Chambers, *Changing Image*, 53.

43. It ought to be noted that for Fontane naming a novel after its heroine does not necessarily mean she is an adulteress. *Frau Jenny Treibel*, for example, *Mathilde Möhring*, and *Stine* do not conform to that trend.

44. Röder-Bolton, *George Eliot in Germany*, 126.

45. Theodor Fontane, *Briefe*, 5 vols., ed. Kurt Schreinert and Charlotte Jolles (Berlin: Propyläen Verlag, 1968–71), 2:306; emphases Fontane's.

46. "A Word for the Germans," in *Selected Critical Writings*, 335.

47. Clifford Alfred Bernd, "Fontane's Discovery of Britain," *Modern Language Review* 87 (1992): 114.

48. Fontane's grandfather's decision is understandable given Prussia's feud with France, especially after Napoleon humiliated the nation at Jena in 1806 (which, incidentally, is the theme of Fontane's second novel, *Schach von Wuthenow*, usually translated in English as *A Man of Honor*).

49. Garland, *The Berlin Novels,* 73.

50. Samuel Beckett, *Krapp's Last Tape and Other Dramatic Pieces* (New York: Grove Press, 2009), 10.

51. Garland, *The Berlin Novels*, 173.

52. Russell A. Berman, *Enlightenment or Empire: Colonial Discourse in German Culture* (Lincoln: University of Nebraska Press, 1998), 135.

53. David Blackbourn, *The Long Nineteenth Century: A History of Germany, 1780–1918* (Oxford: Oxford University Press, 1998), 447.

54. Kopp, *Germany's Wild East*, 2.

55. See, e.g., Christian Grawe, *Theodor Fontane: Effi Briest* (Frankfurt am Main: Diesterweg), 1985.

56. J. P. M. Stern, "*Effi Briest, Madame Bovary, Anna Karenina*," *Modern Language Review* 52 (1957): 374 (in fn. 4).

57. Friedrich Seebaß, ed., *In Freiheit dienen: Briefe von Theodor Fontane* (Munich: Carl Hanser, 1956), 107.

58. Kopp, *Germany's Wild East*, 102; Judith Ryan, "The Chinese Ghost: Colonialism and Subaltern Speech in Fontane's *Effi Briest*," in *Literature and History: Essays in Honor of Karl S. Guthke*, ed. William Collins Donahue and Scott Denham (Tübingen: Stauffenberg Verlag, 2000), 373.

59. Kristen Kopp reads the Chinese ghost thus in *Germany's Wild East*, as does Valerie Greenberg in "The Resistance of *Effi Briest*: An (Un)told Tale," *PMLA* 103 (1988): 770–82.

60. Kopp, *Germany's Wild East*, 120–21.

61. Kopp, *Germany's Wild East*, 117.

62. Nance draws the contrast between Fontane as pro-Polish and Freytag as anti-Polish in *Literary and Cultural Images.*

63. Kopp, *Germany's Wild East*, 105.

64. Quoted in Kopp, *Germany's Wild East*, 104. Original reference in Karl Emil Franzos, *Halb-Asien: Land und Leute des östlichen Europa* (Stuttgart: J. G. Cott'sche Buchhandlung Nachfolger, 1914), 1.

65. Seiler, "Representations," 5.

66. Julian Preece, "Fear of the Foreigner: Chinese, Poles, and Other Non-Prussians in Theodor Fontane's *Effi Briest,*" in *German Studies at the Millenium*, ed. Neil Thomas (Durham, U.K.: University of Durham, 1999), 185.

67. Roswitha speaks a dialect, which highlights her subservient status. I use Hugh Rorrison and Helen Chambers's translation of *Effi Briest* (London: Penguin, 2000) for rendering her speech in English.

68. Helmut Walser Smith, *German Nationalism and Religious Conflict: Culture, Ideology, Politics, 1870–1914* (Princeton, N.J.: Princeton University Press, 1995), 57.

Chapter 3

1. Nikolai Nikolaevich Gusev, *Letopis' zhizni i tvorchestva L'va Nikolaevicha Tolstogo* (Moscow: Gosudarstvennoe izdatel'stvo khudozhestvennoi literatury, 1958–60), 468; emphases Gusev's.

2. Boris Eikhenbaum, *Tolstoi in the Seventies* (Ann Arbor: University of Michigan Press, 1982), 111.

3. Amy Mandelker, *Framing Anna Karenina: Tolstoy, the Woman Question, and the Victorian Novel* (Columbus: Ohio State University Press, 1993); Judith Armstrong, *The Unsaid Anna Karenina* (New York: St. Martin's Press, 1988).

4. Susan Layton's *Russian Literature and Empire: Conquest of the Caucasus from Puskhin to Tolstoy* (Cambridge: Cambridge University Press, 1994), for example, contains a chapter on each of the Tolstoy novellas mentioned above, and the title of Daniel R. Brower and Edward J. Lazzerini's edited collection speaks for itself: *Russia's Orient: Imperial Borderlands and Peoples, 1700–1917* (Bloomington: Indiana University Press, 1997).

5. Eduard Grigor'evich Babaev, *Lev Tolstoi i russkaia zhurnalistika ego epokhi.* (Moscow: Izdatel'stvo Moskovskogo Universiteta, 1978), 133.

6. George Eliot, *The Mill on the Floss*, ed. Hugh Osborne (New York: Modern Library, 2001), 408.

7. Olga Matich, *Erotic Utopia: The Decadent Imagination in Russia's Fin de Siècle* (Madison: University of Wisconsin Press, 2005), 42.

8. In the last paragraph of chapter 39, part 2, volume 3, of the novel, Tolstoy describes the end of the battle of Borodino as "победа нравственная" (a moral victory) for Russia, a victory that "убеждает противника в нравственном превосходстве своего врага" (convinces the opponent of the moral superiorty of his enemy), and ends the chapter with "погибель Наполеоновской Франции, на которую в первый раз под Бородиным была наложена рука сильнейшего духом противника" (the destruction of Napoleonic France, upon which for the first time at Borodino the hand of an opponent mightier in spirit was laid) (*PSS* 11:265).

9. In her book *Unattainable Bride Russia: Gendering Nation, State, and Intelligentsia in Russian Intellectual Culture* (Evanston, Ill.: Northwestern University Press, 2010), Ellen Rutten lists Natasha as one of the nineteenth-century literary heroines that embody the nation. Rutten also notes that Napoleon is described in the same novel as looking upon Moscow as a girl who has lost her virginity (presumably to him). But the most obvious example of the enormous role that the fictional Natasha Rostova has played in representing her nation shows in the title of Orlando Figes's book on the cultural history of Russia: *Natasha's Dance* (New York: Metropolitan Books, 2002).

10. Sofya Andreevna Tolstaya, *Dnevniki*, 2 vols. (Moscow: Khudozhestvennaia literature, 1978), 1:61.

11. Tolstaya, *Dnevniki*, 1:61.

12. Tolstaya, *Dnevniki*, 1:61.

13. Donna Orwin, *Tolstoy's Art and Thought, 1847–1880* (Princeton, N.J.: Princeton University Press, 1993), 144, 215.

14. Tolstoy's answer to Katkov's objections was the following: "В последней главе не могу ничего тронуть. *Яркий реализм*, как вы говорите, есть единственное орудие, так как ни пафос, ни рассуждения я не могу употреблять. И это одно из мест, на котором стоит весь роман. Если оно ложно, то всё ложно" (In the last chapter I cannot touch anything. *Vivid realism*, as you say, is the only tool, such as neither pathos nor reflections could be. And that is one of the places on which the whole novel stands. If it is false, then everything is false) (emphasis Tolstoy's) (*PSS* 62:139).

15. Mikhail Nikiforovich Katkov, ed., *Russkii vestnik: Zhurnal literaturnyi i politicheskii* 129 (1877): 472.

16. For historical information on the Slavonic Question, I have relied on Barbara Jelavich, *Russia's Balkan Entanglements, 1806–1914* (Cambridge: Cambridge University Press, 1991); Peter J. S. Duncan, *Russian Messianism: Third Rome, Holy Revolution, Communism and After* (London: Routledge, 2000); and two books by Jelena Milojković-Djurić, *Panslavism and National Identity in Russia and in the Balkans 1830–1880: Images of the Self and Others* (Boulder, Colo.: East European Monographs, 1994) and *The Eastern Question and the Voices of Reason: Austria-Hungary, Russia, and the Balkan States, 1875–1908* (Boulder, Colo.: East European Monographs, 2002).

17. From a conference paper, titled "Ambiguous Harvest: the Tolstoyan Scythe as a Rhetorical Weapon," delivered at the Annual Meeting of the Association of Slavic, East European, and Eurasian Studies (ASEEES), November 20, 2010—which happened to be the centenary of Tolstoy's death (new calendar)—on the panel "Imagining Peace, Engendering Strife: Russian Pastoral and Its Discontents."

18. Rebecca West, *Black Lamb and Grey Falcon: A Journey through Yugoslavia* (New York: Penguin, 1994), 1009.

19. Aleksandr Nikolaevich Pypin in an article for *Vestnik Evropy*, cited by Milojković-Djurić in *The Eastern Question*, 14, 35.

20. Quoted from Stephen Lukashevich, *Ivan Aksakov, 1823–1886: A Study in Russian Thought and Politics* (Cambridge, Mass.: Harvard University Press, 1965), 120.

21. William E. Gladstone, "Montenegro: A Sketch," *Nineteenth Century* 3 (May 1877): 378.

22. Gladstone, "Montenegro," 359.

23. Fedor Mikhailovich Dostoevsky, *Polnoe sobranie sochinenii* (*PSS*), 30 vols. (Petersburg: Nauka, 1972–90), 23:50, emphasis Dostoevsky's. Further references are to this edition (*PSS*) and will be given by volume and page number in the text.

24. Tolstoy, in fact, names Paris Sodom twice in the same letter addressed (though not sent) to Turgenev from Geneva during the spring of 1857, after having just departed Paris: "Отлично я сделал, что уехал из этого содома. Ради Бога, уезжайте куда-нибудь и вы" (I did very well to get away from that Sodom. For God's sake get away somewhere yourself too); and: "Я прожил 1 ½ месяца в содоме, и у меня на душе уж много наросло грязи, и две девки, и гильотина, и праздность, и пошлость" (I spent 1 and a half months in Sodom, and there is

great accumulation of filth in my soul: two whores, and the guillotine, and idleness and vulgarity) (*PSS* 60:170). I borrow the English translation of Tolstoy's letter from R. F. Christian, *Tolstoy's Letters* (London: Athlone Press, 1978), 97, 98.

25. See Milojković-Djurić, *Panslavism*, 105–11.

26. The title of Momo Kapor's essay is "Serbia—Vronsky's Last Love," and it appears in his collection, *A Guide to the Serbian Mentality* (Belgrade: dereta, 2006). The essay takes the same naive approach to Russian and Serbian brotherhood that is so harshly criticized in the epilogue to *Anna Karenina*.

27. Nikolai Berdiaev, *The Russian Idea* (Boston: Beacon Press, 1962), 6–7.

28. Matich, *Erotic Utopia*, 43.

29. Gusev, *Letopis'*, 384.

30. Matich, *Erotic Utopia*, 43.

31. Renita J. Weems, *Battered Love: Marriage, Sex, and Violence in the Hebrew Prophets* (Minneapolis, Minn.: Fortress Press, 1995), 3.

32. *NOAB*, 357.

33. *NOAB*, 1211–12.

34. For other biblical passages that mention the adulteress's breasts, see Ezekiel 23:3, 8; and Hosea 2:2. In Tolstoy's oeuvre, it is Hélène Bezukhova who is most frequently subjected to similar condemnatory rhetoric, as, for example, when her husband, Pierre, recalls how her own brother, Anatole, "целовал ее в голые плечи" (used to kiss her naked shoulders) and she "позволяла целовать себя" (allowed herself to be kissed) (*PSS* 10:29), or when Natasha recalls, after a night at the opera, how the "голая с спокойною и гордою улыбкою Элен в восторге кричала браво" (naked Hélène, with a calm and proud smile, rapturously shouted "bravo") (*PSS* 10:333).

35. See, e.g., A. Brenner and F. van Dijk-Hemmes, *On Gendering Texts: Female and Male Voices in the Hebrew Bible* (Leiden: Brill, 1993); and Athalaya Brenner, *The Intercourse of Knowledge: On Gendering Desire and "Sexuality" in the Hebrew Bible* (Leiden: Brill, 1997). In *On Gendering Texts* Brenner compares the porno-prophetic texts of Jeremiah with the 1954 French sadomasochistic erotic novel *The Story of O*, which partly inspired my own exploration of Tolstoy's novel in that manner. T. Drorah Setel's "Prophets and Pornography: Female Sexual Imagery in Hosea" was first published in *Feminist Interpretations of the Bible*, ed. Letty M. Russell (Philadelphia, Pa.: Westminster Press, 1985).

36. Isaiah 47:3; *NOAB*, 1043.

37. Critics from Boris Eikhenbaum to Vladimir E. Alexandrov have read the parallels between Anna and Frou-Frou as intended by the author, especially given the similarity of language employed to describe Vronsky's reaction to each "murder": "бледный, с дрожащею нижнею челюстью" (pale, with shivering lower jaw) (*PSS* 18:157) with Anna and "бледный и с трясущеюся нижнею челюстью" (pale and with trembling lower jaw) (*PSS* 18:210) with Frou-Frou. I would like to add, however, that the reaction of Sergei Kasatsky, the future Father Sergei, to finding out that his fiancée had been the tsar's mistress is almost identical: "Он вскочил и бледный как смерть, с трясущимися скулами, стоял перед нею" (He jumped up and pale as death, with trembling cheekbones, stood before her) (*PSS* 30:10). So is Vasily Kuragin's in *War and Peace*, as Pierre

Bezukhov notices in the moment after his wealthy father's death that Vasily, who was hoping for an inheritance, "был бледен и что нижняя челюсть его прыгала и тряслась, как в лихорадочной дрожи" (was pale and that his lower jaw twitched and trembled, as in a feverish shiver) (*PSS* 9:104).

38. Translation by G. S. Smith, from *The Russia Reader: History, Culture, Politics*, ed. Adele Barker and Bruce Grant (Durham, N.C.: Duke University Press, 2010).

39. Ivan Sergeevich Aksakov, *Sochineniia, 1860–1886*, 7 vols. (Moscow: Tip. M. G. Volchaninova, 1886–87), 1:299.

40. Matich, *Erotic Utopia*, 43.

41. Regarding Tolstoy's pacifism, this is another issue in which *Anna Karenina* occupies middle ground. Levin does not so much protest the war per se—though he acknowledges its horrors—as he does its being waged without official government sanction: "Да моя теория та: война, с одной стороны, есть такое животное, жестокое и ужасное дело, что ни один человек, не говорю уже христианин, не может лично взять на свою ответственность начало войны, а может только правительство, которое призвано к этому и приводится к войне неизбежно" (My theory is this: war is, on the one hand, such a beastly, cruel, and terrible thing that no man, to say nothing of a Christian, can personally take upon himself the responsibility of starting a war, but only a government, which is called to it and led into war unavoidably) (*PSS* 19:387).

42. Tolstoy was reading the complete works of the philosopher, and raving about him, at the end of the 1860s. See Eikhenabaum, *Tolstoi in the Seventies*, 145; and Orwin, *Tolstoy's Art and Thought*, 150.

43. Eikhenbaum, *Tolstoi in the Seventies*, 146.

44. Viktor Shklovsky, *Lev Tolstoy* (Moscow: Progress Publishers, 1978), 436. For a more detailed review of the various interpretations of the epigraph, see Mandelker, *Framing Anna Karenina*, 44–47. Noteworthy also is Tolstoy's statement, recorded by his wife, "что задача его сделать эту женщину только жалкой и не виноватой" (that his task was to make that woman only pitiable and not guilty) (*PSS* 20:577).

45. Cited in Eikhenbaum, *Tolstoi in the Seventies*, 145.

46. See Vladimir E. Alexandrov, *Limits to Interpretation: The Meanings of "Anna Karenina"* (Madison: University of Wisconsin Press, 2004), 308 (fn. 3) and chapter 7 for more on the epigraph.

47. Alexandrov, *Limits to Interpretation*, 67, 69. The epigraph ought also to be considered in light of Anna's suicidal motivation, which few scholars have done. As her relationship with Vronsky takes a downward turn, "death, as the sole means of renewing love for her in his heart, of punishing him and of gaining the victory in that fight which the evil spirit that had moved into her heart was waging with him, presented itself clearly and vividly to her" (*PSS* 19:331). Anna's last words to Vronsky are, "You will regret this" (*PSS* 19:333), and a few chapters later she experiences "an uncertain anger and need for revenge" (*PSS* 19:341). Finally, as she considers which part of the train to jump under at the station, she thinks, "There, in the very middle, and I will punish him and escape for everyone and from myself" (*PSS* 19:348). Anna's vengefulness is actually a toned-down version of the one wreaked by her real-life model, who left her

lover the following note: "You are my murderer. Be happy, if an assassin can be happy. If you like you can see my corpse on the rails at Yasenki."

48. The Russian word *inorodtsy* literally means "[those of] other birth," and no English translation is quite satisfactory. Richard Pevear and Larissa Volokhonsky (London: Penguin, 2003) use "racial minorities"; Marian Schwartz (New Haven, Conn.: Yale University Press, 2014), "native populations"; and the classic Constance Garnett (New York: Doubleday, 1944), "native tribes." For a precise historical definition (as well as how the concept changed over time), see John W. Slocum, "Who, and When, Were the *Inorodtsy*? The Evolution of the Category of 'Aliens' in Imperial Russia," *Russian Review* 57 (1998): 173–90.

49. Hosea 1:2; *NOAB*, 1279.

50. Hosea 3:3; *NOAB*, 1282.

51. The phrase is Sofya Andreevna Tolstaya's and is quoted here from Eikhenbaum, *Tolstoi in the Seventies*, 94.

52. For a review of the original serial publication dates in the *Russian Herald*, see William Mills Todd III's article, "The Responsibilities of (Co-)Authorship: Notes on Revising the Serialized Version of *Anna Karenina*," in *Freedom and Responsibility in Russian Literature: Essays in Honor of Robert Louis Jackson*, ed. Elizabeth Cheresh Allen and Gary Saul Morson (Evanston, Ill.: Northwestern University Press, 1995), 159–69. As the dates show, regular monthly publication was interrupted each summer and fall.

53. In manuscript #88, for example, the naive Karenin thinks that Lydia is the only one compassionate toward him because she is the only true Christian among his friends (*PSS* 20:420).

54. Gusev, *Letopis'*, 462.

55. Rutten, *Unattainable Bride Russia*, 24.

56. The *svoi/chuzhoi* binary has become commonplace in Russian studies and is typically employed in discussions of Russia's colonial past. For an excellent example, see Alexander Etkind's article "Russkaia literatura, XIX vek: Roman vnutrennei kolonizatsii," *Novoe Literaturnoe Obozrenie* 59 (2003): 103–24.

57. I am indebted for this insight, as well as a previous one regarding Mitya Levin's recognition of *svoikh*, to Cathy Popkin, whose paper, "Occupy and Cultivate: Foreign Policy and Domestic Affairs (or The Case of *Anna Karenina*)," was presented and discussed at the University of Illinois Russian Reading Circle (*Kruzhok*), Urbana, November 10, 2005.

58. I wish to make a strong case for the specific translation I use for the opening line of the novel, one of the most famous opening lines in world literature. Richard Pevear and Larissa Volokhonsky, who are otherwise lauded for being literal, miss it with their rendition of "alike" for "похожи друг на друга," as does Rosamund Bartlett in her more recent translation (Oxford: Oxford University Press, 2014). Marian Schwartz, however, publishing in the same year as Bartlett, gets it right—as did previously Aylmer and Louise Maude (New York: Oxford University Press, 2008) but not Constance Garnett—and here is, according to my humble opinion, why: "resemble one another" replicates the rhythm of the Russian "похожи друг на друга" to a syllable, while the repetitive sounds produced by "*one ano*ther" mirror the repetitiveness of "друг на друга" and thus reinforce the very concept of resemblance.

59. Morson, *Anna Karenina in Our Time*, 68.

60. Orwin points out the difference in meanings of Levin's and Vronsky's estate names. See *Tolstoy's Art and Thought*, 182.

61. Morson, *Anna Karenina in Our Time*, 70.

62. The idea that Russia had two tsars, one on the throne and the other in Iasnaia Poliana, was wildly popular in the last decade of the author's life, when he had become known worldwide as a great moral authority. The literary critic and publisher Aleksei Sergeevich Suvorin wrote in his diary in 1902, "Два царя у нас: Николай II и Лев Толстой. Кто из них сильнее? Николаи II ничего не может сделать с Толстым, не может поколебать его трон, тогда как Толстой, несомненно, колеблет трон Николая и его династии" (We have two tsars: Nikolai II and Lev Tolstoy. Who among them is the more powerful? Nikolai II cannot do anything with Tolstoy, cannot shake up his throne, whereas Tolstoy, undoubtedly, shakes the throne of Nikolai and his dynasty). A. S. Suvorin, *Dnevnik*, ed. N. V. Potatueva (Moscow: Novosti, 1992), 316.

Chapter 4

1. Šenoa's fifth novel was interrupted by the author's early death, at the age of forty-three, and subsequently completed by Josip Eugen Tomić.

2. Quoted in Vesna Goldsworthy, *Inventing Ruritania: The Imperialism of the Imagination* (New Haven, Conn.: Yale University Press, 1998), 8.

3. Robert William Seton-Watson, *German, Slav, and Magyar: A Study in the Origins of the Great War* (London: Williams and Norgate, 1916), 82.

4. West, *Black Lamb and Grey Falcon*, 52.

5. One might take issue with this argument on forethought in Anna Karenina's case, as her suicide is an act of jealous revenge, with her last words to Vronsky being "вы раскаетесь в этом" (you will regret this) (*PSS* 19:333), but that does not necessarily mean she has his death in mind, especially since it is living with regret that is its punishing aspect.

6. Miroslav Šicel, *Hrvatska književnost 19. i 20. stoljeća*, 2nd ed. (Zagreb: Školska knjiga, 1997), 52.

7. Šenoa mentions, somewhat ironically, the Magyarones' self-designation as "old Croats" in his "Pamflet na Ilirce" (A Pamphlet for the Illyrians), published in *Vienac* 10 (1878): 92–95. Reprinted in and quoted here from *Polemike u hrvatskoj književnosti*, 10 vols. (Zagreb: Mladost, 1982), 4:711.

8. Šicel, *Hrvatska književnost*, 51.

9. Commonly referred to as Gaj's *Pravopis*, the entire title of his work is *Kratka osnova horvatsko-slavenskoga pravopisaña* (A Brief Foundation of Croatian-Slavic Orthography).

10. The translation is taken from the bilingual *Monumenta Serbocroatica* (Ann Arbor: Michigan Slavic Publications, 1980), but I would like to suggest a more literal rendering of "srce ne iskali," which has more cathartic connotations than "appease his anger": "he did not release/empty his heart."

11. Nedjeljko Fabrio, *Vježbanje života* (Zagreb: Večernji list, 2004), 88. In relation to the present chapter, it ought to be mentioned that Fabrio is considered a twentieth-century Šenoa within the Croatian literary canon, focusing the actions of his historical novels in and around the coastal city of Rijeka and thus giving it the literary prominence that Šenoa gave Zagreb. In relation to the pre-

vious chapter, it might be of interest to readers to know that Fabrio's 1994 novel, *Smrt Vronskog—deveti dio Ane Karenjine* (Death of Vronsky—The Ninth Part of Anna Karenina), places the nineteenth-century count and other Russian volunteers in the Croatian town of Vukovar, which fell to Serb forces in November 1991.

12. Two monographs that take up this position are Branimir Anzulović's *Heavenly Serbia: From Myth to Genocide* (New York: New York University Press, 1999) and Michael Anthony Sells's *The Bridge Betrayed: Religion and Genocide in Bosnia* (Berkeley: University of California Press, 1996).

13. As an example of this, Danilo, one of the Christian Montenegro leaders heading the "investigation," is described as a Montenegrin Hamlet in the 1970 *Anthology of Yugoslav Literature*, edited by Vlatko Pavletić.

14. Barbara Jelavich, *History of the Balkans: Eighteenth and Nineteenth Centuries*, vol. 1 (Cambridge: Cambridge University Press, 1983), 168.

15. Julijana Matanović, "August Šenoa između teorije i prakse," *Dani Hvarskoga kazališta* 25 (1999): 270.

16. August Šenoa, *Sabrana djela*, 12 vols., ed. Slavko Ježić (Zagreb: Znanje, 1963–64), 9:522. Most further references, unless otherwise noted, are to this edition (*SD*) and are given by volume and page number in the text.

17. On a personal note, as someone who grew up in the Croatian republic of then-Yugoslavia, I can testify to the middle and high school student's miseries over having to read Mažuranić and the youthful enthusiasm with which Šenoa's novels were greeted in the classroom.

18. Mirko Rogošić, ed., *Ljubavna pisma hrvatskih književnika: Antologija* (Zagreb: Stvarnost, 1984), 67–84.

19. "Švapčić" is the diminutive of the word "Švaba," which would properly speaking be a designation for an inhabitant of the German region of Schwaben (today's Württemberg portion, roughly, of the state of Baden-Württemberg) but is frequently used by speakers of various Yugoslav languages to denote Germans in general. Also, both "Švaba" and "German" have historically been applied to all German-speaking nations, including Austria. Tolstoy, for example, calls the Austrians "Germans" in *War and Peace*, and Šenoa, given Croatia's political dependencies, most often has "Austrian" in mind when he says "German."

20. Dubravko Jelčić, *August Šenoa* (Zagreb: Naklada Slap, 2006), 22.

21. The distinction is a bit tricky, since *jug* means "south"; therefore, Yugoslavia—literally, "Southslavia"—is the land of the South Slavs.

22. Unlike in Russian, the Croatian word *pravo* only means "right" as opposed to "wrong" or "not having rights/being disenfranchised"—the latter being the meaning that the party had in mind—and not "right" as opposed to "left," though the latter would be apt in terms of the party's political bent. The initial split between Pravaši and Narodnjaci, in fact, reemerged in the newly independent Croatia of the 1990s and is described by John Lampe as "the nationalism and liberalism that have survived to the present day in Croatia." See John Lampe, *Yugoslavia as History: Twice there was a Country* (Cambridge: Cambridge University Press, 1996), 60.

23. Seton-Watson, *German, Slav, and Magyar*, 89. The two *bans* who were in power during the writing and publication of *The Goldsmith's Gold* both

came from the Union Party: Levin Rauch (1868–71) and Koloman Bedeković (1871–72).

24. Quoted in Šicel, *Hrvatska književnost*, 81.

25. Jelčić, *August Šenoa*, 27.

26. The Book of Judith mistakenly names the Assyrians as Israel's national enemy of the time, which is one of the reasons it is considered apocryphal. The main reason is that it originates in the Greek Septuagint and does not appear in the Hebrew Bible.

27. Šicel, *Hrvatska književnost*, 81.

28. Rebecca West's strong condemnation of the *Ausgleich* as a "very vulgar" love triangle is worth mentioning in relation to the theoretical framework of this study: "When the Dual Monarchy was framed to placate Hungary, the Croats were handed over to the Hungarians as their chattels. I do not know of any nastier act than this in history. It has a kind of lowness that is sometimes exhibited in the sexual affairs of very vulgar and shameless people: a man leaves his wife and induces a girl to become his mistress, then is reconciled to his wife and to please her exposes the girl to some public humiliation" (*Black Lamb and Grey Falcon*, 54).

29. Jelčić, *August Šenoa*, 22.

30. Antun Barac, *August Šenoa* (Zagreb: Narodna knjižnica, 1926), 55.

31. Eliot, *The Mill on the Floss*, 353.

32. Laza Lazarević, *Sve će to narod pozlatiti i druge pripovijetke*, 6th ed. (Zagreb: Mladost, 1981), 5.

33. Lazarević, *Sve će to narod pozlatiti*, 131.

34. Lazarević, *Sve će to narod pozlatiti*, 119.

35. Lazarević, *Sve će to narod pozlatiti*, 125.

36. Lazarević, *Sve će to narod pozlatiti*, 127.

37. Lazarević, *Sve će to narod pozlatiti*, 136.

38. Lazarević, *Sve će to narod pozlatiti*, 152.

Chapter 5

1. Nance, *Literary and Cultural Images*, 13.

2. Jean-Jacques Rousseau, *The Plan for Perpetual Peace, On the Government of Poland, and Other Writings on History and Politics*, trans. Christopher Kelly and Judith Bush, ed. Christopher Kelly (Hanover, N.H.: Dartmouth College Press, 2005), 217.

3. Wolff, *Inventing Eastern Europe*, 241.

4. Beth Holmgren, *Rewriting Capitalism: Literature and the Market in Late Tsarist Russia and the Kingdom of Poland* (Pittsburgh, Pa.: University of Pittsburgh Press, 1998), 174. Original reference is the Polish *Illustrated Weekly* 52 (1900): 1020.

5. Holmgren, *Rewriting Capitalism*, 174.

6. Stanislaw Eile, *Literature and Nationalism in Partitioned Poland* (New York: St. Martin's Press, in association with School of Slavonic and East European Studies, University of London, 2000), 112.

7. Jerzy J. Maciuszko, review of *With Fire and Sword*, by Henryk Sienkiewicz, trans. W. S. Kuniczak, *World Literature Today* 65 (1991): 514–15.

8. Thomas Napierkowski, "Introduction to *The Deluge*," in *The Trilogy Companion: A Reader's Guide to the Trilogy of Henryk Sienkiewicz*, ed. Jerzy R. Krzyżanowski (New York: Hippocrene Books, 1992), 43. Although the essay primarily concerns, as its title indicates, the second novel of the *Trilogy*, the reference in the line quoted is to its first ("written . . . in 1883").

9. For more on this moral criticism—not unlike the one directed against Njegoš's *Mountain Wreath*, discussed in the previous chapter—see Eile, *Literature and Nationalism in Partitioned Poland*, 115–16, 120–21.

10. Holmgren, *Rewriting Capitalism*, xi.

11. http://www.nobelprize.org/nobel_prizes/literature/laureates/1905/

12. The original statement of Sienkiewicz's was made in French, in a letter to the French writer and critic Auguste Jean Boyer d'Agen, dated January 24, 1912, and published in *Listy* I, 99: "Il est incontestable que les persécutions dont souffrent les Polonais sous le joug de la Prusse et surtout sous le joug de la Russie, ont eu une influence considérable sur mes projets." I came across it in a dissertation by Krzysztof Szymonik, "Romantic-Messianism in the Novels of Henryk Sienkiewicz" (University of Maryland, 1984), 288. The translation from the French is my own.

13. From Michael A. Guzik, "From Soldier to Saint: Ignatian Spiritual Elements in Henryk Sienkiewicz's *Quo Vadis?*," *Polish Review* 53 (2008): 3.

14. This was not only the case for Polish realism, but also for the realist movement in Europe more generally. Bernard Semmel, in *George Eliot and the Politics of National Inheritance*, discusses how heavily George Eliot was influenced by positivism.

15. Berdiaev, *The Russian Idea*, 7.

16. Nikolai Berdiaev, "The Russian and the Polish Soul," trans. Fr. S. Janos, 2009; ellipsis Berdiaev's. This essay, first published in the newspaper *Birzhevye vedomosti* under the title "Russia and Poland" in 1914 (October 10, no. 14610–14424), was reprinted in 1918 in the book *The Fate of Russia*, chapter 18. It is most easily accessible on the following website: http://www.berdyaev.com/berdiaev/berd_lib/1914_178.html

17. See John J. Pilch, "How We Redress Our Suffering: An Exercise in Actualizing Biblical Texts," *Polish Review* 48 (2003): 38.

18. *NOAB*, 441 [New Testament].

19. *NOAB*, 442 [New Testament].

20. Sinead O'Connor has a song on her 1994 album, *Universal Mother* (an album "dedicated as a prayer from Ireland"), titled "Fire on Babylon." It is the first song on the album and, in its reference to England, provides a strong contrast to the title of the album as a whole, which refers to Ireland.

21. My quotations from Sienkiewicz's original Polish *Quo Vadis* come from the following online version: http://wolnelektury.pl/katalog/lektura/quo-vadis.html, 2571, 2578. The numbers identify the paragraph as opposed to the page. Further references are to this edition, henceforth identified as *QV*, and are given by paragraph number in the text.

22. Walicki, *Philosophy and Romantic Nationalism*, 3 and 7, respectively.

23. Holmgren, *Rewriting Capitalism*, 170.

24. See Eile, *Literature and Nationalism in Partitioned Poland*, 114, 115.

25. My information on the early church saints comes from the Catholic Encyclopedia. For Saint Lucina, see http://www.newadvent.org/cathen/09410c.htm; for de Rossi, see http://www.newadvent.org/cathen/04739c.htm.

26. "Warns Prussian Poles," *New York Times*, September 28, 1902; available at http://query.nytimes.com/mem/archive-free/pdf?res=F20E1EFF3F5F12738-DDDA10A94D1405 B828CF1D3

27. The first two stanza's of Blok's lengthy poem are sufficient to convey his satire:

You have millions. We are numberless,
numberless, numberless. Try doing
battle with us! Yes, we are Scythians! Yes,
Asiatics, with greedy eyes slanting!

For you, the centuries; for us, one hour.
We, like obedient lackeys, have held up
a shield dividing two embattled powers—
The Mongol hordes and Europe!

From Aleksandr Blok, *Selected Poems*, trans. Jon Stallworthy and Peter France (Manchester, U.K.: Carcanet Press, 2000), 111.

28. John 8:6b; *NOAB*, 162 [New Testament].

29. *Quo Vadis*, iTunes, dir. Mervin LeRoy (Metro-Goldwyn-Mayer, Hollywood, Calif., 1951), 1:25:28–1:25:33.

30. See Antoni Semczuk, "Échos Polonais à la mort de Tolstoj," *Revue des études slaves* 81 (2010): 47–52.

31. N. N. Gusev, *Dva goda s L. N. Tolstym: Vospominaniia i dnevnik byvshego sekretaria L. N. Tolstogo, 1907–1909* (Moscow: Izd. Tolstovskogo muzeia, 1928), 185. Quoted in *PSS* 77:274.

32. Regarding Tolstoy's abandonment of fiction for spiritual writings, an anonymous assessment in the American *Dial* of "Living Writers of Fiction" placed him in opposition to the rising Sienkiewicz in the following entertaining way: "Of the three or four great novelists that Russia has produced, Count Tolstoi alone is left, and from him there is little reason to expect any further work comparable with "War and Peace," "Anna Karenina, " or even with "The Cossacks." The writer of almost first-rate fiction has become a producer of third-rate tracts, and literature mourns the defection. But the great Slavonic North has sent us of recent years, in the person of Henryk Sienkiewicz, the Polish novelist, a writer of fiction quite the equal of the Russian soldier turned pietist. His magnificent romantic trilogy devoted to the seventeenth-century wars of the Polish Commonwealth, and his subtle piece of psychological analysis called "Without Dogma," are masterpieces in their respective kinds, and with them Polish literature renews the appeal to European attention first made by Mickiewicz half a century ago." (16, no. 192 [June 16, 1894]: 352)

33. Eliot, *Impressions of Theophrastus Such*, 156.

34. Eliot, *Impressions of Theophrastus Such*, 147.

Conclusion

1. Benedict Anderson, Introduction to *Mapping the Nation*, ed. Gopal Balakrishnan (London: Verso, 1996) , 8.

2. The juxtaposition is obvious in the title of Tolstoy's letter, "Патриотизм или мир" (Patriotism or Peace), written in 1896 in response to the English jour-

nalist John Manson's inquiry into Tolstoy's position on the standoff between the United States and the United Kingdom over the Venezuelan crisis.

3. For an informative study on how both Hawthorne from the United States and Gogol from Russia built their national literatures in response to (Western) Europe, see Anne Lounsbery, *Thin Culture, High Art: Gogol, Hawthorne, and Authorship in Nineteenth-Century Russia and America* (Cambridge, Mass.: Harvard University Press, 2007).

4. Kate Chopin, *The Awakening*, ed. Margo Culley (New York: W. W. Norton, 1994), 10.

5. Chopin, *The Awakening*, 18.

6. D. H. Lawrence, *Lady Chatterley's Lover* (London: Penguin Popular Classics, 1960), 22, 24, and 67, respectively.

7. Lawrence, *Lady Chatterley's Lover*, 98, 254, 254, and 98, respectively.

8. Mann, *Gesammelte Werke* 3:322.

9. Mann, *Gesammelte Werke* 8:458.

10. Anderson, Introduction to *Mapping the Nation*, 8.

11. In 1991, when the poem was written, the war had not yet spread to Bosnia, where it began a year later. The Croatian town of Vukovar fell to the Serbian-dominated Yugoslav army in November 1991, which occasioned Ferida Duraković's first war poem. The entire collection is titled, in homage to Joseph Conrad, *Srce tame* (The Heart of Darkness) and was translated into English by Amela Simić and Zoran Mutić (Fredonia, N.Y.: White Pine Press, 1998). The translation of the poem I use in the epigraph, however, is my own.

12. Another instance worth mentioning is a short recitation by the popular Serbian singer Đorđe Balašević, titled "Odjebi, JNA" (Fuck off, JNA). JNA is the acronym for Jugoslovenska narodna armija (the Yugoslav National Army), which led the fight against the seceding republics. Balašević's statement, first made at a concert in Belgrade in 1992, the year in which the war spread from Croatia to Bosnia, was incredibly bold. He starts out by saying, "Dao sam ti jednu dobru godinu života" (I gave you one good year of my life), referring to the obligatory military service every Yugoslav male had to complete, which Balašević did, as his text reveals, in his nineteenth year. He goes on to say, "Ali . . . ja sam bar imao . . . 20-te i 30-te, za razliku od dečaka na čije crno uokvirene fotografije svakodnevno nailazim na predzadnjim stranicama štampe" (But . . . I at least had . . . [my] twenties and thirties, unlike those boys whose black-framed photographs I come accross every day on the second to last pages of the press). https://www.youtube.com/watch?v=KKWRyUTs7-w.

13. My reading of the possible political analogies for the beast is entirely influenced by the analysis of the poem performed by one of my doctoral advisees in her dissertation. The background information about the poem's composition also comes from her. See chapter 2 in Kristine Kotecki, "After the Archive: Framing Cultural Memory in Ex-Yugoslav Collections" (Ph.D. diss., University of Texas at Austin, 2013). Regarding the equation of "homeland" with "nation," rather than the "state," Kotecki points out that Duraković uses "homeland" as a synonym for "nation" by contrasting "homeland" to "state" in another poem (*domovina* and *država* in Bosnian). The world *nacija* can hardly measure up to *domovina* in the feelings of belonging and warmth that it evokes, and the

speakers of former Yugoslav languages, just like the Russians, are more likely to employ *narod* for "nation."

14. http://news.bbc.co.uk/2/hi/europe/348340.stm

15. http://www.vesti.ru/doc.html?id=784205

16. From personal communication with the author I learned the following about her poem (I quote her e-mail in my own translation from Bosnian): "Because it was written then, the direct association is the Yugoslav National Army and the war in Yugoslavia and all that, but my reason was broader and higher (I remembered my own parents, who lost everything in World War II, and then other wars in the world at the time when ours broke out, Palestine, Vietnam, etc.)—I simply realized that ideologies raise boys so that they would die for them. Insofar every war is unjust. In that sense the poem relates to all the wars in the world, before and after ours. My stance in the poem is actually a civilian, powerless, politically unimportant, female perspective." I find the last line of her explanation particularly enlightening regarding both the poem and my project because the female perspective assumes horrendous importance and power when utilized by men, whether it be the Hebrew prophets foretelling Israel's demise for her unfaithfulness to God, Dostoevsky casting Russia in the role of the self-sacrificing mother of all Slavs, or contemporary world leaders and military commanders who keep "the deception of patriotism" alive.

17. http://www.theatlantic.com/international/archive/2014/03/ukrainian-women-have-launched-a-sex-strike-against-russian-men/284614/

18. Clarence A. Manning, trans., *Taras Shevchenko, the Poet of Ukraine: Selected Poems* (Jersey City, N.J.: Ukrainian National Association, 1945), 88. The English translation of the line from Shevchenko's poem is also Manning's.

19. http://www.elle.com/culture/career-politics/news/a19128/ukraine-sex-ban-campaign-interview/

20. Beer, "'Middlemarch' and 'The Woman Question,'" 160.

21. Matanović, "August Šenoa između teorije i prakse," 254.

BIBLIOGRAPHY

Aksakov, Ivan Sergeevich. *Sochineniia, 1860–1886*. 7 vols. Moscow: Tip. M. G. Volchaninova, 1886–87.

Alexandrov, Vladimir E. *Limits to Interpretation: The Meanings of Anna Karenina*. Madison: University of Wisconsin Press, 2004.

Anderson, Benedict. *Imagined Communities: Reflections on the Origin and Spread of Nationalism*. London: Verso, 1983.

———. Introduction to *Mapping the Nation*, edited by Gopal Balakrishnan, 1–16. London: Verso, 1996.

Anonymous. "Living Writer's of Fiction." *The Dial* 192 (1894): 351–53.

———. Review of *Middlemarch*, by George Eliot. *Saturday Review* 34 (December 7, 1872): 733–34.

———. "Warns Prussian Poles." *New York Times*, September 28, 1902.

Anzulović, Branimir. *Heavenly Serbia: From Myth to Genocide*. New York: New York University Press, 1999.

Arendt, Hannah. *Origins of Totalitarianism*. New York: Harcourt, Brace & World, 1966.

Armstrong, Judith. *The Novel of Adultery*. London: Macmillan, 1976.

———. *The Unsaid Anna Karenina*. New York: St. Martin's Press, 1988.

Ashton, Rosemary. *The German Idea: Four English Writers and the Reception of German Thought, 1800–1860*. Cambridge: Cambridge University Press, 1980.

Babaev, Eduard Grigor'evich. *Lev Tolstoi i russkaia zhurnalistika ego epokhi*. Moscow: Izdatel'stvo Moskovskogo Universiteta, 1978.

Bakić-Hayden, Milica. "Nesting Orientalisms: The Case of Former Yugoslavia." *Slavic Review* 54 (1995): 917–31.

Bance, Alan. *Theodor Fontane: The Major Novels*. New York: Cambridge University Press, 1982.

Barac, Antun. *August Šenoa*. Zagreb: Narodna knjižnica, 1926.

Barker, Adele, and Bruce Grant, eds. *The Russia Reader: History, Culture, Politics*. Durham, N.C.: Duke University Press, 2010.

Beaty, Jerome. "The Forgotten Past of Will Ladislaw." *Nineteenth-Century Fiction* 13 (1958): 159–63.

———. *Middlemarch: From Notebook to Novel*. Urbana: University of Illinois Press, 1960.

Beckett, Samuel. *Krapp's Last Tape and Other Dramatic Pieces*. New York: Grove Press, 2009.

Beer, Gillian. *Darwin's Plots: Evolutionary Narrative in Darwin, George Eliot, and Nineteenth-Century Fiction*. Cambridge: Cambridge University Press, 2000.

———. "'Middlemarch' and 'The Woman Question.'" In *Middlemarch, George Eliot*, edited by John Peck, 155–181. Basingstoke: Macmillan, 1992.

Berdiaev, Nikolai. *The Russian Idea*. Translated by R. M. French. Boston: Beacon Press, 1962.

Berman, Russell A. *Enlightenment or Empire: Colonial Discourse in German Culture*. Lincoln: University of Nebraska Press, 1998.

Bernd, Clifford Alfred. "Fontane's Discovery of Britain." *Modern Language Review* 87 (1992): 112–21.

Bjelić, Dušan. "Julia Kristeva: Exile and Geopolitics of the Balkans." *Slavic Review* 67 (2008): 364–83.

Blackbourn, David. *The Long Nineteenth Century: A History of Germany, 1780–1918*. Oxford: Oxford University Press, 1998.

Blake, Kathleen. "*Middlemarch* and the Woman Question." *Nineteenth-Century Fiction* 31 (1976): 285–312.

Blanke, Richard. *Prussian Poland in the German Empire (1871–1900)*. Boulder, Colo.: East European Monographs, 1981.

Blok, Aleksandr. "The Scythians." In *Selected Poems*, translated by Jon Stallworthy and Peter France, 111–13. Manchester, U.K.: Carcanet Press, 2000.

Brenner, Athalya. *The Intercourse of Knowledge: On Gendering Desire and "Sexuality" in the Hebrew Bible*. Biblical Interpretation Series, 26. Leiden: Brill, 1997.

Brenner, Athalya, and Fokkelien van Dijk-Hemmes. *On Gendering Texts: Female and Male Voices in the Hebrew Bible*. Biblical Interpretation Series, 1. Leiden: Brill, 1993.

Brock, Peter. "Polish Democrats and English Radicals, 1832–1862: A Chapter in the History of Anglo-Polish Relations." *Journal of Modern History* 25 (1953): 139–56.

Brower, Daniel R., and Edward J. Lazzerini, eds. *Russia's Orient: Imperial Borderlands and Peoples, 1700–1917*. Bloomington: Indiana University Press, 1997.

Brown, Catherine. "Why Does Daniel Deronda's Mother Live in Russia?" *George Eliot—George Henry Lewes Studies* 58–59 (2010): 26–42.

Butler, Thomas, ed. *Monumenta Serbocroatica: A Bilingual Anthology of Serbian and Croatian Texts from the 12th to the 19th Century*. Ann Arbor: Michigan Slavic Publications, 1980.

Carroll, Alicia. *Dark Smiles: Race and Desire in George Eliot*. Athens: Ohio University Press, 2003.

Carroll, David R. "Unity through Analogy: An Interpretation of *Middlemarch*." *Victorian Studies* 2 (1959): 305–16.

The Catholic Encyclopedia. http://www.newadvent.org/cathen.

Chambers, Helen. *The Changing Image of Theodor Fontane*. Columbia, S.C.: Camden House, 1997.

Chapman, Raymond, and Eleanora Gottlieb. "A Russian View of George Eliot." *Nineteenth-Century Fiction* 33 (1978): 348–65.

Chase, Karen. Introduction to *Middlemarch in the Twenty-First Century*, edited by Karen Chase. Oxford: Oxford University Press, 2006.

Cherry, Conrad, ed. *God's New Israel: Religious Interpretations of American Destiny*. Englewood Cliffs, N.J.: Prentice Hall, 1971.

Chopin, Kate. *The Awakening*. 2nd ed. Edited by Margo Culley. New York: W. W. Norton, 1994.

Christian, R. F. *Tolstoy's Letters*. London: Athlone Press, 1978.

Coogan, Michael, D., ed. *The New Oxford Annotated Bible*. 3rd ed. Oxford: Oxford University Press, 2001.

Costlow, Jane. "Ambiguous Harvest: The Tolstoyan Scythe as a Rhetorical Weapon." Paper presented at the Annual Meeting of the Association of Slavic, East European, and Eurasian Studies (ASEEES), Los Angeles, Calif., November 18–21, 2010.

Craig, Gordon A. *Theodor Fontane: Literature and History in the Bismarck Reich*. New York: Oxford University Press, 1999.

Crowe, David. *A History of the Gypsies of Eastern Europe and Russia*. New York: St. Martin's Press, 1994.

Dostoevsky, Fedor Mikhailovich. *Polnoe sobranie sochinenii*. Edited by V. G. Bazanov. 30 vols. Petersburg: Nauka, 1972–90.

Doyle, Laura. "'A' for Atlantic: The Colonizing Force of Hawthorne's *The Scarlet Letter*." *American Literature* 79 (2007): 243–73.

Duncan, Peter J. S. *Russian Messianism: Third Rome, Holy Revolution, Communism and After*. London: Routledge, 2000.

Duraković, Ferida. *Heart of Darkness*. Translated by Amela Simić and Zoran Mutić. Fredonia, N.Y.: White Pine Press, 1998.

Eikhenbaum, Boris. *Tolstoi in the Seventies*. Ann Arbor: University of Michigan Press, 1982.

Eile, Stanislaw. *Literature and Nationalism in Partitioned Poland*. New York: St. Martin's Press, in association with School of Slavonic and East European Studies, University of London, 2000.

Eliot, George. *Daniel Deronda*. Edited by Terence Cave. London: Penguin Books, 1995.

———. *Impressions of Theophrastus Such*. Edited by Nancy Henry. Iowa City: University of. Iowa Press, 1994.

———. *Middlemarch*. Edited by David Carroll. New York: Oxford University Press, 1997.

———. *The Mill on the Floss*. Edited by Hugh Osborne. New York: Modern Library, 2001.

———. *Scenes of Clerical Life*. Edited by Graham Handley. Ware, U.K.: Wordsworth Editions, 2007.

———. *Selected Critical Writings*. Edited by Rosemary Ashton. Oxford: Oxford University Press, 1992.

———. "Three Months in Weimer." *Fraser's Magazine for Town and Country* 51, no. 306 (June 1855): 699–700.

Etkind, Alexander. "Russkaia literatura, XIX vek: Roman vnutrennei kolonizatsii." *Novoe Literaturnoe Obozrenie* 59 (2003): 103–24.

Everett, Barbara. "Night Air: *Effi Briest* and Other Novels by Fontane." In *Theodor Fontane and the European Context: Literature, Culture and Society in Prussia and Europe*, edited by Patricia Howe and Helen Chambers, 85–94. Amsterdam: Rodopi, 2001.

Fabrio. Nedjeljko. *Smrt Vronskog—Deveti dio "Ane Karenjine" Lava Nikolajeviča Tolstoja*. 2nd ed. Varaždin: Katarina Zrinski, 2004.

———. *Vježbanje života*. Zagreb: Večernji List, 2004.
Figes, Orlando. *Natasha's Dance: A Cultural History of Russia*. New York: Metropolitan Books, 2002.
Finck, Henry T. *Wagner and His Works*. Vol. 1. New York: Haskell House, 1893.
Fontane, Theodor. *Briefe*. Edited by Kurt Schreinert and Charlotte Jolles. 5 vols. Berlin: Propyläen Verlag, 1968–71.
———. *Effi Briest*. Translated by Hugh Rorrison and Helen Chambers. London: Penguin Classics, 2000.
———. *Sämtliche Werke*. Edited by Edgar Gross. 24 vols. Munich: Nymphenburger Verlagshandlung, 1959–1975.
Flaubert, Gustave. *Madame Bovary*. Paris: Gallimard, 1972.
Franzel, Sean. "Cultures of Performance, Gender, and Political Ideology in Fontane's *Vor dem Sturm*." *Colloquia Germanica* 41 (2008): 11–32.
Franzos, Karl Emil. *Halb-Asien: Land und Leute des östlichen Europa*. Stuttgart: J. G. Cott'sche Buchhandlung Nachfolger, 1914.
Furst, Lilian R. "Struggling for Reform in *Middlemarch*." *Nineteenth-Century Literature* 48 (1993): 341–61.
Garland, Henry. *The Berlin Novels of Theodor Fontane*. Oxford: Clarendon Press, 1980.
Gates, Sarah. "'Dim lights and tangled circumstance': Gender and Genre in George Eliot's Realism." *Genre* 31 (1998): 143–58.
Gellner, Ernest. "The Coming of Nationalism and Its Interpretation: The Myths of Nation and Class." In *Mapping the Nation*, edited by Gopal Balakrishnan, 98–145. London: Verso, 1996.
Gladstone, William. "Montenegro: A Sketch." *Nineteenth Century* 3 (1877): 359–79.
Goldstein, Slavko. *1941: The Year That Keeps Returning*. Translated by Michael Gable. New York: New York Review Books, 2013.
Goldsworthy, Vesna. *Inventing Ruritania: The Imperialism of the Imagination*. New Haven, Conn.: Yale University Press, 1998.
Grawe, Christian. *Theodor Fontane: Effi Briest*. Frankfurt am Main: Diesterweg, 1985.
Greenberg, Robert A. "The Heritage of Will Ladislaw." *Nineteenth-Century Fiction* 15 (1961): 355–58.
Greenberg, Valerie D. "The Resistance of *Effi Briest*: An (Un)told Tale." *PMLA* 103 (1988): 770–82.
Gusev, Nikolai Nikolaevich. *Dva goda s L. N. Tolstym: Vospominaniia i dnevnik byvshego sekretaria L. N. Tolstogo, 1907–1909*. Moscow: Izd. Tolstovskogo muzeia, 1928.
———. *Letopis' zhizni i tvorchestva L'va Nikolaevicha Tolstogo*. Moscow: Gosudarstvennoe izdatel'stvo khudozhestvennoi literatury, 1958–60.
Guzik, Michael A. "From Soldier to Saint: Ignatian Spiritual Elements in Henryk Sienkiewicz's *Quo Vadis?*" *Polish Review* 53 (2008): 3–24.
Haight, Gordon S. "George Eliot's 'Eminent Failure', Will Ladislaw." In *This Particular Web*, edited by Ian Adam, 22–42. Toronto: University of Toronto Press, 1975.
Haight, Gordon S., ed. *The George Eliot Letters*. 9 vols. New Haven, Conn.: Yale University Press, 1954–78.

Hardy, Barbara. "The Miserable Marriages in *Middlemarch, Anna Karenina,* and *Effi Briest.*" In *George Eliot and Europe*, edited by John Rignall, 64–81. Brookfield, Vt.: Scolar Press, 1997.

Henry, Nancy. *George Eliot and the British Empire.* Cambridge: Cambridge University Press, 2002.

Hobsbawm, Eric. "Mass-Producing Traditions: Europe, 1870–1914." In *The Invention of Tradition*, edited by Eric Hobsbawm and Terence Ranger, 263–307. Cambridge: Cambridge University Press, 1992.

Holmgren, Beth. *Rewriting Capitalism: Literature and the Market in Late Tsarist Russia and the Kingdom of Poland.* Pittsburgh, Pa.: University of Pittsburgh Press, 1998.

James, Henry. Review of *Middlemarch*, by George Eliot. *Galaxy* 15 (March 1873): 424–28.

———. *The Tragic Muse.* 2 vols. London: Macmillan, 1921.

Jelavich, Barbara. *History of the Balkans: Eighteenth and Nineteenth Centuries.* Vol. 1. Cambridge: Cambridge University Press, 1983.

———. *Russia's Balkan Entanglements, 1806–1914.* Cambridge: Cambridge University Press, 1991.

Jelčić, Dubravko. *August Šenoa.* Zagreb: Naklada Slap, 2006. Originally published as *Šenoa* by Globus in 1984.

Kapor, Momo. "Serbia—Vronsky's Last Love." In *A Guide to the Serbian Mentality*, 264–69. Belgrade: dereta, 2006.

Katkov, Mikahil Nikiforovich, ed. *Russkii vestnik: Zhurnal literaturnyi i politicheskii* 129 (1877).

Koharević, Ojdana. "Nakon 60 godina otkrivena tajna smrti autora pjesme 'Rajska djevo, kraljice Hrvata.'" *Slobodna Dalmacija*, May 15, 2010. Accessed December 10, 2013. http://www.slobodnadalmacija.hr/Split-županija/tabid/76/articleType/ArticleView/ articleId/102669/Default.aspx

Kontje, Todd. "Introduction: Reawakening German Realism." In *A Companion to German Realism, 1848–1900*, edited by Todd Kontje, 1–21. Rochester, N.Y.: Camden House, 2002.

Kopp, Kristin. *Germany's Wild East: Constructing Poland as Colonial Space.* Ann Arbor: University of Michigan Press, 2012.

Kotecki, Kristine. "After the Archive: Framing Cultural Memory in Ex-Yugoslav Collections." Ph.D. diss., University of Texas at Austin, 2013.

Kristeva, Julia. *Strangers to Ourselves.* In *The Portable Kristeva*, edited by Kelly Oliver, 264–94. New York: Columbia University Press, 2002.

Kutolowski, John F. "Mid-Victorian Public Opinion, Polish Propaganda, and the Uprising of 1863." *Journal of British Studies* 8 (1969): 86–110.

Lampe, John. *Yugoslavia as History: Twice There Was a Country.* Cambridge: Cambridge University Press, 1996.

Lawrence, D. H. *Lady Chatterley's Lover.* London: Penguin Popular Classics, 1960.

Layton, Susan. *Russian Literature and Empire: Conquest of the Caucasus from Puskhin to Tolstoy.* Cambridge: Cambridge University Press, 1994.

Lazarević, Laza. *Sve će to narod pozlatiti i druge pripovijetke.* 6th ed. Zagreb: Mladost, 1981.

Levine, George. *Darwin and the Novelists: Patterns of Science in Victorian Fiction*. Cambridge, Mass.: Harvard University Press, 1988.

Lottman, Herbert. *Flaubert: A Biography*. London: Methuen, 1989.

Lounsbery, Anne. *Thin Culture, High Art: Gogol, Hawthorne, and Authorship in Nineteenth-Century Russia and America*. Cambridge, Mass.: Harvard University Press, 2007.

Lukács, Georg. *Theory of the Novel: A Historico-Philosophical Essay on the Forms of Great Epic Literature*. Translated by Anna Bostock. Cambridge: Cambridge University Press, 1971.

Lukashevich, Stephen. *Ivan Aksakov, 1823–1886: A Study in Russian Thought and Politics*. Cambridge, Mass.: Harvard University Press, 1965.

Maciuszko, Jerzy J. Review of *With Fire and Sword*, by Henryk Sienkiewicz. Translated by W. S. Kuniczak. *World Literature Today* 65 (1991): 514–15.

Magocsi, Paul Robert. *Historical Atlas of East Central Europe*. Toronto: University of Toronto Press, 1993.

Malcolm, David. "What Is a Pole Doing in Middlemarch?" *George Eliot Fellowship Review* 17 (1986): 62–69.

Mandelker, Amy. *Framing Anna Karenina: Tolstoy, the Woman Question, and the Victorian Novel*. Columbus: Ohio State University Press, 1993.

Mann, Thomas. *Das essayistische Werk*. Edited by Hans Bürgin. Frankfurt am Main: S. Fischer Verlag, 1968.

———. *Gesammelte Werke*. 12 vols. Frankfurt am Main: S. Fischer Verlag, 1960.

Manning, Clarence A., trans. *Taras Shevchenko, the Poet of Ukraine: Selected Poems*. Jersey City, N.J.: Ukrainian National Association, 1945.

Matanović, Julijana. "August Šenoa između teorije i prakse." *Dani Hvarskoga kazališta* 25 (1999): 251–72.

Matich, Olga. *Erotic Utopia: The Decadent Imagination in Russia's Fin de Siècle*. Madison: University of Wisconsin Press, 2005.

Mayhew, Henry. *London Labour and the London Poor*. London: Penguin Books, 1985.

McLean, Thomas. *The Other East and Nineteenth-Century British Literature: Imagining Poland and the Russian Empire*. Basingstoke: Palgrave Macmillan, 2012.

Meyer, Priscilla. "*Anna Karenina*: Tolstoy's Polemic with *Madame Bovary*." *Russian Review* 54 (1995): 243–59.

Mickiewicz, Adam. *Pan Tadeusz or the Last Foray in Lithuania: A Story of Life among Polish Gentlefolk in the Years 1811 and 1812*. Translated by George Rapall Noyes. New York: Mondial, 2009.

Milojković-Djurić, Jelena. *The Eastern Question and the Voices of Reason: Austria-Hungary, Russia, and the Balkan States, 1875–1908*. Boulder, Colo.: East European Monographs, 2002.

———. *Panslavism and National Identity in Russia and in the Balkans, 1830–1880: Images of the Self and Others*. Boulder, Colo.: East European Monographs, 1994.

Mittelmann, Hanni. *Die Utopie des weiblichen Glücks in den Romanen Theodor Fontanes*. Bern: Peter Lang, 1980.

Morson, Gary Saul. *Anna Karenina in Our Time: Seeing More Wisely*. New Haven, Conn.: Yale University Press, 2007.

Müller-Seidel, Walter. "Fontane und Polen: Eine Betrachtung zur deutschen Literatur im Zeitalter Bismarcks." In *Studien zur Kulturgeschichte des deutschen Polenbildes, 1848–1939*, edited by Hendrik Feindt, 41–64. Wiesbaden: Harrassowitz, 1995.

Nance, Agnieszka Barbara. *Literary and Cultural Images of a Nation without a State: The Case of Nineteenth-century Poland*. New York: Peter Lang, 2008.

Napierkowski, Thomas. "Introduction to *The Deluge*." In *The Trilogy Companion: A Reader's Guide to the Trilogy of Henryk Sienkiewicz*, ed. Jerzy R. Krzyżanowski, 42–48. New York: Hippocrene Books, 1992.

Nord, Deborah. *Gypsies and the British Imagination, 1807–1930*. New York: Columbia University Press, 2006.

Novalis. "Die Christenheit oder Europa." In *Europa: Analysen und Visionen der Romantiker*, edited by Paul Michael Lützeler, 57–79. Frankfurt: Insel, 1982.

Orwin, Donna. *Tolstoy's Art and Thought, 1847–1880*. Princeton, N.J.: Princeton University Press, 1993.

Overton, Bill. *The Novel of Female Adultery: Love and Gender in Continental European Fiction, 1830–1890*. Basingstoke: Macmillan, 1996.

Pavletić, Vlatko, ed. *100 djela književnosti jugoslavenskih naroda*. Zagreb: Stvarnost, 1970.

Paxton, Nancy L. *George Eliot and Herbert Spencer: Feminism, Evolutionism, and the Reconstruction of Gender*. Princeton, N.J.: Princeton University Press, 1991.

Pilch, John J. "How We Redress Our Suffering: An Exercise in Actualizing Biblical Texts." *Polish Review* 48 (2003): 21–42.

Pinney, Thomas. "Another Note on the Forgotten Past of Will Ladislaw." *Nineteenth-Century Fiction* 17 (1962): 69–73.

Popkin, Cathy. "Occupy and Cultivate: Foreign Policy and Domestic Affairs (or The Case of *Anna Karenina*)." Paper presented at the University of Illinois Monthly Russian Reading Group (*Kruzhok*), Urbana, November 10, 2005.

Prażmowska, Anita J. *A History of Poland*. Houndmills, U.K.: Palgrave Macmillan, 2004.

Preece, Julian. "Fear of the Foreigner: Chinese, Poles, and Other Non-Prussians in Theodor Fontane's *Effi Briest*." In *German Studies at the Millennium*, edited by Neil Thomas, 173–95. Durham, U.K.: University of Durham, 1999.

Riasanovsky, Nicholas, and Mark Steinberg. *A History of Russia*. 7th ed. New York: Oxford University Press, 2005.

Ritter, Naomi. Review of *Adultery in the Novel: Contract and Transgression*, by Tony Tanner. *Comparative Literature Studies* 19 (1982): 390–93.

Roberts, Clayton, David Roberts, and Douglas R. Bisson. *A History of England*. Vol. 2: *1688 to the Present*. Upper Saddle River, N.J.: Prentice Hall, 2002.

Rogošić, Mirko, ed. *Ljubavna pisma hrvatskih književnika: Antologija*. Zagreb: Stvarnost, 1984.

Rousseau, Jean-Jacques. *The Plan for Perpetual Peace, On the Government of Poland, and Other Writings on History and Politics*. Edited by Christopher Kelly. Translated by Christopher Kelly and Judith Bush. Hanover, N.H.: Dartmouth College Press, 2005.

Röder-Bolton, Gerlinde. *George Eliot in Germany, 1854–55: "Cherished Memories."* Burlington, Vt.: Ashgate, 2006.

Runciman, John F. *Richard Wagner: Composer of Operas*. Charleston, S.C.: BiblioBazaar, 2007.

Rutten, Ellen. *Unattainable Bride Russia: Gendering Nation, State, and Intelligentsia in Russian Intellectual Culture*. Evanston, Ill.: Northwestern University Press, 2010.

Ryan, Judith. "The Chinese Ghost: Colonialism and Subaltern Speech in Fontane's *Effi Briest*." In *Literature and History: Essays in Honor of Karl S. Guthke*, edited by William S. Donahue and Scott Denham, 367–84. Tübingen: Stauffenberg Verlag, 2000.

Said, Edward. *Culture and Imperialism*. New York: Knopf, 1993.

———. *Orientalism*. New York: Vintage Books, 1979.

Sammons, Jeffrey L. Review of *The Truth of Realism: A Reassessment of the German Novel 1830–1900*, by John Walker. *Monatshefte* 104 (2012): 130–33.

Schiller, Friedrich. "Letter on the Aesthetic Education of Man." Translated by E. M. Wilkinson and L. A. Willoughby. In *Critical Theory Since Plato*, rev. ed., edited by Hazard Adams, 415–27. Fort Worth, Tex.: Harcourt Brace Jovanovich College Publishers, 1992.

Schmitt, Cannon. *Alien Nation: Nineteenth-Century Gothic Fictions and English Nationality*. Philadelphia, Pa.: University of Pennsylvania Press, 1997.

Seebaß, Friedrich, ed. *In Freiheit dienen: Briefe von Theodor Fontane*. Munich: Carl Hanser, 1956.

Seiler, Christiane. "Representations of the Loving, Hateful and Fearful Wife in Flaubert's *Mme Bovary*, Fontane's *Effi Briest*, and Tolstoy's *Anna Karenina*." *Germanic Notes and Reviews* 25 (1994): 3–7.

Sells, Michael Anthony. *The Bridge Betrayed: Religion and Genocide in Bosnia*. Berkeley: University of California Press, 1996.

Semmel, Bernard. *George Eliot and the Politics of National Inheritance*. New York: Oxford University Press, 1994.

Semczuk, Antoni. "Échos Polonais à la mort de Tolstoj." *Revue des études slaves* 81 (2010): 47–52.

Setel, T. Drorah. "Prophets and Pornography: Female Sexual Imagery in Hosea." In *Feminist Interpretations of the Bible*, edited by Letty M. Russell, 86–95. Philadelphia, Pa.: Westminster Press, 1985.

Seton-Watson, Robert William. *German, Slav, and Magyar: A Study in the Origins of the Great War*. London: Williams and Norgate, 1916.

Shklovsky, Viktor. *Lev Tolstoy*. Translated by Olga Shartse. Moscow: Progress Publishers, 1978.

Sienkiewicz, Henryk. *Quo Vadis*. http://wolnelektury.pl/katalog/lektura/quo-vadis.html.

Simcox, Edith. Review of *Middlemarch*, by George Eliot. *Academy* 4 (January 1, 1873): 2–4.

Slocum, John W. "Who, and When, Were the *Inorodtsy*? The Evolution of the Category of 'Aliens' in Imperial Russia." *Russian Review* 57 (1998): 173–90.

Smith, David L. "Will Ladislaw's Polish Ancestry." *Polish Anglo-Saxon Studies* 3–4 (1992): 55–63.

Smith, Helmut Walser. *German Nationalism and Religious Conflict: Culture, Ideology, Politics, 1870–1914*. Princeton, N.J.: Princeton University Press, 1995.

Spencer, Herbert. *The Factors of Organic Evolution*. New York: D. Appleton and Co., 1895.

———. *The Principles of Biology, Vol. I*. New York: D. Appleton and Co., 1904.

Stern, Joseph Peter Maria. "*Effi Briest*, *Madame Bovary*, *Anna Karenina*." *Modern Language Review* 52 (1957): 363–75.

Stump, Reva. *Movement and Vision in George Eliot's Novels*. Seattle: University of Washington Press, 1959.

Suvorin, Aleksei Sergeevich. *Dnevnik*. Edited by N. V. Potatueva. Moscow: Novosti, 1992.

Szymonik, Krzysztof. "Romantic-Messianism in the Novels of Henryk Sienkiewicz." Ph.D. diss., University of Maryland, 1984.

Šenoa, August. *The Goldsmith's Treasure*. Translated by Neven Divjakinja. Zagreb: Spiritoso, 2015.

———. "Pamflet na Ilirce." In *Polemike u hrvatskoj književnosti*, edited by Ivan Krtalić. 10 vols. Zagreb: Mladost, 1982.

———. *Sabrana djela*. Edited by Slavko Ježić. 12 vols. Zagreb: Znanje, 1963–64.

Šicel, Miroslav. *Hrvatska književnost 19. i 20. Stoljeća*. 2nd ed. Zagreb: Školska knjiga, 1997.

Tanner, Tony. *Adultery in the Novel: Contract and Transgression*. Baltimore, Md.: Johns Hopkins University Press, 1979.

Thompson, Andrew. *George Eliot and Italy: Literary, Cultural and Political Influences from Dante to the Risorgimento*. New York: St. Martin's Press, 1998.

Todd III, William Mills. "The Responsibilities of (Co-)Authorship: Notes on Revising the Serialized Version of *Anna Karenina*." In *Freedom and Responsibility in Russian Literature: Essays in Honor of Robert Louis Jackson*, edited by Elizabeth Cheresh Allen and Gary Saul Morson, 159–69. Evanston, Ill.: Northwestern University Press, 1995.

Todorova, Maria. *Imagining the Balkans*. New York: Oxford University Press, 1997.

Tolstaya, Sofya Andreevna. *Dnevniki*. Edited by S. A. Rozanova. 2 vols. Moscow: Khudozhestvennaia literatura, 1978.

Tolstoy, Lev Nikolaevich. *Polnoe sobranie sochinenii* (*PSS*). Edited by V. G. Chertkov. 90 vols. Moscow: Gosudarstvennoe izdatel'stvo khudozhestvennoi literatury, 1929–65.

Tolstoy, Leo. *Anna Karenina*. Translated by Constance Garnett. New York: Doubleday, 1944.

———. *Anna Karenina*. Translated by Louise and Aylmer Maude. New York: Oxford University Press, 2008.

———. *Anna Karenina*. Translated by Marian Schwartz. New Haven, Conn.: Yale University Press, 2014.

———. *Anna Karenina*. Translated by Richard Pevear and Larissa Volokhonsky. London: Penguin, 2003.

———. *Tolstoy's Letters*. Edited by R. F. Christian. 2 vols. London: Athlone Press, 1978.

Vaziri, Fritz Hubertus, et al. *Fontane's "femme fragiles": Effi Briest, Cécile und Frau Jenny Treibel*. Munich: Science Factory, 2013.

Walicki, Andrzej. *Philosophy and Romantic Nationalism: The Case of Poland*. New York: Clarendon Press, 1982.

Watt, Ian. *The Rise of the Novel: Studies in Defoe, Richardson, and Fielding*. Berkeley: University of California Press, 1964.

Weems, Renita J. *Battered Love: Marriage, Sex, and Violence in the Hebrew Prophets*. Minneapolis, Minn.: Fortress Press, 1995.

West, Rebecca. *Black Lamb and Grey Falcon: A Journey through Yugoslavia*. New York: Penguin, 1994.

Wolff, Larry. *Inventing Eastern Europe: The Map of Civilization on the Mind of the Enlightenment*. Stanford, Calif.: Stanford University Press, 1994.

Wormald, Mark. "Microscopy and Semiotic in *Middlemarch*." *Nineteenth-Century Literature* 50 (1996): 501–24.

Zimmermann, Gisela. "The Civil Servant as Educator: *Effi Briest* and *Anna Karenina*." *Modern Language Review* 90 (1995): 817–29.

INDEX

Adam Bede (Eliot), 27, 52
L'Adultera (Fontane), 58, 65, 66–71, 90
Adultery: in *L'Adultera*, 66–71; in *Anna Karenina*, 93–94, 101, 108–9, 111–13, 119; in *Cécile*, 71–77; in *Effi Briest*, 13, 20, 58, 66–71, 77–78, 85, 90; in *The Goldsmith's Gold*, 151; as literary trope, 3–5, 7, 10–11, 181, 183, 185–87; as metaphor for national betrayal, 112; in *Middlemarch*, 22–23; and Pan-Slavism, 108; in *Quo Vadis*, 170, 178
Adultery in the Novel: Contract and Transgression (Tanner), 7
Aksakov, Anna Fedorovna, 122–23
Aksakov, Ivan Sergeevich, 103, 114–15, 122
Aleksandr II (tsar), 104
Anderson, Benedict, 11, 133, 181, 184
Anna Karenina (Tolstoy), 92–127; *L'Adultera* compared with, 70; adultery trope in, 3, 4; bourgeois reading of, 7; cuckolded husband-statesman in, 116–18; death of heroine in, 66; friends of Anna in, 118–20; hair color in, 148; idealization of family in, 63; love as battlefield in, 99–101; Madonna/whore imagery in, 109–16; Pan-Slavism in, 101–6; publication of, 20; Serbia in, 106–9; Siberia in, 14; and statelessness, 182; *War and Peace* links to, 92–93, 99; women Slavophiles in, 120–23
Arendt, Hannah, 9, 10
Aristophanes, 186
Ashton, Rosemary, 38, 39
Augustine (Saint), 67
Austria: annexation of Bosnia and Herzegovina, 126, 174; and Austro-Hungarian empire, 14; in *The Goldsmith's Gold*, 147; and Poland, 32, 160; and Prussia, 74
The Awakening (Chopin), 3, 183

Babaev, Eduard Grigor'evich, 92, 127
Bakić-Hayden, Milica, 21
Balkan uprisings (1875), 103, 122, 123
Balzac, Honoré de, 30, 87
Bance, Alan, 57, 58
Beaty, Jerome, 31, 44
Beer, Gillian, 39, 187
Berdiaev, Nikolai, 109, 159, 183
Beware of the Senj Hand (*Čuvaj se Senjske ruke*) (Šenoa), 136
Biblical references: Judges 2:17, 112; Ezekiel 16, 113; Ezekiel 23, 112, 113, 203n34; Hosea 2, 117–18, 203n34; John 8:1–11, 66–67; Revelation 17:6, 161; Revelation 18:3, 161; on adultery, 111–12; and Polish messianism, 159–66; on vengeance, 115–16
Bismarck, Otto von, 14, 16–17, 61, 65, 78, 93
Blok, Aleksandr, 167, 210n27
Bosnia: annexation by Austria, 126, 174; ethnic cleansing in, 185; language in, 134; Muslim population in, 135; and Pan-Slavism, 103, 104
Britain. *See* England

The Carnation from the Poet's Grave ("Karanfil s pjesnikova groba") (Šenoa), 138
Catherine the Great, 30, 81, 156, 182

Catholicism: in Austria, 74; in *Effi Briest*, 88–89; in France, 140; in Italy, 164; in *Middlemarch*, 50–52, 54; in Poland, 50, 160; in *Quo Vadis*, 160
Cécile (Fontane), 58, 66, 70, 71–77
Central Europe: geography and identity of, 21–22. *See also specific countries*
Chambers, Helen, 57, 70, 200n67
Chekhov, Anton, 152
Cherniaev, Mikhail Grigor'evich, 103
China, German colonial interest in, 84
Chopin, Kate, 183
Christ: and Polish messianism, 159–66; as romantic rival, 170–72
Class boundaries. *See* Social class
Colonialism, 11–14, 28, 30, 55, 84, 87, 182. *See also* Empire literature
Congress of Berlin (1878), 139
"Considerations on the Government of Poland" (Rousseau), 155–56
The Cossacks (Tolstoy), 92, 98
La Cousine Bette (Balzac), 30, 87
Craig, Gordon A., 59–60, 62, 65, 70
Crimean War (1853), 97, 114
Croatia: anthropomorphizing of, 16; Illyrian movement in, 133–37; language in, 134; realism in, 131–32, 144; and statelessness, 182
Čuvaj se Senjske ruke (*Beware of the Senj Hand*) (Šenoa), 136

d'Albert-Durade, François, 34, 37
Dalmatian Renaissance, 143, 144
Daniel Deronda (Eliot), 4, 27–28, 36, 45–47, 52, 182
Darwinism, 39–40
The Death of Ivan Il'ich (Tolstoy), 62, 190n26
The Death of Smail-aga Čengić (*Smrt Smail-age Čengića*) (Mažuranić), 134–35
Defoe, Daniel, 8, 27
The Deluge (*Potop*) (Sienkiewicz), 155
Denmark, Prussia's victory over, 84–85
Der Stechlin (Fontane), 62, 63, 75
Deutscher Kolonial-Atlas (Langhans), 78, 143
Disraeli, Benjamin, 104, 196n63
"Do Matki Polki" (Mickiewicz), 16
Dostoevsky, Fedor Mikhailovich, 103–6, 110, 115, 119, 126, 160
Dukhobortsy (Christian sect), 96
Duraković, Ferida, 8, 175, 184, 211n11, 211n13

Eastern Crisis, 92, 102–3, 185. *See also* Slavonic Question
Eastern Europe: contemporary scholarship on, 29–32; geography and identity of, 21–22. *See also specific countries*
Effi Briest (Fontane), 57–91; adultery trope in, 3, 4, 11–12, 13, 15, 66–71; bourgeois reading of, 7; death of heroine in, 66; publication of, 20; and Slavic world, 60–65
Eikhenbaum, Boris, 92, 115, 203n37
Eliot, George, 27–56; doctrine of sympathy of, 79; and German intellectual thought, 73, 74; and historical novels, 142; and Kovalevskaya, 196n68; language use by, 143; on nationalities, 11, 19, 181; and Slavic world, 22; and Tolstoy, 93, 98. *See also specific works*
Empire literature: *Anna Karenina*, 92–127; *Effi Briest*, 57–91; *Middlemarch*, 27–56; terminology of, 14
England: anthropomorphizing of, 16; in *Cécile*, 72–73; as empire, 14, 30; First Reform Bill (1832), 27, 32, 51–52, 55; Fontane in, 73–74; imperialism of, 80; in *Middlemarch*, 27–56; "Polish Fever" in, 32–37; Russia's imperial competition with, 55–56; Second Reform Bill (1867), 27–28, 43
Enlightenment, 30, 156
Ethnicity. *See* Race and ethnicity
Euromaidan Revolution (Ukraine, 2014), 186

Fabrio, Nedjeljko, 135, 206n11
Fathers and Children (Turgenev), 63
Father Sergei (Tolstoy), 101
Felix Holt, the Radical (Eliot), 27, 45
Fet, Afanasy Afanas'evich, 97, 98, 122
Fichte, Johann Gottlieb, 41, 44
Fielding, Henry, 8
Fire in the Steppe (*Pan Wołodyjowski*) (Sienkiewicz), 155
First Morning Service with Father ("Prvi put s ocem na jutrenje") (Lazarević), 152
First Reform Bill (England, 1832), 27, 32, 51–52, 55
Flaubert, Gustave, 3, 70, 101, 189n2
Fontane, Theodor: and historical novels, 4, 142; language use by, 143; and Slavic world, 22, 60–65; on unification of Germany, 16. *See also specific works*
France: anthropomorphizing of, 17; Catholics in, 140; imperialism of, 80; nationalism in, 10; and Poland, 32
Franco-Prussian War (1870), 10, 14
Frau Jenny Treibel (Fontane), 63, 75

Gaj, Ljudevit, 133, 134, 139, 141, 143
Garland, Henry, 57, 64, 75, 77, 88, 199n35
Gates, Sarah, 52–53, 54
Gellner, Ernest, 9, 11, 93
George Eliot's Selected Critical Writings (Ashton), 39
The German Girl ("Švabica") (Lazarević), 6, 152–53
Germany: anthropomorphizing of, 16, 17; and China, 84; in *Effi Briest*, 57–91; as empire, 14; imperialism of, 80; in *Middlemarch*, 37–39; nationalism in, 10, 11; and Poland, 160, 164–65; realism in, 57–58; romanticism in, 46; unification (1871), 61, 74
Gladstone, William, 104, 132
Goethe, Johann Wolfgang von, 7, 57, 58–59, 88
The Goldsmith's Gold (*Zlatarovo zlato*) (Šenoa), 131–54; hair color in, 148; as historical novel, 5, 142, 145–51; and Illyrian movement, 133–37; publication of, 20; Serbian perspective, 152–54
Gorski vijenac (*Mountain Wreath*) (Njegoš), 135–36, 150
Gubec, Matija, 137, 146
Gusev, N. N., 174

Hadji Murat (Tolstoy), 92
Haight, Gordon S., 34, 35
Hair color, 149–50, 176
Halliday, Andrew, 33
Hardy, Thomas, 59
Hawthorne, Nathaniel, 183, 211n3
Hegel, G. W. F., 41
Henry, Nancy, 36, 47, 60, 197n94
Herder, Johannes Gottfried, 41, 167
Herzegovina: annexation by Austria, 126, 174; language in, 134; and Pan-Slavism, 103, 104; uprising (1875), 120
Hobsbawm, Eric, 9, 10, 17, 18, 77
Hungary: and Austro-Hungarian empire, 14; Croatia influenced by, 134; and Illyrian movement, 141

Illyrian movement, 133–37, 141
Imperialism. *See* Colonialism; Empire literature
Impressions of Theophrastus Such (Eliot), 49
In the Registry (*U Registraturi*) (Kovačić), 145
Israel, anthropomorphizing of, 18–19, 20

James, Henry, 31, 46, 52, 59, 83
Jelavich, Barbara, 136, 148
Jesus: and Polish messianism, 159–66; as romantic rival, 170–72
Jews: in *L'Adultera*, 90; in *Middlemarch*, 19, 44–50
John Paul II (pope), 158
Julie, ou la nouvelle Héloïse (Rousseau), 7

Karadžić, Vuk, 134

"Karanfil s pjesnikova groba" (The Carnation from the Poet's Grave) (Šenoa), 138
"Kateryna" (Shevchenko), 186
Katkov, Mikhail Nikiforovich, 102, 103, 104, 106, 112
Kerr, Deborah, 157, 176
Khomiakov, Aleksei Stepanovich, 114, 115, 122, 125, 152
Klaczko, Julian, 35, 45–46
Kopp, Kristin, 61, 78, 84, 86, 87, 182
Kościuszko, Tadeusz, 63, 64
Kosovo: ethnic cleansing in, 185; Muslim population in, 135
Kovačić, Ante, 145
Kovalevskaya, Sofia, 46, 196n68
The Kreutzer Sonata (Tolstoy), 62
Kristeva, Julia, 21, 54–55
Krzyżacy (*The Teutonic Knights*) (Sienkiewicz), 158
Kulturkampf (Germany), 61, 62, 64, 93, 158

Lady Chatterley's Lover (Lawrence), 22, 183
Langhans, Paul, 78, 143
Lawrence, D. H., 22, 183
Lazarević, Laza, 6, 152–54
Lebed', Anatoly, 185
Lewes, George Henry, 34, 35
Lewes, Herbert (Bertie), 36–37
Lewes, Thornton, 34, 36–37, 98
The Life of Jesus (Strauss), 38, 49
Liszt, Franz, 45, 46, 195n62
Ludwig, Otto, 58, 80
Lukács, Georg, 6, 189n7
Luther, Martin, 161
Lysistrata (Aristophanes), 186

Madame Bovary (Flaubert): adultery trope in, 3, 4–5, 10; death of heroine in, 66; lawsuit regarding indecency of, 101, 190n26; publication of, 57
Madonna imagery, 109–16
Magyarization, 133, 141
Malcolm, David, 32, 34, 36, 39, 50
Mann, Thomas, 57, 58, 62, 184, 197n7
Matich, Olga, 93, 110, 111, 115
Mayhew, Henry, 33
Mažuranić, Ivan, 133, 134–35, 136, 141, 146
Meine Kinderjahre (Fontane), 60
Mickiewicz, Adam, 15, 16, 159, 161–62
Middle class, 8–9, 27, 152, 190n26
Middlemarch (Eliot), 27–56; adultery trope in, 4, 11, 15, 187–88; bourgeois reading of, 7; Catholic role in, 50–52; *Cécile* compared with, 72–73; critical reviews of, 30–31; disinherited individual and nation in, 52–56, 182; and Eastern Europe scholarship, 29–32, 183; and Germany, 37–39; hair color in, 148; Jewish role in, 19, 44–50; and nineteenth-century science, 39–44; and "Polish Fever," 32–37; publication of, 20, 57; *Quo Vadis* compared with, 178
The Mill on the Floss (Eliot), 93, 149–50
"The Modern Hep! Hep! Hep!" (Eliot), 19
Montenegro: Gladstone on, 132; language in, 134; Pan-Slavism in, 103, 104; war with Turkey, 122
Morson, Gary Saul, 52, 125–26
Motherhood, 109–16
Mountain Wreath (*Gorski vijenac*) (Njegoš), 135–36, 150

Nance, Agnieszka, 62, 65, 155
Napoleon Bonaparte, 10, 97
Napoleon III (France), 161
Narodnjaci (Croatian political party), 141, 145, 207n22
"Naša književnost" ("Our Literature") (Šenoa), 137
Nation literature: anthropomorphizing of nations, 15–20; *The Goldsmith's Gold*, 131–54; *Quo Vadis*, 155–79; terminology of, 14–15
"The Natural History of German Life" (Eliot), 49

Njegoš, Petar Petrović, 135–36
Nord, Deborah, 31, 48, 52, 181

O'Connel, Daniel, 50
O'Connor, Sinead, 161, 209n20
Ogniem i mieczem (*With Fire and Sword*) (Sienkiewicz), 155, 156, 157, 158
Orientalism, 12, 21, 29–30, 82, 92
Orientalism (Said), 12, 197n94
Orthodox Church, 96, 102, 113, 124, 160
Orthography (Gaj), 134, 141
Ottoman Empire: in literature of Southern Slavs, 5–6; and Orthodox Church, 102; Russia's war with, 22, 61, 135
"Our Literature" ("Naša književnost") (Šenoa), 137

Pacifism, 96, 174, 204n41
Pan-Slavism, 101–6, 108, 109, 120–23, 139
Pan Tadeusz (Mickiewicz), 16
Pan Wołodyjowski (*Fire in the Steppe*) (Sienkiewicz), 155
The Peasant Revolt (*Seljačka buna*) (Šenoa), 136, 137, 142, 144, 146
Peloponnesian War, 186
Petar I (*vladika* of Montenegro), 135
Peter the Great, 169
Peter III, 81
Petrarca, Francesco, 144
Pirogova, Anna Stepanovna, 111
Pius X (pope), 158
Pochaev Icon of the Virgin, 109
Poland: adultery trope involving, 22–23; anthropomorphizing of, 15–16, 90–91, 160; and Austria, 32, 160; Catholicism in, 50, 160; in *Cécile*, 71–77; in *Effi Briest*, 60, 77–91; and France, 32; and Germany, 160, 164–65; January Uprising (1863), 159; Jews in, 44–50; in *Middlemarch*, 32–37, 50–52; and Prussia, 32; realist novels in, 5, 159; romanticism in, 35, 37, 159, 182; and Russia, 32, 158, 160, 168; and statelessness, 182; in *War and Peace*, 97
Polish messianism, 159–66
Porno-prophetic motifs, 109–16, 117
Postcolonial theory, 12, 78
Positivism, 162
Potop (The Deluge) (Sienkiewicz), 155
The Power of Darkness (Tolstoy), 62
Pravaši (Croatian political party), 141, 207n22
Pravopis (Gaj), 134, 141
Preece, Julian, 88, 186
Prešeren, France, 139
Protestantism, 19, 139
Prussia: and Austria, 74; and *Cécile*, 74; and Denmark, 84–85; in *Effi Briest*, 61, 79; as empire, 14; Franco-Prussian War (1870), 10, 14; and Poland, 32; political climate in, 74; Protestantism in, 139
"Prvi put s ocem na jutrenje" (First Morning Service with Father) (Lazarević), 152
Punch (magazine), 104

Quo Vadis (Sinkiewicz), 155–79; adultery trope in, 5; and barbarians, 167–70; Christ as romantic rival in, 170–72; hair color in, 176; happy ending in, 177–79; *Middlemarch* compared with, 178; Polish messianism in, 159–66; publication of, 20; Whore of Babylon in, 175–77

Race and ethnicity: in *L'Adultera*, 69, 90; and adultery trope, 22; in the Balkans, 185; in *Cécile*, 72; colonialism and, 14, 30; in *Der Stechlin*, 75; in *Effi Briest*, 86, 87; in France, 11; in Germany, 10; in *The Goldsmith's Gold*, 148, 150; in *Middlemarch*, 36, 39–45, 48–49, 54–55; and social class, 11
Rape, 12, 13, 191n30
Realism: and adultery trope, 3–6; in Croatia, 131–32, 144; in France, 57; in Germany, 57–58; poetic, 84, 87; in Poland, 159; in Russia, 102, 110, 112; vivid, 102, 110, 202n14

Replacement theology, 18
Resurrection (Tolstoy), 95–96, 99, 121, 172–73
Richardson, Samuel, 8, 27
Ristich, Jovan, 121
Röder-Bolton, Gerlinde, 73, 195n62
Roman Empire, 163–64, 169
Romanticism: end of, 57; in Germany, 46; in Poland, 35, 37, 159, 182; and Rousseau, 156; in Russia, 30, 125–26 Rousseau, Jean-Jacques, 7, 155–56
Rubis, Irina, 186
Russia: in *Anna Karenina*, 92–127; anthropomorphizing of, 15–16, 17; and colonialism, 13; in *Daniel Deronda*, 47; and *Effi Briest*, 61; England's imperial competition with, 55–56; imperialism of, 80; Ottoman Empire's war with, 22, 135; and Poland, 32, 158, 160, 168; romanticism in, 30, 125–26; and Serbia, 106–9, 185; Turkey's war with, 109, 114; and Ukraine, 184, 185–86
Rutten, Ellen, 123, 201n9

"The Sad Fortunes of the Rev. Amos Barton" (Eliot), 28, 33
Said, Edward, 12, 21, 29–30, 82, 92, 197n94
The Scarlet Letter (Hawthorne), 183
Scenes of Clerical Life (Eliot), 33
Schiller, Friedrich von, 9
Schopenhauer, Arthur, 115, 116
Science in *Middlemarch*, 39–44
Scott, Walter, 155, 179
Second Reform Bill (England, 1867), 27–28, 43
Seljačka buna (*The Peasant Revolt*) (Šenoa), 136, 137, 142, 144, 146
Semicolonialism, 12, 13, 78, 87
Šenoa, August, 131–54; and historical novels, 141–52; and Illyrian movement, 133–37; language use by, 143; and Russian identity, 13; on statelessness, 6, 20, 182. *See also specific works*
Serbia: in *Anna Karenina*, 106–9; language in, 134; Pan-Slavism in, 103, 104, 124; realist novels in, 5–6; and Russia, 106–9, 185; war with Turkey, 122
Serbo-Turkish War (1876–78), 126, 152
Seton-Watson, Robert, 132, 141
Shevchenko, Taras, 186
Sienkiewicz, Henryk, 155–79; historical novels of, 141–42; and statelessness, 182; and Tolstoy, 172–75. *See also specific works*
Silas Marner (Eliot), 27, 52
Slavic Benevolent Committee, 102, 103, 114, 120
Slavonic Question, 92–127, 196n76
Smith, David L., 34, 37, 50
Smrt Smail-age Čengića (*The Death of Smail-aga Čengić*) (Mažuranić), 134–35
Social class: adultery trope and, 3, 7–9; in *Anna Karenina*, 103, 107, 121; in *Effi Briest*, 64–65, 83; in *The Goldsmith's Gold*, 138, 143, 147–48, 151–52; middle class, 8–9, 27, 152, 190n26; in *Middlemarch*, 27–29, 32–33, 42, 48; and national status, 5, 9–10, 11; in *Quo Vadis*, 161, 171, 177; and race and ethnicity, 11
Solidarity movement (Poland), 32
Spencer, Herbert, 29, 40–41, 43, 195n50
Starčević, Ante, 141
Statelessness, 6, 20, 182
Strangers to Ourselves (Kristeva), 21, 54
Strauss, David Friedrich, 38, 49
Strossmayer, Josip Juraj, 141
"Švabica" (The German Girl) (Lazarević), 6, 152–53

Tanner, Tony, 7–8, 10, 12, 13, 58, 111
Tennyson, Alfred, 104

Tess of the D'Urbervilles (Hardy), 59
The Teutonic Knights (*Krzyżacy*) (Sienkiewicz), 158
Tintoretto, 66, 68
Tiutchev, Fedor Ivanovich, 103, 122
Todorova, Maria, 12, 13, 21, 78
Tolstoy, Lev: and Dostoevsky, 106; and Eliot, 93, 98; on imperialism, 3, 79; isolationist politics of, 115; language use by, 143; on nationalism, 4, 10; on patriotism and peace, 181; and Sienkiewicz, 172–75; and Turgenev, 109. *See also specific works*
Train imagery, 109
Turgenev, Ivan, 63, 106, 109, 198n26
Turkey: and Balkan uprisings, 103, 122, 123; in *The Goldsmith's Gold*, 146; and Pan-Slavism, 103, 104; Russia's war with, 109, 114; Serbo-Turkish War, 126, 152

Ukraine conflict (2014), 184, 185–86
Unattainable Bride Russia (Rutten), 123, 201n9
U Registraturi (*In the Registry*) (Kovačić), 145
Uspensky, Gleb Ivanovich, 107–8

Vengeance, 115–16
Venzhik, Katerina, 186
Victorian domesticity, 52, 53–54
Vienac (journal), 131, 176
Vischer, Friedrich Theodor, 16, 17
Vivid realism, 102, 110, 202n14
Voltaire, 30, 155
Vor dem Sturm (Fontane), 4, 57–58, 62–63, 65, 71, 90, 199n35

Wahlverwandtschaften (Goethe), 7, 58–59, 67
Walicki, Andrzej, 15, 16–17, 161
War and Peace (Tolstoy): *Anna Karenina* links to, 92–93, 99; idealization of Russia in, 95, 101; love as battlefield in, 99–101; nationalism in, 10, 96–99; as novel of empire, 4; publication of, 57; war as crime in, 113, 126
Watt, Ian, 8, 10
West, Rebecca, 103, 132, 208n28
Wharton, Edith, 183
Whore imagery, 109–16, 160–61, 175–77
With Fire and Sword (*Ogniem i mieczem*) (Sienkiewicz), 155, 156, 157, 158
Wolff, Larry, 12, 13, 21, 22, 29, 30, 41, 87, 156
Woman Question, 11, 29, 43, 56, 58, 84, 190n8
"A Word for the Germans" (Eliot), 38, 49, 55
Writer's Diary (Dostoevsky), 119

Yugoslavia: anthropomorphizing of, 184; creation of, 182; dissolution of, 8, 15, 50, 184–85; Duraković on, 132, 184; and Illyrian movement, 133; and orientalism, 21; Šenoa on, 141; West on, 103

Zlatarovo zlato (Šenoa). *See The Goldsmith's Gold*